GENDER AND CULTURE
IN AMERICA

SECOND EDITION

GENDER AND CULTURE
IN AMERICA

Linda Stone

Washington State University

Nancy P. McKee

Washington State University

Prentice
Hall

UPPER SADDLE RIVER, NEW JERSEY 07458

Library of Congress Cataloging-in-Publication Data

Stone, Linda.
   Gender and culture in America/Linda Stone, Nancy P. McKee.—2nd ed.
      p. cm.
   Includes bibliographical references and index.
   ISBN 0-13-061328-2
      1. Sex role—United States—History.   2. United States—Social conditions.   I. Title.

HQ1075.5.U6 S765 2002
305.3'0973—dc21

2001053264

VP, Editorial director: Laura Pearson
AVP, Publisher: Nancy Roberts
Editorial assistant: Lee Peterson
Marketing manager: Chris Barker
Editorial/production supervision: Kari Callaghan Mazzola
Prepress and manufacturing buyer: Ben Smith
Electronic page makeup: Kari Callaghan Mazzola and John P. Mazzola
Interior design: John P. Mazzola
Cover director: Jayne Conte
Cover design: Kiwi Design
Cover art: Farida Zaman/Stock Illustration Source, Inc.

This book was set in 10/12 Meridien by Big Sky Composition
and was printed and bound by Courier Companies, Inc.
The cover was printed by Phoenix Color Corp.

© 2002, 1999 by Pearson Education, Inc.
Upper Saddle River, New Jersey 07458

All rights reserved. No part of this book may be
reproduced, in any form or by any means,
without permission in writing from the publisher.

Printed in the United States of America
10   9   8   7   6   5   4   3   2

ISBN 0-13-061328-2

Pearson Education LTD., London
Pearson Education Australia PTY, Limited, Sydney
Pearson Education Singapore, Pte. Ltd
Pearson Education North Asia Ltd, Hong Kong
Pearson Education Canada, Ltd., Toronto
Pearson Educación de Mexico, S.A. de C.V.
Pearson Education—Japan, Tokyo
Pearson Education Malaysia, Pte. Ltd
Pearson Education, Upper Saddle River, New Jersey

To the memory of my mother, Mary Driscoll McKee,
and my aunt, Martha McKee Keehn,
who coped in their own ways
with gender and culture in America
through challenging times.

—Nancy P. McKee

To my niece, Julie Bradley-Hart,
for whom the challenges
of gender and culture in America lie ahead.

—Linda Stone

CONTENTS

PREFACE

"More time should be spent on gender in the United States." This is a student evaluation we both frequently received from our respective sections of the anthropology course Gender and Culture, a class that focuses on the anthropology of gender in non-Western societies. Although this course inevitably draws contrasts between gender in non-Western societies and in the United States, students over a ten-year period eventually convinced us that devoting more class time specifically to gender in America was a good suggestion that reflected a genuine concern on the part of students. It was to meet this need that we wrote this book. There is, of course, a rich literature on gender in the United States from a variety of disciplines. There are also edited readers covering anthropological works on gender in the United States. *Uncertain Terms: Negotiating Gender in American Culture* (Ginsburg and Tsing 1990) and *Situated Lives: Gender and Culture in Everyday Life* (Lamphere, Ragoné, and Zavella 1997) are two that come to mind. But we felt that a single book on gender in the United States written specifically for undergraduates and from an anthropological perspective was absent.

We sought to write a book that did not focus primarily on contemporary gender issues in the United States (sexual harassment, violence against women, gender inequity in the workforce, and so on), all of which are well covered in innumerable other texts. We wanted, rather, a book that focuses on cultural constructions of gender, one that invites the reader to see America as a set of interacting cultural beliefs and values, much as students of our Gender and Culture classes are encouraged to view societies of Asia, Africa, or Latin America. The book is intended to open a new perspective for students, moving attention away from American gender inequality as a problem to be dealt with through new legislation or policy reform, into a deeper view of American gender as enmeshed in our own distinctive and varied cultural traditions. The book seeks to challenge students to consider that addressing gender inequality in

America involves not just activism or new laws and policies, but new modes of thought, a rethinking of our deepest, most accepted premises about the world.

Our book, then, is designed for undergraduate anthropology courses like our own Gender and Culture. We recommend it especially for the last few weeks of such a class, after students have been exposed to the study of gender in any number of non-Western societies, and after they are familiar with basic concepts and theories in the anthropology of gender. Students can then approach gender in American culture comparatively, within a framework of the cross-cultural study of gender already developed in the course. The book will also be useful in sociology, history, or women's studies courses that cover the United States.

The book approaches American gender through a historical and multicultural framework. Two chapters following the introductory chapter focus on the culturally dominant white middle class. These two chapters also present material on alternative gender constructions among gay men and lesbians. The next two chapters cover a history of gender constructions among ethnic minorities (specifically Native Americans, African Americans, Hispanic groups, and Asian Americans).

Chapter 6 then moves to a subject we think will be of particular interest to students, "Gender on the College Campus." In this chapter we include results of our own study of gender and students' perceptions of their futures on a campus in the Northwest, as well as the results of a smaller subsequent study we conducted on eight other campuses around the country. This study shows important variation by gender in how students perceive and plan for their future world of work, marriage, and reproduction. As part of this research we administered a questionnaire to students on all campuses. Appendix A provides the questionnaire we used. Instructors using our book might like to have their students fill out this questionnaire in order for students of their classes to see how their own responses conform to or vary from those of the students in our study.

The book's first few chapters introduce a number of themes that recur later in the book. A central theme is American individualism. The book discusses how gender constructions of the white middle class have been shaped by the different positions that women and men have had with respect to this central value of mainstream American life. The chapters covering ethnic minorities show how other groups have reacted to individualism and how these reactions fit in with their own constructions of gender. Another theme is gender in relation to the body. We discuss how gender constructions are related to ideal body images and notions of health and illness. A connection between religion and gender is another theme, mostly developed in Chapters 2 and 3. A final important theme that runs through all chapters implicitly or explicitly concerns the interconnections among the inequalities of gender, ethnicity, and class in America. A final chapter draws together the various themes of the book and provides a summary and conclusion.

Like all textbooks, this one has limitations. One is that we do not, and could not, cover all ethnic or social groups that play relevant roles in American gender construction. As noted, we selected for attention the categories of white middle-class Americans, Native Americans, African Americans, Hispanics, and Asian Americans, and thus we have excluded many other categories. For example, Jewish Americans, elderly Americans, poor whites, Polish Americans, and so on are not mentioned individually. Similarly, in a book of this size, the vast cultural variation within the categories we have chosen could not be covered in great detail. And though we use a historical framework, no one historical period is covered in the depth it deserves. Finally, although we have tried to maintain an objective tone in the book, we are well aware that our personal, professional, and gender biases seep through. If one were to read this book without knowing the identity of the authors, it would come as no surprise to learn that they are women, academics, feminists, and anthropologists. Our aim, however, has been not to promote a particular theoretical position but to offer students a view of the many contributions that varied anthropological perspectives can make to our understanding of gender in the United States.

In this second edition of *Gender and Culture in America* we have added a section on gender theory in anthropology in Chapter 1 and more material on gender and the body in Chapter 3. Throughout the book we have included more works by anthropologists on gender in the United States. We have also added discussion questions at the end of each chapter. Finally, we have included some useful Web sites for further information on issues we cover in the book. These Web sites are listed at the end of Chapter 7.

For their comments on earlier drafts of the book manuscript, we would like to thank Susan Armitage, Edward C. Joyce, Jane R. Millard, Jill M. Wagner, and Miranda Warburton. We are grateful to the Spencer Foundation for financial assistance with the research reported in Chapter 6. The data presented there, the statements made, and the views expressed are solely the responsibility of the authors. For their interviewing on that project we thank our graduate assistants, Jennifer Strauss and Towako Masuda, and we thank Louis Olsen for his help with analysis of data. Special thanks go to Diana Ames, Karl G. Heider, and Karen Sinclair for their assistance with the project. We are also grateful to the many students around the country who participated in the research. Linda Stone would like to thank her husband, Paul F. Lurquin, for his help and support throughout the preparation of the book. Nancy P. McKee would like to thank her husband, George E. Kennedy, and her daughter, Hannah McKee-Kennedy, for their assistance and encouragement. Finally, we thank the following reviewers, who gave many helpful suggestions: Judith Krieger, Western Washington University; Susana M. Sotillo, Montclair State University; Barbara D. Miller, George Washington University; and Ann Corinne Freter-Abrams, Ohio University.

Linda Stone
Nancy P. McKee

REFERENCES

Ginsburg, Faye, and Anna Lowenhaupt Tsing, eds. 1990. *Uncertain Terms: Negotiating Gender in American Culture*. Boston, MA: Beacon Press.

Lamphere, Louise, Helena Ragoné, and Patricia Zavella, eds. 1997. *Situated Lives: Gender and Culture in Everyday Life*. New York: Routledge.

GENDER AND CULTURE
IN AMERICA

INTRODUCTION

In 1956, anthropologist Horace Miner reported some customs and beliefs of a group of people known as the Nacirema:

> In the hierarchy of magical practitioners, and below the medicine man in prestige, are the specialists whose designation is best translated "holy mouth-men." The Nacirema have an almost pathological horror and fascination with the mouth, the condition of which is believed to have a supernatural influence on all social relationships.... The daily body ritual performed by everyone includes a mouth rite.... In addition ... the people seek out a holy mouthman once or twice a year. These practitioners have an impressive array of paraphernalia, consisting of a variety of augers, awls, probes and prods. The use of these objects in the exorcism of the evils of the mouth involves almost unbelievable ritual torture of the client. (Miner 1956, 504–505)

A fundamental Nacirema belief is that the body is ugly and tends toward decay and illness, tendencies that only certain stringent rituals can avert. Along with their treatments of the mouth, Miner described their daily private body rituals. Nacirema keep shrines in their houses devoted to the performance of these rituals, and the more such shrines a house contains, the more opulent it is considered to be. As for Nacirema gender, Miner wrote that "a distinctive part of the daily body ritual which is performed only by men ... involves scraping and lacerating the surface of the face with a sharp instrument," while women occasionally "bake their heads in small ovens for about an hour" (1956, 506). To this we might add that about half of all Nacirema parents perform a birth ritual where a masked medicine man slices off some skin of the penis of a newborn male, amid the infant's howling protest, so that it will enter the world with even greater promise of a lifetime of sanitary living.

The Nacirema do not live in a remote, little-known region of the globe. Needless to say, perhaps, they are a majority group in the United States (Nacirema is American spelled backward) and Miner was writing a spoof on middle-class American practices concerning the care and maintenance of human bodies. While it is clearly humorous, Miner's work also invites Americans to take a new look at themselves, to see themselves as a culture. By taking only small, playful liberties in his descriptions of behavior, Miner helps his audience to see itself as a group with its own peculiar beliefs and practices. Too often we take our own ways of life, and the assumptions on which they are based, for granted; we assume that our way of doing things is perfectly natural, and that it is always other people who engage in "exotic" practices or hold "strange" ideas.

This book on the anthropology of gender in America also invites the reader to see America as a culture, or more precisely, a plurality of cultures. Although we do not take Miner's linguistic liberties, we hope to expose American ideas on gender to be as enmeshed in particular cultural assumptions and traditions as that of any other group of people. We maintain, along with most other social scientists, that gender is everywhere largely culturally constructed. Gender does not automatically take shape out of our male and female biologies; gender is rather something that all of us invent, modify, and reinvent as we go about the business of leading our individual and collective lives.

Many books that deal with gender in America focus on contemporary gender issues—sexual harassment, gender discrimination in the workplace, abortion debates, rape, and so on—in an effort to increase awareness of the issues and find solutions to problems. We discuss a few such issues in a concluding chapter (Chapter 7), but most of the book deals not with current gender issues but with what lies behind them, such as the question of how and through what cultural ideas and practices these gender issues have arisen in the first place. The book uncovers what is distinctive about gender in America and relates those distinctions to broader cultural themes. This is done through the book's organization around the following topics: the cultural history of American gender, focusing on the white middle class (Chapters 2 and 3), gender in relation to ethnic and class diversity (Chapters 4 and 5), and a special section on gender among American college students (Chapter 6).

Along with our premise that gender is a cultural construction we also maintain that gender, in the United States and in many other industrial societies, is thoroughly interwoven with the social divisions of ethnicity and class. But making these starting points clear and specifying what we mean by the cultural construction of gender and what is involved in the relationships between gender, ethnicity, and class requires that we first discuss a few basic concepts in both anthropology and gender studies.

Culture and Gender

This book, like many other anthropology texts, adopts a broad and flexible use of the term *culture* to refer to the learned behaviors and ideas that characterize particular groups of people. *Behaviors* can include just about anything—from religious rituals to clothing styles to conventional forms of greeting; *ideas* can include knowledge, language, beliefs, and values. Even more broadly, *culture* can be understood as a people's *way of life* or *traditions*.

The United States, which in this book is often referred to simply as America, can for many purposes be considered one society, sharing a common political and economic organization as well as many social institutions. It is also *multicultural*, by which it is meant that the many ethnic groups within it orient themselves to the country's political, economic, and social organization through their own distinctive cultural traditions. This multicultural dimension of American society has received a great deal of attention in recent times as different ethnic groups have asserted their rights and fought to preserve their own identities. In America we can also speak of innumerable *subcultures*, including, for example, a student subculture, a working class subculture, or even a subculture of stamp collectors or tennis buffs.

It is tempting to see culture as a static set of ideas and behaviors, transmitted over the generations, that we internalize from birth and that deeply, often unconsciously, shape our lives. This view, however, misses the fact that while we are all born into a culture, we also act within and so affect it. Culture is better seen as sets of ideas and behaviors that human actors themselves continually generate. Each actor is in a dynamic relationship with his or her culture; as a result, all cultures undergo change.

This dynamic dimension of culture is related to the fact that all cultures express some internal tensions. People of one group may recognize a set of cultural categories in common, but this does not mean that they necessarily agree about what the categories mean or feel the same way about them. For example, nearly all Americans will recognize categories such as baseball, skyscrapers, jazz, Marilyn Monroe, the Easter Bunny, Donald Duck, a Confederate flag, and McDonald's Golden Arches as distinctively American, but they may respond and relate to these categories in very different ways. Thus, for example, some people see the skyscraper as epitomizing American economic glory; to others it represents a dehumanized world and an environmental eyesore. Children may "believe in" the Easter Bunny in a way that adults do not. For most adults the Easter Bunny is a harmless figure, but to some Christian groups it represents a dangerous lapse into paganism. For many, Marilyn Monroe is an ultimate in feminine beauty; to others, she represents the objectification of women as "sex objects." To be sure, some cultural categories, such as Donald Duck, elicit less widely ranging reactions or controversy.

People may, then, attach quite different meanings to common cultural symbols. Indeed, as in all societies, Americans have a variety of visions about what life should be like and about how their own cultural categories should be evaluated. As in all societies, the meaning and evaluation of many cultural categories is disputed. Very often a dominant set of ideas or practices exists within one society, supported by a majority or by a powerful elite. But other people within the society resist these ideas or challenge the validity of these practices. Much of culture, then, is not agreed upon by all but is contested between different individuals and groups. As we will see throughout this book, gender is a hotly contested cultural category in America today.

Gender refers to the different ways that men and women are culturally defined and evaluated. Earlier, it was common for social scientists to distinguish *gender* from *sex*. *Sex* was understood as referring to the biological differences between men and women, whereas *gender* was seen as the way those differences are interpreted and evaluated. Thus biological sexual differences were considered universal in all human groups, whereas gender was seen as highly variable between different groups. For example, the fact that women menstruate is, in this view, a matter of "sex" or biology. But the idea that a menstruating woman is "unclean" or "dangerous" (an idea found in many cultures) is a matter of gender.

This distinction between gender and sex was, admittedly, a handy way to look at human gender variation. It preserved the notion of universal biological sexual differences without invoking the argument that "biology is destiny" or the idea that men and women behave differently or should be evaluated differently because of their biological differences. More recently, however, many scholars have pointed out that biological sexual differences themselves are understood differently within various cultures. For example, Thomas Laqueur (1990) points out that medical authorities in ancient Rome did not view women and men as biologically or even anatomically different; rather they saw women's sexual organs as merely smaller versions of male ones. Thus the clitoris was seen not as a unique female organ but as a very small penis. The contrast in men and women was one of degree, not kind, and was attributed to men's having greater "heat" in their systems. Again, when we hear that a group of people in Malaysia believe that pregnancy begins in a father's brain, that a liquid fetus then travels through the man's sperm into the woman's womb through sexual intercourse (Laderman 1991), we can appreciate that it is not just gender but also ideas about human biology that are culturally conditioned.

Modern biological science does offer an unequivocal and universal definition of human sexual difference based on genetic determinations: Individuals carrying two X chromosomes are female while those carrying one X and one Y chromosome are male. However, even this clear-cut definition becomes a little slippery in certain human contexts. Thus, rare genetic defects affecting the X or Y chromosomes can drastically alter the external appearance of afflicted individuals. One striking example involving a mutation of the Y chromosome yields individuals that, though having X and Y chromosomes, look completely female—they lack external male organs and have well-developed breasts. These individuals cannot reproduce as females because they lack ovaries, nor as males because they lack testicles and a penis. This example shows that alterations in X or Y chromosomes can produce persons with, biologically speaking, an ambiguous sexual status. These persons are anatomically more like females yet genetically more like males.

However we view the biological issues of human sexual difference, gender is a cultural construction, learned and internalized, often debated, and ever changing as human actors undergo life experiences and interact with one another. To show in this book how gender in America has been and is being constructed and debated, it is helpful to introduce the following additional concepts and distinctions.

ETHNOCENTRISM AND CULTURAL RELATIVISM

Ethnocentrism is the notion that one's own group or culture (Greek: *ethnos*) is the ideal or standard for human behavior and values, and that to the extent that other groups or cultures diverge from one's own, they are defective, weird, sick, evil, bad, silly, or unnatural. Actually, most peoples of the world are afflicted by ethnocentrism to some extent; it is not a problem confined only to Americans or to Western or industrial cultures. But Western and industrial cultures are likely to have wealth, advanced technology, and power, so when they act on their ethnocentrism they may do substantial damage. As colonial powers they told indigenous (native) peoples that they were sinners to have multiple wives, expose their bodies, worship supernaturals other than God, or eat human flesh. And in many cases they destroyed the indigenous cultures.

To counter the power of ethnocentrism, anthropologists advance the principle of *cultural relativism*. This is the idea that human needs can be met by an infinite variety of cultural systems and that it is counterproductive to make value judgments about cultures other than one's own.

Does this mean that we have to accept Nazi Germany as just another culture that works fine for its own participants? Does it mean that a culture that fosters grinding poverty for large numbers of participants is perfectly acceptable? Are societies in which women are blatantly subjugated to men acceptable? Anthropology offers no standard answers to these questions, but one suggestion may help to deal with them: No matter what the culture, it is useful to consider whether it permits most of its participants to construct generally rewarding lives for themselves on their own terms.

PATRIARCHY AND MATRIARCHY

Many discussions of gender invoke the idea of *patriarchy*. The term *patriarchy* originally referred to societies in which strong authority and control over resources was vested in senior males. In these societies, women and children were seen as legal minors with little or no control over property and virtually no voice in political affairs. The upper classes of ancient Rome are an example, as is Afghanistan in modern times. In the nineteenth century, anthropologists and others debated whether the first human societies were patriarchal or the opposite, *matriarchal*. Today most anthropologists agree that there is no evidence that truly matriarchal societies have ever existed. On the other hand, many anthropologists have argued that some societies exhibit near gender equality (Shostak 1981) or gender complementarity (Ackerman 1982; Lepowsky 1993).

Today the term *patriarchy* is more often used in a looser sense to mean male dominance in certain social spheres, for example, politics or economic decision making. It is in this sense that we use the term in this book. It would be difficult to classify whole societies or cultural groups as thoroughly male dominant since women in nearly all societies exercise some power, even if informally, and have some authority in at least a few spheres of life.

FEMINISM

The word *feminism* is by now loaded with many different meanings and connotations. A dictionary definition of the term calls it "a doctrine that advocates or demands for women the same rights granted men, as in political and economic status." This is what we mean by *feminism* whenever the term is used in this book. With this definition, the authors declare themselves "feminists" and readily admit to all the biases that this position brings. Others define and use *feminism* or *feminist* in different ways and many see these terms in quite a negative light. As we will see in Chapter 6, for example, many American college students, male and female, interpret *feminist* as "bra-burning radical," "political extremist," or "man hater." All of this testifies to the extent to which gender itself is a very sensitive and controversial topic in the country today. For this reason we wish to be clear about our use of the term *feminism*, to openly state our position, and to disavow any associations with either man hating or, as feminists, any political agenda beyond gender equality in our own society.

GENDER EQUALITY

The concept of gender equality is neither inevitable nor obvious. It does not necessarily occur to people to ask whether gender equality exists. In some cultures it is assumed that such equality does not and cannot exist, so questions about it do not develop. In other cultures men's and women's roles are considered complementary rather than competitive; thus the question of equality fails to arise in these cultures, too. In late-twentieth-century America, however, gender equality is of compelling interest, particularly to women.

But what do we mean by "equality"? How will we recognize it when we see it? We may feel that we will just "know" it, but such intuitive guesses are not very useful, since one person's gut recognition of equality is completely lost on another. One useful approach to this dilemma is to analyze "gender equality" as the degree to which men and women have similar kinds or degrees of power, status, autonomy, and authority.

Power can be thought of as the ability to make people do what one wants and to acquire what one desires. Status (a Latin word meaning *standing*, or *position*) refers to one's position in society. Often status and power go hand in hand, but not always. An organized crime boss, for example, has power but very little status outside of his crime family. And the Queen of England has plenty of status, but virtually no power at all, at least in the political sphere (it's hard to be a completely powerless billionaire).

Autonomy is the ability to control one's own actions, a fairly straightforward concept though sometimes difficult to determine. Authority is the most difficult of all the components of equality to pin down. Basically it has to do with access to legitimacy, either because of one's own nature or by right of association with a particular role, institution, or individual, natural or supernatural. The pope, for example, has authority because of his role and implicit association with the supernatural. This is not quite the same thing as power, though, as the millions of birth control–practicing Catholics amply demonstrate, or the heads of state who proceed with executions, despite papal pleas for clemency.

Looking at gender in terms of women and men's relative power, status, autonomy, and authority is a useful exercise but it does not solve all the problems of assessing gender equality. One problem is that a people within a culture may interpret their own gender situation very differently from the way an outside researcher might interpret it. For example, an outsider visiting a conservative Islamic region might see women as "oppressed" because they are usually secluded in the home or heavily veiled when they go out. But the women of this region may have an entirely different view. They may see the home as an area where they exercise a lot of power, and they may see veiling as a good and necessary protection of their persons in the world outside, as well as a symbol of their own self-respect. They may see veiling as a practice that eases their lives in public spaces rather than a restriction that oppresses them. On what basis can the outside researcher say that her or his interpretation is correct or superior to that of the Islamic women themselves? To state this problem another way, can researchers define "female oppression" in such a way that it is free of their own cultural biases?

Another problem is that in all societies men and women play a variety of roles that change over their lifetimes, and their power, autonomy, status, and authority may vary according to these roles. Thus, for example, men of one society may exercise clear authority in their roles as religious leaders but very little in their roles as fathers or husbands. Or women of a particular society may have significant political power but no official authority in the political realm.

Another way to approach the concept of gender equality is to consider the way in which items of general value in a society are distributed among its population according to gender. Of course, one needs to know what a particular society values and to select items that are in some way measurable. Thus, "happiness" is valued in America, but it would be difficult to determine whether males or females are happier. On the other hand, money, good health, and education are generally valued in this country and are easily quantified. Using these measures, we take a look at gender equality in America in Chapter 7.

Two important terms we use throughout this book are *race* and *ethnicity*, terms that can easily cause confusion. Like the terms *sex* and *gender* that we discussed earlier, race and ethnicity run into debates over what is biological, or "natural," and what is cultural, or "constructed." Usually people think of a *race* as a group of people who share some common physical characteristics, such as skin color. We are all familiar with terms such as *white* and *black* that are used to designate "racial" categories. We will return to the idea of race in a moment, but first we will distinguish the term *race* from *ethnic group*. An ethnic group is a group of persons who in some contexts set themselves apart from others based on their own distinctive cultural, linguistic, or other characteristics. Often the phrase *ethnic group* is used for distinctive minority populations within a modern nation. In this sense, the term *black* can refer to an ethnic group in the United States. Thus *race* is a designation that categorizes human beings according to some idea of biological differences, while *ethnic group* usually refers to people's identifications with particular subcultural groups.

It is easy to understand ethnic groups as, like gender, cultural constructions. People create cultural categories and construct labels such as "Bosnian," "Basque," "Native American," or "Hispanic" to indicate their, or other's, social identifications. But what about race? When people use this term, they usually do not have cultural constructions but rather biological, or genetically transmittable, attributes in mind. Yet today many anthropologists claim that, biologically speaking, there are no scientifically valid categories of human races. Some of these people argue that human physical variations are better understood as variations in distributions of gene frequencies. Thus the genes responsible for dark skin gradually become more frequent as one moves southward from Northern Europe to Central Africa. But the variation is gradual, and there are no clear divisions we could use to demarcate neatly bounded categories of people (Harris 1988, 104). At the same time, we find that the variation in some gene frequencies within any one human population is as great as or greater than the variation between populations.

Others argue that, even though there are demonstrable differences in gene frequencies in human populations, the way most people employ the idea of "race" is so unscientific, and so socially dangerous, that it is better to do away with the term altogether. They feel there is no way to talk about race without invoking racism. Yet another point of view is that all discussions of biological variations in human groups, even presumably scientific, objective ones, are cultural. In a way similar to those who argue that biological "sex," like "gender," is culturally constructed, these people hold that any biological concept of race is itself a cultural construct.

Whether *race* is or is not a valid scientific concept is today being debated in anthropology, and we will not enter into that controversy here. Our book is concerned with "race," not in relation to biological science, but in everyday social usage—in other words, as a pure cultural construction. In the book we try to use "race" and "ethnic group" in a way that best fits the semantic context of the discussion at hand. Thus when we refer to contemporary African Americans or Native Americans, we usually use the term *ethnic group*. Sometimes we use *race* rather than *ethnic group* to follow the usage of other writers whose work we discuss. This is particularly true when we refer to nineteenth-century writers or when we discuss nineteenth-century ideas of "racial" inequality.

THEORETICAL PERSPECTIVES

In anthropology, gender is a fairly recent topic, largely inspired by the women's movement in the United States in the 1960s and early 1970s. A number of women anthropologists brought a "raised consciousness" from the women's movement into their profession. They began to ask new questions about anthropology and, in the process, transformed it. For one thing they noticed a "male bias" in the discipline. They saw that very few ethnographies included accounts of the activities or interests of women. Or, when these accounts did include women, they presented them as quietly taking care of children or cleaning huts in the background of the more important and more interesting male activities, such as hunting, warfare, politics, and public ritual. These women anthropologists began to question the validity of ethnographic portraits that excluded or backgrounded women, as well as some of the theories that were based on these reports.

One theory that was particularly significant had to do with human evolution; it was known as "the hunting hypothesis." In this hypothesis, our early hominid ancestors (*Australopithecines*) descended from the trees and developed hunting of large prey as an adaptation to ground-dwelling in open country (Washburn and Lancaster 1968). This adaptation promoted the invention of tools for the hunt, a process that in turn stimulated an increase in the size and complexity of the human brain. Hunting also promoted bipedal-ism, since it is easier to walk upright with the arms and hands free to use tools. In short, it was hunting that turned us into bipedal, intelligent crea-tures, soon capable of language and culture. And it was males, not females, who hunted. Women and their children were dependent on men to pro-vide them with valuable meat from the hunt. Later archaeological evidence challenged this hypothesis with the finding that these early hominids were still semi-arboreal, unlikely to have hunted with tools and more likely to have, in fact, been the prey of hyenas and other animals (Brain 1981). Even with this, the hunting hypothesis lived on. Along with a few other adjust-ments, the time frame was merely shifted forward to the period of later ho-minids, *Homo erectus* (as seen, for example, in the work of Robin Fox [1980]).

But another challenge to the hunting hypothesis was formulated by a woman anthropologist, Sally Slocum (1975), who argued that this hypoth-esis was full of male bias and countered it with the "gathering hypothesis." According to the gathering hypothesis, the diet of hominid big-game hunters was probably similar to that of modern gatherer-hunters, and thus consisted primarily of plant foods gathered by women. Slocum further suggested that the earliest human tools were probably those invented to facilitate gathering, the carrying of children while gathering, and the transportation of gathered food. The gathering hypothesis was not only more in line with the ethno-graphic evidence, it showed that ignoring the activities of women could pro-duce distortions in the study of human evolution.

Looking at gender from another perspective, many women anthropolo-gists began to consider that women are virtually everywhere subordinate to men and to ask why this is so. A landmark book addressing this issue was Michelle Rosaldo and Louise Lamphere's *Woman, Culture and Society* (1974). A number of theories accounting for women's universal subordination (some of which are discussed later) were first presented in this book. Since that time many things have changed in the anthropology of gender. First, female sub-ordination is no longer assumed to be universal. Although some people argue that it is, many anthropologists feel that a focus on general female subordi-nation over-simplifies the issues. As discussed earlier, female subordination has been a difficult concept to apply cross-culturally since it is hard to define "female subordination" in a way that is free of cultural biases. Second, gen-der studies now include the study of men as well as of women, and male an-thropologists as well as female anthropologists are now conducting research on gender. Third, gender inequality is now approached through a broader framework that includes other kinds of social inequality, such as race and class (an issue we explore more fully in a later section of this introduction). Fourth, greater attention is now given to the particular historical contexts through which each society has constructed gender. Finally, more emphasis is now given to the diversity of ideas about and perspectives on gender with-in any society or within any group of people.

Today, theoretical approaches to gender in anthropology are diverse and debates continue to abound. Here we present a brief sketch of the main currents.

BIOLOGICAL APPROACHES

Within anthropology, most of the ideas linking gender with biology have to do with human evolution. Some major theoretical perspectives, for example those of evolutionary ecology and evolutionary psychology, draw from the idea that human males and females have evolved significantly different mating strategies. As with all animal species, according to this line of thinking, human males and females are (or were in our evolutionary past) biologically oriented to maximize their "fitness" or reproductive success. They adopt strategies, then, to maximize the transmission of their genetic material to subsequent generations. For this, the best male strategy is to impregnate as many females as possible. For females, by contrast, the best strategy is not to get pregnant and give birth as often as physically possible, as this would weaken the mother and endanger the survival changes of offspring, but rather to aim for fewer offspring who can then be cared for properly so they can survive and themselves reproduce. A woman does not need numerous men to maximize her fitness, but only one (or maybe a few) to impregnate her. Thus, compared to women, men are interested in sexual activity with a number of partners, or are inherently more promiscuous, since this will help to maximize their fitness. Women are more interested in securing just one or maybe a few good mates, especially ones who will be good providers and protectors. Thus males go for "mate quantity" whereas females go for "mate quality" (Smuts 1995, 5). Notice that this set of ideas retains the assumption of female dependency on males for resources and protection in human evolution, an assumption made in the hunting hypothesis. Some researchers, for example, assert that, in contrast to other primates, early human mothers were unable to provision their children alone given that human children require feeding and care for a much longer period of life. Hence evolving women needed to solicit the help of males (Lancaster and Lancaster 1987).

Complicating the picture further is the idea that women and men differ not only in mating strategies but also in how and how much they invest in (care and provide for) offspring in order to enhance the offspring's survival and eventual reproduction (and hence the parents' own fitness). Women always know who their offspring are, so for them parental investment is much simpler. Investing in her offspring will increase a woman's fitness, although she will have to adopt different strategies under certain circumstances. For example, if a woman is in a situation of poor resources and so cannot provide for all her children, she may need to favor those who are more likely to survive and neglect those who are less likely to survive. But for men, the investment in offspring is also contingent on "paternity certainty"—the extent to which a man can be reasonably certain that a particular child is biologically his own. The higher the paternity certainty, the greater the male parental investment. Further, paternity certainly will be higher where there are greater restrictions on female sexuality, or where female exhibitions of "chastity" are greatest. Thus some have argued that the many ideas and institutions found throughout the world to restrict female sexuality (chastity belts, female seclusion, the double sexual standard, and so on) developed to increase paternity certainty (Wilson and Daly 1992). In this line of argument, women themselves support the restrictions because they "know" that exhibiting chastity or offering a higher paternity certainty will increase the chances that men will provide for and protect them and their children.

Evolutionary psychologists hold that male and female mating and parental investment strategies evolved during what they call the "Environment of Evolutionary Adaptation," roughly the Paleolithic period in human prehistory. These evolved strategies, they contend, continue to shape human behavior, even though our current environment is now quite different. Thus David Buss (1994) claims that men everywhere are attracted to women who show signs of good fertility—namely those who look young and healthy. Women care less about looks and youth in a mate (less attractive, older men may still be good impregnators), but are rather attracted to men who exhibit wealth and power, since these men are likely to be good providers. In addition, Buss holds that men evolved greater sexual jealousy than women. A woman's fitness is not really threatened if her mate sleeps around with other women (so long as the other women do not draw away the man's valuable resources). But if a woman is unfaithful to a man, this directly threatens his fitness because it reduces his paternity certainty.

These approaches to gender from evolutionary biology are very controversial today. Many feminists contend that these biological approaches are merely an attempt to make male philandering and societal restrictions of female sexuality seem "natural" and so to perpetuate gender inequality (Tang-Martinez 1997). They reject theoretical approaches that imply that "biology is destiny" and that gender relationships and inequities cannot really be changed. On another level they criticize the assumption that women were dependent on men for resources in human evolution and seriously question the evidence for the idea that men naturally seek greater variety in sexual partners than do women (Mageo and Stone n.d.). On the other hand, a few of those who do take these biological approaches to gender claim they are themselves feminists. Some, such as evolutionary ecologist Barbara Smuts (1995), hold that these evolutionary approaches do not necessarily amount to biological determinism, and thus gender inequality is not inevitable and can be changed. Human evolution, in Smut's view, has only fostered certain tendencies that may or may not be expressed, depending on environmental circumstances. But as a result of all the controversies it is very difficult for researchers in cultural anthropology and biological anthropology to work together toward any kind of theory that incorporates both biological and cultural dimensions of gender.

SOCIALIZATION THEORY

Challenging biological explanations of gender patterns and difference have been other explanations that make use of the concept of socialization, or how we learn particular behaviors and attitudes as we grow from infants to adults. Gender patterns, sex roles, and differential evaluations of men and women are all learned, and societies differ in how they condition their male and female members to assume adult roles. The impact of giving Barbie dolls to girls and toy military weapons to boys is one simple example of how male and female children are socialized differently in the United States.

There are many different theoretical perspectives that draw from the concept of socialization. One particularly intriguing theory important in anthropology was put forth by Nancy Chodorow, a sociologist influenced by Freudian psychology. Chodorow (1978) noted that nearly everywhere it is women who are primarily involved in child care. Thus both male and female children are largely raised by mothers; but their experience of mothering is quite different because of their separate destinies as adult men and women. In her view both male and female children initially have a strong attachment to and identity with the mother. For female children this identity continues smoothly as they develop and grow; the little girl retains a sense of connection with others and is socialized to eventually become a mother herself. But male children must learn to distinguish themselves from the mother in order to develop a male identity. They must detach themselves from the mother, and in so doing they develop greater independence and self-reliance. As a result, males, according to Chodorow, universally tend to be more detached and autonomous whereas females feel a stronger connection to others. Further, Chodorow suggested that to help him break away from the mother, the child learns to devalue the feminine. In this respect, Chodorow's theory was one that aimed to account for the near universal devaluation of women.

MATERIALISM

Materialist approaches understand the cultural construction of gender as resulting from the material conditions of life. *Material conditions* refers to the physical resources available for survival, and the technological and economic arrangements by which these resources are distributed and used. In this view the position of men and women in any given society will depend to a large extent on the sexual division of labor, the relative contributions of men and women to subsistence, and the control that women and men have over the means and distribution of production. Cultural ideas about gender are the outcome of these economic arrangements, often generated and promoted by those who benefit from them in terms of power and wealth.

Materialist approaches to gender are, of course, rooted in the works of Karl Marx and Frederick Engels, social and economic theorists of the nineteenth century. Engels ([1884] 1942) postulated that human history showed a decline in the status of women. In early human society, he suggested, resources were communally owned and private property did not exist. Women and men both contributed to production for use, which created an economic basis for a state of gender equality. In this society women were also especially highly valued for their roles as mothers. Later, as population expanded and new technologies of food production developed, private property and, with it, wealth differences and socioeconomic classes emerged. This became male private property; regrettably, Engels did not speculate just how private property came to be in the hands of men rather than women, or both. In any case, these new developments led men into production for exchange, not just production for use. Women, however, were left back in the realm of production for use, which confined them to domestic tasks and child care. In the realm of production for exchange, men were competing for power and wealth, fostering economic and political inequality, and in the process establishing patriarchy or male dominance.

Marx ([1867] 1930) concentrated on a later stage of economic transformation—Western industrial capitalism. He showed how capitalism is inherently exploitative of the worker with his theory of labor value. In capitalism there are two important categories of people—those who own the means of production, the capitalists, and the workers (proletariat) who sell their labor for a wage. To survive in this system, the capitalist must make a profit. But there is one and only one way to do so, and that is to underpay the worker for his or her labor. For example, let's say that a capitalist produces a bushel of strawberries that sells on the market for $20.00. Let's say that for this bushel the capitalist pays out $5.00 to purchase a growing plot, seeds, etc. What, then, does he pay the workers he hires to actually grow the strawberries? To be fair, he should pay them $15.00 since in a free market that is the true value of their labor (the price of a commodity minus the capital needed to produce it). But if he did so, he would make no profit. Hence he underpays them, giving them $10.00 and making a profit of $5.00 for himself. In this way the worker is forever exploited and economic inequality is perpetuated.

Together with Engels, Marx also saw that the exploitation of the worker by the capitalist encompasses the subordination of women to men. In the upper or capitalist classes, women are (or were until recently) excluded from production, leaving them with little power. Their only important activity in the system is to produce heirs to men's property. In the working classes they either serve capitalists by providing unpaid domestic services for the workers and reproducing the working class itself; or, when needed, by selling their own labor even more cheaply than do men (Zaretsky 1973; Bonvilliam 1998).

While later scholars have not necessarily agreed with all that Mar____
Engels proposed, the ideas of these men produced a wealth of research on gender inequalities in relation to economic factors. Over the twentieth century,
researchers covered the globe asking whether indeed women's status is higher in those societies where their contribution to subsistence is substantial.
They compared gender under different modes of production, such as foraging, horticulture, agriculture, and industrial capitalism. In one recent review
of this literature, Frances Mascia-Lees and Nancy Johnson Black remark that
"while women's contribution to subsistence does not necessarily guarantee
high status, it seems to be a prerequisite for it" (2000, 60).

One anthropologist who advanced materialist approaches to gender in
anthropology was Eleanor Leacock. Leacock (1983) focused on gender in relation to class, political power, and changes in the mode of production. She
argued that Engels was essentially right, that gender equality obtained in
those societies where, prior to Western contact, men and women made equal
contributions to production. Gender relations are unequal in many of these
societies today but that, she argued, is the result of their subjugation under
Western colonialism.

STRUCTURALISM

Materialist approaches see cultural ideas as arising out of a material base,
often with these ideas fostered and manipulated by those in power as a means
to maintain the status quo. Thus, for example, a materialist approach inter-
prets the cultural idea that "a woman's place is in the home" as arising from
a particular economic arrangement that keeps women out of production and
serves as a justification for this arrangement. Male capitalists, as we have
seen, benefit from this arrangement and so promote the cultural idea that
legitimizes it. So-called structuralist approaches take a reverse stand and see
cultural ideas as entities in and of themselves that, however they came to be,
powerfully shape human behavior. People act according to their ideas about
the world. The word *structure* refers to the notion that cultural ideas are just
that—structured in a certain way, providing a framework for action and a
framework by which we can understand human action. The founder of struc-
turalism, French anthropologist Claude Lévi-Strauss, believed that the structure of human thought was based on an underlying structure to the human
brain itself—that the human brain thinks in terms of binary oppositions.

Lévi-Strauss (1969) himself came up with a very interesting theory that
by implication addresses the origin of gender inequality. He started with the
opposition between "nature" and "culture," an opposition he presumed to
be made in all cultures. In addition, whatever has to do with human culture
is universally considered to be on a higher plane than animal "nature." He
then proposed that to distinguish themselves from mere animal nature, early
humans invented a cultural rule, the incest taboo, which prohibited mating

between primary kin (mother-son, father-daughter, brother-sister). By doing this, humans forced themselves to look outside their own group for mates, setting up the potential to form intergroup alliances and cooperation. Men, then, exchanged women with one another. For example, males in two different groups could exchange their sisters. Like Engels in his discussion of the emergence of male private property, Lévi-Strauss did not spell out why men came to exchange women rather than women to exchange men. In any event, with the exchange of women, marriage (and not mere animalistic mating) was born, alliances between men were created, and, most important of all, women became items of exchange, mere pawns in a male political game where males controlled access to female sexuality and reproductive capacity. Thus, the origin of male dominance and gender inequality was part and parcel of the origin of human culture itself (Rubin 1975). Lévi-Strauss presented an abundance of ethnographic data on kinship and marriage in aboriginal societies to support his theory, but his ideas were still highly speculative. We have no idea how Paleolithic societies organized mating or how marriage or incest taboos actually arose. But we do know that in contemporary societies, political matchmaking is a game in which both women and men participate (Stone 2000).

The structuralist ideas of Lévi-Strauss influenced a later anthropological theorist, Sherry Ortner (1974). Ortner, too, used the opposition between nature and culture and, like Lévi-Strauss, she presumed the opposition to be cross-culturally universal. Emphasizing that in all societies the realm of culture is regarded as superior to that of nature, Ortner suggested that everywhere males are more closely associated with culture, whereas females are more closely associated with nature. Hence, women are universally devalued. Women are more closely associated with nature, she maintained, because of their roles as mothers and childrearers. Lacking these "natural" roles, men moved beyond into a higher sphere of creativity—into politics, art, and public ritual, leaving women stuck back in mere nature.

This provocative idea was later criticized for its presumptions of the universality of female subordination and the universality of a nature/culture opposition (McCormack and Strathern 1980). Ortner (1996) later retreated from the position that male dominance is universal, although she upheld the nature/culture opposition in the sense that all cultures must in some way come to terms with the restrictions that nature imposes.

Another anthropologist who developed a structuralist approach to gender was Michelle Rosaldo (1974). Rosaldo focused on the opposition between the public and private (or domestic) spheres of life and used this opposition to account for what she saw as the universal subordination of women to men in all cultures. She held that women are everywhere subordinate because, given their childbearing roles, women are associated with the domestic sphere of housework and child care. This sphere, she argued, is universally valued less than the public world dominated by men—the world of politics, leadership, and extradomestic economic activity. Thus as every culture devalues the domestic sphere, it devalues the women within it.

Rosaldo's work was criticized from many angles. Some critics argued, for example, that in some societies women do play prominent public roles; others insisted that the domestic world of women is not so strongly devalued in all societies; still others pointed out that not all societies make a sharp division between public and private spheres of life in the first place (Lamphere 1993). Rosaldo (1980) agreed with much of this criticism but maintained that although the public/male, domestic/female dichotomy is not universal, it is relevant to the construction of gender and to female subordination in the Western world. As we will see, this dichotomy is an important theme in the cultural history of gender in America.

PRACTICE, PROCESS, AGENCY

In her later (1984) work, Sherry Ortner moved to a *practice theory* approach, which stresses that social systems and human agency are in dynamic interaction, such that social systems are as much constructed and changed by human action as they, in turn, shape it. This approach has been quite popular in contemporary anthropology. Without labeling it as *practice theory*, our discussion of the concepts of gender and culture earlier in this chapter incorporated this perspective. A practice theory approach has also supported the view of gender as a social process. In this view gender is seen less as a static cultural construction that shapes our thoughts and behavior and more as something we all continually construct, often in different ways, as we go about our daily lives. Gender, then, is to a certain extent negotiated in specific, everyday social settings (Lamphere, Ragoné, and Zavella 1997). For example, as we will see later in this book, some immigrant women to the United States have been able to negotiate greater autonomy in their gender roles within their everyday marriage and family lives as they found paid employment outside the home.

NEW APPROACHES, NEW CONCERNS

In the closing decades of the twentieth century, theory in the social sciences was greatly influenced by some broader intellectual currents, sometimes collectively referred to as *postmodernism*. In the social sciences, postmodernism challenges the presumptions of objectivity, rationalism, claims to "truth," and valid representation that governed "modern" social science from roughly 1920 to 1975 (McGee and Warms 2000). Postmodern currents led to a "crisis of representation" in anthropology. On what basis, or by what authority, can an anthropologist claim that his or her written descriptions of another people validly represent them? By extension, how can anyone claim to truly represent the sociocultural realities of others, whether these others are headhunters of New Guinea or the neighbors next door? This concern led to a "reflexive" approach in anthropology. The idea is that without continual and vigilant self-reflection and self-criticism, anthropological analysis is loaded with personal, cultural, and professional biases. Perhaps these biases are ultimately inescapable but at least they might be reduced or put in perspective with continual reflexive thinking.

Another postmodern trend that influenced anthropology theory followed upon the work of the French philosopher, Michel Foucault. Foucault (1980) was concerned with power relationships and wrote about how those in power construct a "discourse" through which they seek to maintain power. For example, he wrote about how medical science constructed a "discourse of homosexuality" through which "the homosexual" became a new, distinct social category and through which homosexuality was formulated as "abnormal." In Foucault's view, all knowledge(s) can be seen as "discourses of power." From his work, a concern with power struggles behind the construction of knowledge has penetrated far into gender studies.

If some of these postmodern currents are taken to an extreme, they result in the position that an anthropology of gender (or any other topic for that matter) is impossible. In less extreme form they result in a more cautious, self-critical, and modest anthropology of gender that still seeks to study gender across ethnic groups, cultures and nations, but is aware of the limitations of doing so and grants that claims of total objectivity are not valid. At the same time, postmodernism has not entirely derailed other theoretical perspectives. So far, the impact of postmodernism has been more reformative than destructive. Biological, materialist, and structuralist approaches to gender continue, and many scholars reject postmodernism (e.g., D'Andrade 1995).

Yet, in the wake of postmodern critiques, rather than attempting grand comparisons or applying conceptual abstractions, today's gender studies are more focused on the historical particularities of each group, the diversity of perspectives (sometimes called "voices") within any group, and the construction, reconstruction, and negotiation of gender through everyday practice (Lamphere, Ragoné, and Zavella 1997). Another trend is a movement away from work that is strictly within one theoretical perspective and "toward studies that combine the strengths of particular theoretical orientations while eschewing some of their weaker points" (Mascia-Lees and Black 2000, 105). In this book, although we may favor materialist perspectives in some sections, and although we do not make use of biological approaches, we include contributions from a variety of theoretical perspectives to promote an understanding of gender in America.

AMERICAN GENDER IN THE WHITE MIDDLE CLASS

History helps us to see a certain arbitrariness in contemporary American ideas about gender, which we otherwise too easily regard as simply "natural." For example, from American history we find that when colors were first associated with male and female children, the popular preference was pink for boys and blue for girls (Kimmel 1996). This book opens in the next two chapters with a cultural history of American gender, covering the culturally dominant white middle class. Chapters 4 and 5 focus on other ethnic groups and also maintain historical referents.

In the next two chapters, we organize our discussion of gender around a set of common cultural themes that have been and continue to be important in middle-class American life. One of these, perhaps the most important, is American individualism, introduced in Chapter 2. Individualism, strongly valued in America and promulgated especially by the dominant white middle class, has permeated all aspects of American life and thought. We discuss how the pervasive value of individualism has affected gender relationships in the white middle class and, in later chapters, how other ethnic groups have reacted to it. A second theme we cover in Chapters 2 and 3 is religion. Here we discuss gender in relation to elements of America's Christian heritage, the rise of particular Protestant movements, and, in more recent times, the rise of a variety of religious cult movements.

Another theme in Chapters 1 and 2 has to do with the physical body, with our images of ideal female and male body types and our cultural notions of male and female bodily processes. Like religion, ideas about the physical body express ideas about gender in all cultures. Perhaps the association is particularly close in middle-class America, where concern with the physical body (as seen today in eating disorders, idealization of female thinness, male muscularity, and a near obsession with diet and physical fitness for everyone) has long been pronounced. As we have seen, Miner (1956) documented this cultural concern among the Nacirema more than forty years ago. Even then, as he put it, there were special women's rituals to make small breasts larger and large breasts smaller.

GENDER, ETHNICITY, AND CLASS: VARIATIONS, COLLISIONS, AND COLLUSIONS

This book follows a current concern that in most societies gender cannot be understood in isolation from other forms of social inequality. In the United States, the 1960s women's "liberation" movement was largely inspired and led by white, middle-class women. Many of them assumed that women of other classes and ethnic groups would join in the struggle, since they saw it as a struggle for all women as women. But largely, other groups did not join. Many black women, for example, felt that they experienced more oppression as members of an ethnic minority than as women in a male-dominated society. While certainly aware of sexism and male dominance, they expressed greater allegiance to all persons within their ethnic group than to women outside it. Similarly, many working-class women, who had from necessity worked outside the home all their lives, were alienated from the movement when they heard middle-class women root their oppression in the doldrums of full-time housework. When women of these other ethnic and class groups responded this way, it forced everyone to recognize a salient fact of American life, namely that there are several dimensions of social inequality—gender, ethnicity, class, and age, to name the ones currently most discussed—and that a person's experiences and interests will vary according to her identity along not just one dimension but several.

With this, a new question was raised: How are the different dimensions of social inequality interrelated? In what ways do they intersect? And how can we understand gender within this broader social mosaic? Innumerable studies are now focused on this problem, and theorists are struggling to develop models that will encompass different dimensions of social inequality. Among the many different approaches to this problem currently being discussed and debated, we will draw attention to two primary ways in which social scientists are now seeing the intersection of gender, ethnicity, and class. One of these we call the *collision* model; the other is a model of *collusion*. In the collision model, different social hierarchies are seen to "bump into" each other in a number of contexts, usually reinforcing one another when they do. A good example concerns the collision of ethnic and gender divisions in the workplace following the Civil War. At this time, freed black males sought new jobs. They were barred from many kinds of jobs simply because they were black (based on a policy of racial discrimination), but in addition they were denied access to jobs that would place them close together with white women (Spain 1992), women who were themselves already segregated into lower paying, less prestigious positions.

Instances of this kind of collision of social hierarchies are informative, but many people have felt that the intersection of inequalities based on ethnicity, class, and gender goes deeper. Some of these researchers have developed a collusion model that imputes a more intimate interlocking between hierarchies of social inequality. Some researchers have based the connection on economic organization. Adopting Marxist approaches, they asserted that capitalism generates and links both class and gender inequality (Hartmann 1976). In this view, the capitalist class exploits the male worker, but the same system exploits women who serve capitalism by maintaining the male workers through unpaid domestic labor, reproducing the working class for capitalism's next generation and, when needed, supplying a source of labor even cheaper than that provided by male workers. Thus the oppression of women is the other side of the coin of class oppression.

Other researchers follow a collusion model that specifies that hierarchies of gender, ethnicity, and class are mutually constructed within the development of a larger cultural worldview. For example, as we cover in greater detail in Chapter 2, a dominant American ideology of colonialism in the nineteenth century invoked and linked ethnicity, gender, and class in one

sweeping cultural construction of America's role in the ʻ
lization (Bederman 1995).

Chapters 4 and 5 explore gender among ethnic minc
mensions. First, how does gender operate in traditional ʂ
where minorities are (or were) the majority? Second, wʰ__ ____ₚ__ ___
majority Euro-American society had on traditional gender roles and institutions, and how have ethnic minorities responded through time in forging
an accommodation to mainstream demands of individualism and assimilation? Third, what is the current state of affairs? How does contemporary
gender among ethnic minorities reflect traditional roles and values; how is
it the result of historical struggles; and how are the inequities of contemporary social and economic life affecting the lives, loyalties, and choices of
today's ethnic minorities?

GENDER AND THE COLLEGE EXPERIENCE

How does what we learn about gender from the social sciences apply to the
world of the college student? More specifically, how do American cultural
constructions of gender operate in the student subculture? Chapter 6 covers
this topic. Much of what we present here is the result of our own three-year
study of students' ideas about gender and their own futures, at our university and on a few other campuses around the country. Here we discuss the different choices men and women college students are making (about their
majors, careers, marriage, and children) and what these choices mean for
gender equality, or inequality, in the years ahead. The discussion leads into
the ways in which students are constructing their own ideas about sexual
differences, love and romance, marriage and divorce, the family, motherhood, fatherhood, and a particular problem nearly all students will soon
face—the balancing of career and family.

DISCUSSION QUESTIONS

1. Many anthropologists have told students about the Nacirema (always
   hoping to snare as many as possible into believing that this group is an
   "exotic" population in a land far, far away). Aside from the fun of dis-
   covering that the Nacirema are actually Americans, what is the value of
   Miner's presentation of the familiar in such a clinical or "objective" way?
   Do you think that taking this kind of approach with one's own population can help in developing new insights? Why? How?

2. The terms *sex* and *gender* seem fairly easy to define. Give it a try yourself: Define both terms in your own words. Now that you have these two
   definitions, consider why the two terms exist. That is, try to come up
   with a situation or issue in which it is useful, interesting, or productive

to discuss *both* sex *and* gender. Many Americans tend to feel that sex and gender are isomorphic (identical in form). Do you feel this way? After reading this chapter do you still think it is true? If it were true, what do you think would be the point of two words for the same phenomenon? We will revisit this issue when we discuss alternative gender identities in middle-class white America in Chapter 3 and alternative constructions of gender among Indian peoples in Chapter 4.

3. Many American women (including many of our students) frequently say something like, "I'm not a feminist, but of course I believe in equal rights for men and women, and equal pay for equal work." According to the definition of feminism we provide in this book, would the speakers cited above be feminists? Why or why not? Why do you think so many American women are so eager to distance themselves from feminism? Do you think that the acceptance of notions like equal pay for equal work would have developed without feminism? What about men? Can they be feminists? Explain your answer.

4. Students sometimes complain that discussions of theory are irrelevant and boring because they do not deal with anything "real." Besides, they say, theories are always changing, so what is the point of discussing them? At first this seems like a plausible objection. But when we consider the enormous impact of theory on the way we think, we realize that the practical reverberations of theory are very real indeed. Galileo was nearly burnt at the stake because his view that the earth revolved around the sun did not accord with the official Christian scientific theory of his day. And graveyards are full of people who died prematurely because the germ theory of disease had not yet been developed.

One of the most productive ways to examine competing theories is to use two or more different theories to account for a particular phenomenon, and to pit one of them against another in an attempt to determine which theory provides the most useful or plausible account of the data. Give this a try. Consider the development of the second wave of feminism in the late 1960s and 1970s (the first wave occurred in the late nineteenth and early twentieth centuries). Now select two different theoretical perspectives on gender described in this chapter and use each one to account for why feminism developed as and when it did. Then pit each perspective against the other, in an attempt to see which one you think provides the best explanation. Why do you prefer one perspective over the other? Be prepared to use this system to explore other important gender issues raised throughout the book.

REFERENCES

Ackerman, Lillian. 1982. Sexual Equality in the Plateau Culture Area. Ph.D. dissertation, Washington State University, Pullman, Washington.

Bederman, Gail. 1995. *Manliness & Civilization: A Cultural History of Gender and Race in the United States, 1880–1917.* Chicago, IL: University of Chicago Press.

Bonvillain, Nancy. 1998. *Women and Men: Cultural Constructions of Gender*. 2nd ed. Upper Saddle River, NJ: Prentice Hall.

Brain, C. K. 1981. *The Hunters or the Hunted? An Introduction to African Cave Taphonomy*. Chicago, IL: University of Chicago Press.

Buss, David M. 1994. *The Evolution of Desire: Strategies of Human Mating*. New York: Basic Books.

Chodorow, Nancy. 1978. *The Reproduction of Mothering: Psychoanalysis and the Sociology of Gender*. Berkeley, CA: University of California Press.

D'Andrade, Roy. 1995. "Moral Models in Anthropology." *Current Anthropology* 36(3): 399–408.

Engels, Frederick. [1884] 1942. *The Origin of the Family, Private Property and the State*. New York: International Publishers.

Foucault, Michel. 1980. *The History of Sexuality, Volume I: An Introduction*. Trans. Robert Hurley. New York: Vintage.

Fox, Robin. 1980. *The Red Lamp of Incest*. New York: E. P. Dutton.

Harris, Marvin. 1988. *Culture, People, Nature: An Introduction to General Anthropology*. New York: Harper & Row.

Hartmann, Heidi. 1976. "Capitalism, Patriarchy, and Job Segregation by Sex." Pp. 137–170 in *Women and the Workplace: The Implications of Occupational Segregation*, ed. Martha Blaxall and Barbara B. Regan. Chicago, IL: University of Chicago Press.

Kimmel, Michael S. 1996. *Manhood in America: A Cultural History*. New York: Free Press.

Laderman, Carol. 1991. *Taming the Wind of Desire: Psychology, Medicine, and Aesthetics in Malay Shamanistic Performance*. Berkeley, CA: University of California Press.

Lamphere, Louise. 1993. "The Domestic Sphere of Women and the Public Sphere of Men: The Strengths and Limitations of an Anthropological Dichotomy." Pp. 67–77 in *Gender in Cross-Cultural Perspective*, ed. Caroline B. Brettell and Carolyn F. Sargent. Englewood Cliffs, NJ: Prentice Hall.

Lamphere, Louise, Helena Ragoné, and Patricia Zavella. 1997. "Introduction." Pp. 1–19 in *Situated Lives: Gender and Culture in Everyday Life*, ed. Louise Lamphere, Helen Ragoné and Patricia Zavella. New York: Routledge.

Lancaster, Jane B., and Chet S. Lancaster. 1987. "The Watershed: Change in Parental-Investment and Family-Formation Strategies in the Course of Human Evolution." In *Parenting across the Life Span: Biological Dimensions*, ed. Jane B. Lancaster, Jeanne Altmann, Alice S. Rossi, and Lonnie R. Sherrod. New York: Aldine de Gruyter.

Laqueur, Thomas. 1990. *Making Sex: Body and Gender from the Greeks to Freud*. Cambridge, MA: Harvard University Press.

Leacock, Eleanor. 1983. "Interpreting the Origin of Gender Inequality: Conceptual and Historical Problems." *Dialectical Anthropology* 7(4): 263–284.

Lepowsky, Maria. 1993. *Fruit of the Motherland: Gender in an Egalitarian Society*. New York: Columbia University Press.

Lévi-Strauss, Claude. [1949] 1969. *The Elementary Structures of Kinship*. Trans. James Harle Bell, John Richard von Strarmer, and Rodney Needham. Boston, MA: Beacon Press.

Mageo, Jeannette Marie, and Linda Stone. n.d. "The Trope of Orgasm in Science and Social Science." Unpublished ms.

Marx, Karl. [1867] 1930. *Capital: A Critique of Political Economy*. 4th ed. Trans. Paul Eden and Paul Ceder. New York: E. P. Hutton.

Mascia-Lees, Frances E., and Nancy Johnson Black. 2000. *Gender and Anthropology.* Prospect Heights, IL: Waveland Press.

McCormack, Carol, and Marilyn Strathern, eds. 1980. *Nature, Culture and Gender.* Cambridge, MA: Cambridge University Press.

McGee, R. Jon, and Richard L. Warms. 2000. *Anthropological Theory: An Introductory History.* 2nd ed. Mountain View, CA: Mayfield Publishing.

Miner, Horace. 1956. "Body Ritual among the Nacerima." *American Anthropologist* 58(3): 503–507.

Ortner, Sherry B. 1974. "Is Female to Male as Nature Is to Culture?" Pp. 67–87 in *Woman, Culture and Society*, ed. Michelle Zimbalist Rosaldo and Louise Lamphere. Stanford, CA: Stanford University Press.

Ortner, Sherry B. 1984. "Theory in Anthropology since the Sixties." *Society for Comparative Studies in Society and History* 26(1): 126–165.

Ortner, Sherry B. 1996. "So, Is Female to Male as Nature is to Culture?" Pp. 173–180 in *Making Gender: The Politics and Erotics of Culture*, ed. Sherry B. Ortner. Boston, MA: Beacon Press.

Rosaldo, Michelle Zimbalist. 1974. "Woman, Culture and Society: A Theoretical Overview." Pp. 17–42 in *Woman, Culture and Society*, ed. Michelle Zimbalist Rosaldo and Louise Lamphere. Stanford, CA: Stanford University Press.

Rosaldo, Michelle Zimbalist, and Louise Lamphere, eds. 1974. *Woman, Culture and Society.* Stanford, CA: Stanford University Press.

Rosaldo, Michelle Zimbalist. 1980. "The Use and Abuse of Anthropology: Reflections of Feminism and Cross-Cultural Understanding." *Signs: Journal of Women in Culture and Society* 5(3): 389–417.

Rubin, Gayle. 1975. "Traffic in Women: Notes on the 'Political Economy' of Sex." Pp. 157–210 in *Toward an Anthropology of Women*, ed. Rayna Reiter. New York: Monthly Review Press.

Shostak, Marjorie. 1981. *Nisa: The Life and Words of a !Kung Woman.* New York: Random House.

Slocum, Sally. 1975. "Woman the Gatherer: Male Bias in Anthropology." Pp. 36–50 in *Toward an Anthropology of Women*, ed. Rayna Reiter. New York: Monthly Review Press.

Spain, Daphne. 1992. *Gendered Spaces.* Chapel Hill, NC: The University of North Carolina Press.

Smuts, Barbara B. 1995. "The Evolutionary Origins of Patriarchy." *Human Nature* 6(1): 1–32.

Stone, Linda. 2000. *Kinship and Gender: An Introduction.* 2nd ed. Boulder, CO: Westview Press.

Tang-Martinez, Zuleyma. 1997. "The Curious Courtship of Sociobiology and Feminism: A Case of Irreconcilable Differences." Pp. 116–150 in *Feminism and Evolutionary Biology: Boundaries, Intersections and Frontiers*, ed. Patricia Adair Gotway. New York: Chapman and Hall.

Washburn, Sherwood L., and C. Lancaster. 1968. "The Evolution of Hunting." Pp. 293–303 in *Man the Hunter*, ed. Richard B. Lee. Chicago, IL: Aldine.

Wilson, Margo, and Martin Daly. 1992. "The Man Who Mistook His Wife for a Chattell." Pp. 289–326 in *The Adapted Mind: Evolutionary Psychology and the Evolution of Culture*, ed. Jerome H. Barkow, Leda Cosmides, and John Toby. New York: Oxford University Press.

Yanagisako, Sylvia J., and Jane F. Collier. 1990. "The Mode of Reproduction in Anthropology." Pp. 131–141 in *Theoretical Perspectives on Sexual Difference*, ed. Deborah L. Rhode. New Haven, CT: Yale University Press.

Zaretsky, Eli. 1973. "Capitalism, the Family, and Personal Life." *Socialist Revolution* 13–14:69–125.

CHAPTER 2

A CULTURAL HISTORY
OF AMERICAN GENDER:
1600–1900

"I, personally, had imagined, from all reports, that the women of this country would astound me by their independence: American women seemed synonymous with free women." Thus wrote Simone de Beauvoir (1953, 287), French scholar and among the best-known writers on the topic of gender, on her visit to America in the late 1940s. But then she reported what she actually saw: "Their dress amazed me with its violently feminine, almost sexual character. I read in American women's magazines long articles on the art of fishing and hunting for husbands and on the art of snaring men. I saw that college girls cared only about men...." What is interesting here is the discrepancy between de Beauvoir's expectations and what she saw. Why had she expected American women to astound her with their independence, and why hadn't they? This chapter and the next will offer a number of suggestions about how gender in America has taken the peculiar turns that it has and how it has developed the particular contradictions that so impressed de Beauvoir and others.

These two chapters trace the cultural history of American gender with a focus on the white middle class. The white middle class is singled out in this historical treatment because this class has been culturally dominant. Possibly this has been more true in America than elsewhere; author Henry James once claimed that America is the most middle-class culture in the world. White middle-class values and ways of life have dominated the media and American popular culture; other groups, whether emulating the middle class or contesting its privilege, have had to contend with its cultural power, with its vision not only of what it means to be an American, but also what it means to be a man or a woman. Here we will take a close look at how white, middle-class Americans came to define, and themselves dispute, gender before the twentieth century.

In this chapter the term *middle class* is intentionally used rather loosely. Probably only the very rich and the very poor would be excluded from our descriptions of middle-class ways of life. No boundaries drawn by economic indicators or occupation are implied in our use of the term. Rather, we use "middle class" as a cultural category to include all those who see (or saw) themselves as middle class, who feel that they participate in the construction of middle-class values and ways of life.

The historical treatment of gender in this and the subsequent chapter revolves around a number of American cultural themes. There are three particularly important themes that crop up again and again in our discussion. One concerns relationships between religion and gender. We show how religion in certain cases both shaped ideas about gender and became an arena in which some of these ideas were challenged. Another theme concerns images of the body, or how middle-class Americans have expressed gender patterns in their ideas about ideal male and female bodies and in ideas about physical health and illness. A third theme, perhaps the most important one of all, is American individualism.

What we mean by religion and ideas about the body is no doubt already self-evident, but a few more words need to be said about American individualism. Individualism has been cited by many as a core American value or the centerpiece of an American worldview, but what exactly does individualism mean? There are many legitimate meanings of the term, but here we are referring to something fairly specific. First, to clarify what we do not mean, *individualistic* as used here does not mean "selfish," "egotistical," or "nonconformist." Although some Americans certainly could be described with these terms, they hardly characterize the American middle class, much less express middle-class American values. Terms like "independent," "autonomous," and "self-reliant" come much closer. But we can go beyond these and move to the heart of the issue by drawing from the work of French anthropologist, Louis Dumont (1970, 4), who articulated the meaning of individualism in the Western cultural tradition. To him, Western individualism is a view that

> humanity is made up of men [today we would say persons], and each man is conceived as presenting, in spite of and over and above his particularity, the essence of humanity.... This individual is quasi-sacred, absolute; there is nothing over and above his legitimate demands; his rights are limited only by the identical rights of other individuals.

In Western culture the "essence of humanity" is contained within each person. The individual is complete unto him or herself. In some other cultural traditions, by contrast, the "essence of humanity" is located not in an individual person but in the relationships between persons or in the way that persons are integrated to form larger social wholes. The lone individual is incomplete. Dumont saw that all societies contain individuals, of course, but not all societies value the individual. In some non-Western cultures the value is placed on the larger social whole—that is, the marriage, the family, the community, the tribe or ethnic group—of which individuals are a part. These societies can be called *holistic*, rather than *individualistic*.

Dumont also saw that individualism is connected to another Western value: equality. Western culture came to incorporate the principle that all individuals are equal. This value is expressed, for example, in the French Rights of Man and in the American Declaration of Independence (although gender, class, and race inequalities continued despite these historic documents). By contrast, holistic societies are hierarchical; people have hierarchical relationships with one another so that, in various contexts, some are subordinate to others. Thus we can see Western culture as expressing an "egalitarian individualism" in contrast to a "holistic hierarchy" found elsewhere.

Individualism has deep roots in the European tradition, roots that stem from Christianity and through the development of certain political and economic philosophies, all of which spread to America. What, then, is distinctive about American individualism? A few things come to mind. First, compared with Europe, Americans are often seen as more individualistic in the sense of being more autonomous and striving for greater self-reliance. Thus Americans are more likely to tackle problems through individual rather than collective action.[1] Second, in our view, individualism is expressed slightly differently in America than in Europe. Europe has stayed with an older tradition, also present in America, in which individualism is expressed in philosophical or intellectual terms—for example, literature and art depict a lone individual confronting his or her own conscience, God, or the meaning of existence. In America, in addition to this tradition, individualism came also to be expressed as a striving for success in the world or achievement in the public sphere. In American popular literature the true individualist is often a self-made economic giant or someone who achieves an extraordinary publicly acclaimed feat. Finally, America has in more recent times developed a new expression of individualism, not seen in Europe: individualism as "free choice." We will return to this facet of American individualism in Chapter 3.

The reader may be wondering, rightfully, what any of this has to do with gender. We suggest that while individualism is a cardinal American value, men and women historically came to assume very different positions with respect to it. These differences were related to specific ways of defining manhood and womanhood and to dynamic tensions between the genders that have been and continue to be unique to American culture. To return to Simone de Beauvoir's observation in the late 1940s, it may be that she had assumed that what she had heard about the American spirit of independence would apply to both women and men equally. But let's start at the beginning, in the seventeenth century, at a time when American individualism was barely born and hardly at the forefront of cultural values.

The Colonial Era

The British and other Europeans who migrated to America in the seventeenth century were a motley crew of religious dissidents, profit seekers, adventurers, indentured laborers, and convicts. Although people crossing the Atlantic had a variety of motives, most came largely for economic gain or to practice and promote their religion, or both. Some succeeded and some failed but all left their mark: Despite four hundred years of vast social, political, and economic changes, making money and religious proselytization have remained prominent themes in American life to the present time.

Those who came for profit went mostly to the South, where the first English settlement was established in 1607. The South soon developed a plantation economy based on tobacco and, later, on cotton. Compared with northern migrants, many who went to the South arrived as single individuals and from a wide variety of social classes—from the upper classes to a sizable number of indentured laborers who bound themselves to another for a few years of service in exchange for payment of their passage to the New World. Northern migrants more often came in family groups and in religious communities, the most prominent being the Puritans who settled in New England. Puritans, so called because they had sought to purify the Church of England of its Catholic remnants, had faced persecution and even execution in England. Those who fled to the New World were primarily middle-class farmers and artisans.

European settlers to North America brought with them a whole host of ideas and practices that were to influence their gender systems for decades, even centuries, to come. Among the most salient of their European traditions were identification with state governments and interests in private property (Coontz 1988), socioeconomic inequality, and Protestant Christianity. In addition, the European settlers brought with them one very important idea, that women are subordinate to men, which we will explore in some depth here.

THE PURITANS

For many early colonists in the New World, gender was intimately bound up with their religion, both in terms of religious beliefs and in terms of the particular social structures that these beliefs encouraged. This was especially true of one group for whom religion was extremely important, the New England Puritans. The Puritans sought to establish morally regulated communities that, in their view, would be manifestations of the will of God and models of godliness for the rest of the world eventually to follow. These people espoused the Calvinist doctrine of predestination, according to which a person's fate in the afterlife, whether salvation or eternal damnation, has already been determined by God. No amount of prayer or good works could alter one's fate.

One should nevertheless lead an ordered moral existence and seek to experience God's grace in this life. The experience of grace, along with other worldly signs such as material prosperity and achievement of high social status, gave one assurance of God's favor and, hence, salvation. Only those who had personally experienced grace and who could give evidence of it in some way could be true members of Puritan churches. These favored Puritans, male and female, were called "saints." It was largely saints who were the first settlers in New England. In each new settlement they drew up a "covenant" binding all residents together in religious and social unity. In these settlements church attendance was mandatory for all, but only saints could take communion and only male saints could vote in church affairs. Although both males and females could be saints, public authority in these communities, vested in a body of elected village and church officials, was strictly a male affair.

Women and men were spiritually equal, or equal in the eyes of God, and yet in religious contexts the Puritans expressed some ambivalence toward women. On the one hand, Puritan leaders rejected an association of woman with the sinful Eve. One minister in New Hampshire, John Cotton,[2] told an audience in 1694 that women were not a "necessary evil" but a "necessary good." They were needed by men and good for men as "helpmeets." Yet the specter of Eve and her role in the fall of humans from God's grace were in the background of Puritan consciousness, so there was some "suspicion of women" (Demos 1987, 9). In addition, the Puritans took quite literally St. Paul's injunction to "Let your women keep silence in the Churches; for it is not permitted unto them to speak" (1 Corinthians 14:34–35). And most people took for granted that women's minds and bodies were weaker than men's. Yet for all this, the bottom line was clear: "New England preachers knew that woman's soul—that part of her which God alone saw—was the equal of any man's" (Kamensky 1995, 83). Evidently women felt so too since, as we will see, it was primarily through religion that women on occasion asserted themselves in ways normally only approved for men.

Socially, however, there was no question but that women were subordinate to men, and this can be seen by situating Puritan gender within its religiously inspired social structure. Colonists lived in households consisting not only of nuclear families of parents with children but also of servants and apprentices. Apprentices were children or youths sent out to live for a time with another family to learn housework or a trade, a practice also common in Europe in this period. It was this household, and not the nuclear family, that was the fundamental economic and social unit in these communities (Coontz 1988). These households were thoroughly interdependent with one another in a daily sharing of work, trade, and neighborly exchange of goods and services. Men carried out a more formal trade in items like grain; but the informal sharing of work and the trade in items like milk and cheese that took place between households day to day was in the hands of women.

"Borrowing tools and commodities, working in other women's kitchens and yards, exchanging products and children, early American housewives were bound to each other through the most intimate needs of every day" (Ulrich 1980, 398).

Over each household presided a male head who owned the house and land and held undisputed authority over all its dependents, his wife and children, servants and apprentices. This strong, rightful authority of male heads of households was expressed in many ways and through many symbols. One symbol was a rather ordinary material artifact, the chair. In early colonial America, as in England, there were few wooden, straight-backed chairs, but in households that had them they were thrones of male heads, even though the cushions, benches, or stools on which others sat were probably more comfortable (Deetz 1996).

That wives were subject to the rule of their husbands was a paramount fact of colonial life. People heard of the duty of wifely submission from the pulpit and taught it to their children. In the colonial view, a wife's subordination was first and foremost seen as a practical necessity, a way to bring about order, for social order was what these pioneers sought desperately to establish in their New World of wilderness, hardship, and Protestant values. As historian Stephanie Coontz (1988, 98) writes, "The subordination of women and the dominance of men were based less on ideas about gender than on ideas about the need for hierarchy in all relations."

Female subordination also expressed a worldview of male encompassing female. Many references are made in the period to women as "Adam's rib" (Ryan 1975). The Puritan minister Cotton Mather expressed the ideal husband–wife relationship as being "One Mind in Two Bodies" (cited in Ryan 1975, 54), and we can be sure that Mather meant the husband's mind to rule the two bodies. That husbands encompassed wives was also reflected in the fact that, legally speaking, a woman at marriage ceased to exist, becoming subsumed within her husband's legal status. Without her husband's permission, she could not own property, sign a contract, or write a will (Salmon 1979). With time, however, American courts came to grant women greater legal autonomy (Friedman, Shade, and Capozzoli 1987). Colonial women could acquire property through inheritance. A woman was also entitled to one-third of her husband's estate at his death; however, if the husband had heirs she only held the property in trust for them.

Inside the household, male heads ruled over all persons, but wives of heads governed children and servants. The household was a social hierarchy, and outside the household males and females were involved in equally hierarchical relationships with one another. Older and wealthier male household heads assumed upper ranks within a hierarchy of church and village officials. A woman's status was set by that of her father or husband. There was not really a class system in this period but rather a fluid gradation of ranks based on age, wealth, social position, and gender. In virtually any social context, people knew who was "higher" and "lower" than whom and behaved accordingly, with appropriate displays of deference or authority. As within the household, this wider social hierarchy was seen as both natural and necessary to the achievement of an ordered community (Coontz 1988).

Female subordination was thus one aspect of a much larger social order and cultural ideology. This situation brings up a theme we will encounter again: In America, as in all societies, concepts of gender never exist in isolation. They are a part of broader definitions of social relationships that tie individuals to groups and groups to one another. Among the Puritans, this connection is particularly clear. Colonists expressed the idea that the household was a microcosm of the larger community: As each house should submit to the authority of the community, so should household members submit to the authority of the male head. On a higher level, all of this ordered submission was the will of God. Not only this, but the authority of male household heads was directly supported by the broader community authority. If a male household head failed to keep his house in order and his dependents obedient, community officials freely intervened to force their submission. Male household heads could themselves be punished for failing to exercise their domestic authority or for abusing their power (Coontz 1988). In New England, this external monitoring and regulation of the internal affairs of households was the job of special public officers called tithingmen.

In the popular imagination Puritans are often thought to have had peculiarly repressive ideas about sex. But the idea that these people were "puritanical" about sex is one of many myths about American colonial life, another being that Puritans wore drab clothing (Deetz 1969). It is true that in Puritan communities dancing, immodest or extravagant clothing, and clandestine meetings between unmarried men and women were forbidden. It is true that adulterous women and men could be executed and that a few were. More often, and especially after 1650, less drastic but no doubt grossly humiliating forms of punishment were meted out, such as flogging, dunking, or branding of foreheads with the letters "AD." But it was not sex that was the problem; it was merely sex outside marriage (Hunt 1994). Within marriage sex was considered perfectly appropriate, indeed praiseworthy. To be sure, one was to be sexually moderate even within marriage, with the idea that sex should be geared toward reproduction. Still, the notion that sex would bring closeness between husband and wife and pleasure to both was acknowledged (D'Emilio and Freedman 1988). In fact there was a widespread idea that a woman had to have an orgasm in order to conceive. Courts upheld women's rights to marital sex as much as men's; a woman could, for example, divorce her husband for impotence (Demos 1987). In Boston, one man, James Mattock, was expelled from his church for his refusal to have sexual relations with his wife (he claimed he was abstaining from sex as punishment for his sins [Hunt 1994, 234]).

If anything, the Puritans were rather frank and open about sex. The facts of sex were not hidden from children. Indeed, children regularly saw and heard sex between adults, as they slept in the same rooms and even beds of parents (D'Emilio and Freedman 1988). The many restrictions on sex or circumstances promoting sexual temptations outside marriage were publicly discussed; violators of the rules were publicly punished. Court records reveal neighbors happening upon cases of adultery taking place in houses and barns, interrupting the couples in the act, and calmly testifying in court about what they had observed in some detail (Cott 1976). Using court records, D'Emilio and Freedman (1988, 29) report the following:

> When Susanna Kenneth and John Tully of Virginia heard snoring in the next room, they stood on a hogshead of tobacco and peered over the wall to see that "Richard Jones Laye snoring in her plackett [a slit in her skirt] and Mary West put her hand in his Codpis [what today is called a 'fly']." Kenneth then pried loose a board to observe Mary West "with her Coats upp above her middle and Richard Jones with his Breeches down Lying upon her."

There were laws against adultery, fornication, and illegitimate births in every colony. However, they were there to keep sex properly within marriage and so preserve social order. Moreover, the rules governing sex applied equally to men and women, with one exception. Adultery for a man was defined as sex with a married woman. The term did not apply to a married man having sex with an unmarried woman. For a married woman, though, adultery meant sex with any man, married or not, other than her husband (Demos 1987).

Even premarital sex was dealt with lightly if it led to marriage. This can be seen, for example, in a curious custom called "bundling," practiced in New England in the eighteenth century and perhaps earlier. Here, parents allowed a courting couple to sleep together in one bed provided they kept their clothes on or placed a "bundling board" between them. It was thought that the clothes or the board would help prevent sexual intercourse. It is, of course, unlikely that this was a naive attempt at birth control; rather, the idea was that if a pregnancy did occur, a marriage would soon follow (D'Emilio and Freedman 1988; Coontz 1988). Except in some rural areas, bundling was no longer practiced by the nineteenth century.

Not just sex but love as well was ideally considered vital to marriage. Love was discouraged as a basis for a union, but it was expected to come after marriage. Though parents did not actually arrange marriages for their children, fathers had a great deal of influence over children's courtship and selection of spouses. In part this was because fathers controlled the sons' use or inheritance of land and the dowries of daughters (D'Emilio and Freedman 1988). Spouses were to be selected on the basis of certain characteristics such as piety or family status; but once married, husband and wife were to develop affection and become companions, however much the wife was to submit to the husband.

OTHER COLONIAL EXPERIENCES

The constructions of gender among European colonists varied somewhat by region and religious group. White settlers in the South, mostly Anglicans, had come primarily for economic profit. This, combined with the fact that southern farms were more spread out and isolated, meant that church control over individuals and households was less stringent. As a result, southern women may have been more autonomous and less subordinate to men than was the case in Puritan New England. There is evidence, however, that servant girls (those immigrating as indentured servants) may have been exploited by men. Court records show that many of these girls "had been made pregnant by their masters. Thousands of miles from their families back in England, isolated on small plantations, impoverished adolescent girls were easy prey for aggressive and unscrupulous men" (Kamensky 1995, 55).

Some religious groups constructed gender in ways notably different from the Puritans and other Protestants. A good example is the Society of Friends, or Quakers. Quaker preachers came from England to America in the mid-seventeenth century. Nearly half of these preachers were women. The Quaker religion focused on the conversion experience, which it described as being reborn and so receiving the Divine Light, or grace. Ideas about the sin of Eve and God's curse on her no longer applied to those reborn in the Light, since after rebirth men and women returned to the equality they had known before the Fall. Quaker women played extraordinarily active roles in the Society, including participation in the lay ministry. Quakers also tolerated a woman's decision to remain unmarried (Dunn 1979). Partly on account of the public role of women in their faith, the Quakers were condemned in New England and banished from many colonies. Many Quaker women were accused of being witches. This persecution led them to seek refuge to the south in Pennsylvania. Another example of a Christian group that developed unconventional connections between gender and religion was the Shakers, who arrived in America from England in 1774. Their founder, Ann Lee, was seen by her followers as the second coming of Christ; Shakers also spoke of God as both Mother and Father (Procter-Smith 1993).

The seventeenth-century experiences of the other important ethnic groups—Native Americans and, later, black slaves—were entirely different from those of the white colonists (see Chapter 4). As we will see in this and later chapters, white Americans wove their ideas about Native Americans and black people into their own gender constructions.

Among most white groups, female subordination is clear throughout the colonial period. Some earlier historians, however, argued that the colonial era was in fact a "Golden Age" for women, a time when women were held in higher esteem and had greater power than in later eras (e.g., Ryan 1975; Lerner 1987). Supporting this argument was, first, the observation that in colonial America white women were scarce. Most of the European migrants to the New World were male, and it was not until the eighteenth century that sex ratios evened out. Yet men needed to marry, establish themselves as householders, and reproduce; in a word, men needed women in order to achieve their own manhood. This must have, the argument went, given a woman some bargaining power while men competed for her hand in marriage. A second point was that women's labor was vitally important in the colonial economy. The economy revolved around agriculture and home-based production, largely for subsistence. Men worked the fields but women performed a great number of tasks beyond the housecleaning, cooking, and child care that women nearly everywhere have always done. Colonial women did carding and spinning for cloth, preserved food, tended gardens, milked livestock, knitted, sewed, baked bread, and made butter, ale, and candles. Even those women who had servants worked at managing and supervising a complex household and participated in cloth production and other tasks. Indeed there were practically no occupations deemed inappropriate for women. Some women worked as blacksmiths, tavern keepers, barbers, healers, and in innumerable other businesses and trades. Women's substantial economic contribution, according to some, must have given them an edge over their sisters of later centuries.

One historian who challenged this view of the Golden Age was Mary Beth Norton (1979). She claimed that an imbalanced sex ratio did not favor women. What it did was lower the age of marriage for women (colonial women were marrying on average in their early twenties, slightly earlier than European women). She argued that these young women were unlikely to wield much power over their marriages; instead, once married, women were subordinate to husbands and were set on a tortuous path of childbearing and childrearing for many years. It is true that colonial women gave birth to many children, especially in the North; that childbirth was a risky, frightening business; and that infant mortality was high. Norton also counters the argument that women's economic contributions gave them power by saying that although women made important economic contributions, they did not have control over the distribution of family resources; these resources were owned and controlled by men.

Today the Golden Age view of colonial women receives little support. But this whole debate bypassed a larger question, namely, by what criteria can we determine whether women's status is relatively high or low? (Coontz 1988). As we discussed in Chapter 1, there is no agreed way to measure gender status. Also, we saw in Chapter 1 that it is difficult to construct a monolithic "status" of women or men in any society because men and women play such a variety of roles and occupy different social positions throughout their lives. Finally, the issue is complicated by the fact that we do not know much about the views of colonial women; that is, how they saw themselves as women, what they thought of their conditions, or the range of variation in their perceptions.

What we can, perhaps, suggest as a generalization about colonial women is that they lived at a time when there was no sharp separation between the domestic and public spheres, or between "home" and "work." Within this context they could assume virtually any economic activity without being seen as unwomanly, competing with men, neglecting their children, or stepping out of their proper place. By contrast, when women did try to assume public leadership roles, a definite male terrain, they were discouraged and punished. The case of Anne Hutchinson comes to mind. Anne was a British woman who immigrated with her husband to Boston in 1634. There she was active in the religious life of the community, but soon she became critical of the Boston clergy. She felt the clergy failed to inspire any real faith in congregations, being too concerned with mere form and appearances. She openly aired her views and also criticized women's limited voice in the church. She began to hold prayer sessions in her own home, helping her followers achieve a more direct, immediate communication with God. When she drew a sizable following, the colony's clergy condemned her. One minister explicitly said that she had stepped out of her place as a woman; he drew a direct parallel between gender and public roles by charging Anne with seeking to be like a husband rather than a wife, a preacher rather than a listener. In 1637 Anne Hutchinson was excommunicated from the church and banished from Massachusetts.

In most respects the colonial era was culturally about as far removed from a spirit of American individualism as it could be. European colonial communities were founded upon hierarchy. Individuals in households were subordinate to its male head. Individuals were subordinate to the larger community authorities, and their Protestantism emphasized the submission of all to God. Especially in the North, these God-fearing people bound themselves to community rules and regulations affecting all aspects of their lives. These people were practically and ideologically interdependent. They defined themselves and their society in terms of an ordered interdependence.

The American colonial emphasis on hierarchy and holism rather than individualism can be seen in the way children were raised. Children were individually dealt with, of course, but, culturally speaking, they were not treated as individuals. They were not given special parts of the house to occupy. Children were loved and cared for, but parents put them to work and treated them much like servants. Often they were not given new, unique names at birth but were called by the names of their dead siblings (Coontz 1988). They were taught how to fit into the community, not how to stand on their own two feet. They were told to submit themselves to God's will, not to assert their own. They were taught to know their place, not to be all that they could be.

Everyone was a part of wider and wider "wholes" within which they found their identities. They fit themselves hierarchically into marriages, households, local communities, and communities of the faithful. With regard to gender, this hierarchical holism of the colonial era can perhaps tell us something about how men and women saw themselves. This is admittedly a bit speculative, but it looks as though colonial manhood was relatively secure. Manhood was established through marriage and setting up a household, which most men managed to do. Men were in cooperative hierarchical relationships with one another, not in egalitarian competition. Wives were clearly subordinate. There was not much to threaten or challenge one's manhood once secured, and certainly it does not appear that manhood was something men needed to "prove" over and over again in rapidly changing contexts, as we see in later periods.

What about women? As mentioned earlier, little is known about how they really felt or what their view of the situation was. Our suggestion, however, is that even though they were so clearly subordinate to men and lacked political power or control over economic resources, they nevertheless may have felt a wholeness that women of later periods lacked. However they defined themselves, their "selves" were in all likelihood comfortably integrated with their other dimensions, their work, their fertility, and their sexuality. It was accepted that women could be both sexual beings and mothers, something that was, as we will see, denied to nineteenth-century Victorian ladies. And we can presume that they saw their economic activities as comfortably integrated with their roles as mothers, in contrast with many twentieth-century American women who struggle to balance careers with motherhood, and face social criticism in the attempt.

None of this is to say that either men or women were happier in colonial times or that colonial society always functioned smoothly. Indeed, at least in New England, witchcraft accusations indicate that there were rifts in the social fabric. As these were primarily made by women against other women, with men presiding over court trials and sentencing, questions of gender arise.

WITCHCRAFT IN COLONIAL AMERICA

Witchcraft and execution of witches was of course nothing new; New England colonists merely brought a set of witchcraft beliefs and practices with them from the Old World. In New England there were widespread beliefs that witches, usually women, were people who harmed others through supernatural means, acquiring this power through a pact, or covenant, with Satan. Witches could bring any manner of misfortune to their victims: illness, death, miscarriages, deformed births, spoiling of beer, memory loss, or the wandering off of livestock, to name a few (Karlsen 1987). Their motive was envy or greed or merely the desire to do the work of Satan. Witches were also believed to control animal familiars (supernatural companions) that fed off their bodies.

Some connection between witchcraft and gender is seen not only in that witches and their victims were primarily women, but also in that the ideas and practices surrounding witchcraft were infused with images of female sexuality. Female witches were believed to have sexual intercourse with Satan. Evidently this was not for his pleasure but theirs, merely Satan's way of luring women into his diabolical covenant. (Interestingly, another way he did this was to promise women that he would do their tiresome domestic chores for them!) A witch was believed to have a mark, the "witches' teat," showing where her animal familiar sucked on her body for nourishment. Inevitably, during a search, these were found near women's breasts or genitals. And some men reported strange attacks by witches in the night. Their descriptions of these attacks strongly imply that the witches forced them to have sex (Karlsen 1987).

Various ideas have been proposed that interpret New England witchcraft as either a mass venting of Puritan sexual repression, a male fear of women, or a grim women's protest against their own oppression. There may be grains of truth in all these speculations. Less tantalizing but more convincing insights come from the detailed research of a few historians. Carol Karlsen's (1987) study found that most of the accused females were women who didn't quite fit the Puritan ideals of proper women or who in some way challenged the Puritan social order. Most of the women were over forty and known to be assertive, outspoken, quarrelsome, or ill-tempered. Interestingly, she found that many were without husbands, brothers, or sons; these women, lacking these male relatives, stood to inherit or control land, going against the patriarchical norm. They were women who "stood in the way of the orderly transmission of property from one generation of males to another" (Karlsen 1987, 116). It may also have been relevant that these women had no male kin to defend them.

An intriguing question is not why most of the accused witches were women (as is generally true the world over) but why most of the accusers and professed victims of witches were also women. This fact tends to discredit ideas that Puritan witchcraft expressed a male fear of women or a female protest against male oppression. John Demos (1982) drew attention to the fact that witch accusers (excepting those of the famous Salem trials) were the very closest neighbors of the accused, those who were in daily contact with the witch and her household, exchanging goods and services. Accused witches were often those women who in some way strained these important neighborly relationships, for example by asking for too many favors. Very often witch accusers were those who refused to give something to the alleged witch, and then feared retribution. Coontz (1988, 103) reports: "One victim lent her cup to a witch and was afflicted when she took it back refusing to sell it to the borrower. Another was struck in the back (as 'with a clap of fire') when she refused to lend a pound of cotton." Thus women initiated witchcraft accusations against other women because it was primarily women who were engaged in the informal but easily threatened process of sharing, exchange, and reciprocity in these close-knit New England communities.

To these ideas Elizabeth Reis (1997) has added an analysis of the religious reasons linking women and witchcraft in Puritan New England. Her work shows how Puritan religious ideas were interwoven with perceptions of the human body and how these notions together affected constructions of gender. Reis points out that Puritans perceived the body as a kind of enemy—it was indeed through the body (by tempting the flesh or even possessing the body) that Satan worked his way into the soul. As we pointed out earlier, Puritans also insisted that women's bodies, along with their minds, were weaker than men's. Thus, whereas the Puritan faith officially saw men and women as equal in the eyes of God, "Women's feminine souls were seen as unprotected in their weaker female bodies, vulnerable to the devil's molestations" (1997, 5). In connection with this perception, lay women and men related somewhat differently to the concepts of sin, guilt, and depravity so prominent in their Puritan faith: Men focused more on their particular sins and the need to repent for them, whereas women saw their essential natures as utterly depraved.

Reis's work is interesting not only for drawing out the ideas through which colonial women were believed to be, and believed themselves to be, more vulnerable to Satan, but also for highlighting a central theme—the body as one's enemy—that appears to have long outlived Puritanism in American culture. The body is still an enemy in mainstream America, not for its vulnerability to Satan but for its vulnerability to weight gain and flab. Here we see how the Nacirema aversion to the body, as noted in Chapter 1, has its roots in Puritanism. Even today people use religious rhetoric (the "sin" of eating chocolates, for example) to discuss their modern battles with the human body, their enemy.

SEEDS OF CHANGE, TIMES OF TRANSITION

Even though the colonial period was founded on hierarchy, we may presume that for two reasons the early settlers to America already carried within them a nascent spirit of individualism. First, their religion had taught them, as well as generations of their ancestors in Europe, that to be Christian was not a matter of birth, family, or tradition, but, ultimately, a matter of individual commitment. Second, the settlers were likely expressing a new individualism of their own in the very act of breaking with the Old World and venturing to America. These people were, after all, boldly settling down where few Europeans had gone before. Some came on their own, some came with spouses and children. Either way, they were breaking off from the wider groupings and networks of kinship that, in Europe, continued to greatly influence the life choices and options of individuals.

These seeds of individualism were about to germinate in American soil. Many forces of change were at work in early-eighteenth-century America that transformed the colonial way of life. A more specialized commercial market economy was developing. Commercial centers were beginning to grow. The population expanded through reproduction and the arrival of new groups of immigrants. A class system, and sometimes class hostilities, began to emerge. The new ideas of the Enlightenment, praising science and reason, were already stirring in Europe and about to drift across the Atlantic. Most notably, parents were exerting less control over their children. Population growth eventually forced sons to move outside their parents' communities in order to secure land. This broke the hold of fathers over sons through the promise of land inheritance. Young people increasingly came to select their own spouses. By one measure, premarital sex undoubtedly increased: In New England the number of pregnant brides rose from less than 10 percent in the seventeenth century to more than 40 percent in the mid-eighteenth century (Mintz and Kellogg 1988, 19).

As part of these social and cultural changes, this period saw a steady growth of individualism and the shaping of American culture around it. One interesting example of this rise of individualism can be seen in the changing styles of tombstones throughout the seventeenth and eighteenth centuries in New England. In the seventeenth century, tombstones showed a grim, winged death's head with vacant eyes. Epitaphs gave a chilling view of life and death. Archaeologist James Deetz (1996, 98) records the following example:

> My youthful mates both small and great
> Come here and you may see
> An awful sight, which is a type
> Of which you soon must be

Increasingly in the 1700s the death's head was replaced with a more cheerful, personal-looking cherub, and epitaphs gave a description of the deceased individual. By the end of the century, tombstones showed a willow tree over an urn and epitaphs were personalized memorials, some of which "lauded the individual in terms of his worldly achievements" (Deetz 1996, 99–100).

Women and men had very different parts to play in the rise of American individualism and were affected by it in different ways. One event that was entangled with a rising individualism and that expressed gender tensions was the Great Awakening. This was a Protestant religious revival that swept over the colonies, reaching its peak in the 1730s and 1740s. Itinerant preachers, some from England, spurred the movement, inviting converts to break away from society and seek a personal salvation on their own. Preaching a new, individualistic message in "hellfire and brimstone" sermons, often out in the open fields, they attracted eager crowds and many converts. This is the first time we see expressed the idea that "Christ is your personal Savior," an individualistic theme of evangelical religion that emerges again in later centuries. This expression of religious individualism was, interestingly, occurring right at the time when cherubs were replacing impersonal death's heads on New England tombstones (Deetz 1996).

The cornerstone of the Awakening was individual conversion, or rebirth (sometimes referred to as New Light). By this time the Puritan congregations had lost touch with their earlier idea of "saints" who had experienced grace,[3] and the Puritans themselves were concerned about a lack of religious vigor and piety in their own communities. Also critical of the lack of religious zeal and the inattention to the conversion experience that had developed in orthodox churches, the revivalists sought to help their followers to an immediate experience of God's grace. In these crowds, individuals often swooned or fell into ecstatic fits, later testifying to the utter joy and release they experienced. Followers were told to seek salvation on their own, to abandon family and friends and join a new spiritual community.

Among converts to the Awakening, a distinct majority were women. The Awakening, in stark contrast to the Puritan churches, encouraged women to speak out and testify in church and to play active roles in church affairs. Indeed the new faith, especially in its early, intense phase, saw its own spirituality as beyond the earthly distinctions of male and female. It combined individualism with gender equality: "Alone before God, the sinner stood naked, stripped of all conventional attributes, from sex to caste. 'In Christ there is neither Jew nor Greek, slave nor free, male nor female,' insists the scripture, and evangelicals heeded the word" (Juster 1994, 46).

With so many women converts and with a new women's voice in Awakening revivals, the movement is sometimes described as an example of a religious "feminization" in American Protestantism. But it is not just the presence and voices of women that give the revivals this label. According to Susan Juster (1994), the Awakening movement was expressed through a feminine discourse. Thus converts, both male and female, described themselves as "Brides of Christ." Even more telling, and more sexual, was the blatantly "feminine" position both male and female converts assumed in relation to God: They described themselves as vessels to be impregnated with God's seed (Greven 1977; Juster 1994).

The movement did not last long. It was opposed by orthodox churches, but more important, in order to survive in a new political climate—namely, the union of the colonies and the American Revolution against Britain— Awakening groups eventually came to resemble the established churches in organization and doctrine. They moved from being radical sects to becoming conventional denominations. At the same time, they supported the American War of Independence. Juster (1994, 119) shows how during the era of the Revolution the movement switched its imagery from feminine to masculine: "Once 'brides of Christ,' evangelicals now became 'soldiers of Christ'...." Instead of encouraging individuals to leave their families and join a new spiritual community, these groups now supported stable families with male heads. The movement adopted the mainstream American rhetoric of the Revolution, which saw males as manly warriors for the nation and pa- triarchal heads of families. Women were now discouraged from being active and vocal in church affairs, and they were positively encouraged to tend to their familial duties at home.[4]

Sociologist Michael Kimmel (1996) also analyzes the American Revolu- tion as a masculinized expression and shows further how the Revolution brought in a new male identity, at least in the North. The Revolution was not only a denial of British rule but also a renunciation of aristocracy. Aris- tocracy and the social hierarchy on which it was based were to be replaced with an American spirit of equality and liberty. In revolutionary America the British enemy was denounced as "foppish" and "effeminate," as were any "aristocratic behaviors or manners." Now it was manly to be an individual- istic self-made man. Aristocratic values and lifestyles did, however, live on in the South until the Civil War.

THE VICTORIAN PERIOD[5]

By the 1830s individualism was an important part of the American cultural landscape. In 1832 Henry Clay had remarked in a Senate speech that "We are a nation of self-made men." From 1831 to 1832 the French aristocrat Alexis de Tocqueville visited the United States to observe its egalitarian democracy. Pitting this new democracy against an older tradition of aristocracy, de Toc- queville (1898, 121) articulates the essence of American individualism:

> Aristocracy had made a chain of all the members of the community, from the peasant to the king: democracy breaks that chain, and severs every link of it.... They owe nothing to any man, they expect nothing of any man; they acquire the habit of always considering themselves as standing alone, and they are apt to imagine that their whole destiny is in their own hands. Thus not only does democracy make every man forget his ancestors, but it hides his descendants, and separates his contemporaries from him; it throws him back forever upon himself alone, and threatens in the end to confine him en- tirely within the solitude of his own heart.

Severed links in a chain, standing alone, a man's destiny in his own hands—these are all potent images of the spirit of individualism that infused American culture, finding reflection in religion, art, literature, and lifestyles over the next 170 years. In the late twentieth century, an Italian observer, Luigi Barzini, contrasted the hurried American approach to life with a more leisured European one. His remarks reveal an American individualism in a way that echoes de Tocqueville:

> Most Americans believe ... that all achievements must be completely accomplished ... within a person's lifetime. A man must perform what he has set out to do before he dies or consider his existence wasted. This is not so in Europe, or at least it wasn't so until a few years ago. Each man in the Old World knew that he was merely a link in a chain between ancestors and descendants.... Each man received the rod from his father or teachers and passed it on to his sons or followers. If a man didn't make it, his sons or grandsons might. (Barzini 1983, 241)

But notice that in de Tocqueville's account, "in the end" this democratic individualism "threatens" to confine man to "solitude." This is where women come in. In the nineteenth century, women's role in the new American individualism was not to embrace it themselves, but to help men bask in its glories without succumbing to a desolate solitude or suffering the hardships of struggling as lone individuals in an increasingly impersonal world. They were to do this within the family by embracing the very opposite of individualism—connection to others, self-sacrifice, a nurturing orientation—and so counterbalance the competitive individualism of the male public sphere. Alexis de Tocqueville saw this part of American family life very well. Somewhat chauvinistically, he attributed the strength of American democracy to the superiority of its women; but American women are superior, he wrote, because they know their place and do not use democracy to contest the natural authority of husbands over wives!

For all that, some women did come to argue for more autonomy and individualism for women during the nineteenth and twentieth centuries, as we will explore more fully in the next chapter. In the view of historian Carl Degler (1980), this posed a real challenge to the American family, which in these centuries was founded on hierarchical relationships and the subservience of individuals to the group, values antithetical to individualism.

THE IDEAL MAN

To explore the relationship between individualism and gender we can first take a look at American manhood in relation to individualism in the nineteenth century. The "effeminate" British of the "mother" country had been defeated. Industrial capitalism was rapidly expanding. Men were moving off the farms and into cities to work for wages or salaries. A self-conscious middle class was taking shape. And manhood came to be increasingly defined in terms of individual success in the industrial, capitalist economy. Manhood was "no longer fixed in land or small property ownership or dutiful service. Success must be earned, manhood must be proved and proved constantly" (Kimmel 1996, 23). For middle-class white men, manhood was no longer something that came along with adulthood and inherited property; it had to be achieved by the self-reliant individual.

From the early 1800s the self-made man was above all to be a successful "breadwinner." This meant he was to support a dependent wife and children. His ability to do so was a measure of his manhood, and a nonworking wife was a symbol of his middle-class status. Only in the lower classes would wives have to work. Basically, this idea was retained until the 1960s.

Once in the workplace, middle-class men had to keep up the struggle. Economic setbacks, loss of jobs, or even periods of serious inflation that made "breadwinning" difficult were now direct affronts to manhood, as was any failure in achieving expected new rewards or promotions. Manhood had to be continually demonstrated through public success.

An important aspect of middle-class manhood in this period was self-control. Exerting self-control was both a sign of manhood and a strategy for achieving it. It was a virtue a man cultivated in order to become self-made (Kimmel 1996). Self-control meant, for one thing, control over emotions: "Real men held their emotions in check, the better to channel them into workplace competition" (Kimmel 1996, 128). Self-control also meant restraint or "control over impulse" (Bederman 1995, 11) and, in particular, sexual impulse. Medical theory of the time held that humans had only a finite supply of "nervous energy," which could be irreversibly lost through certain activities and particularly through sex. Thus sperm loss depleted a man's energy, while conserving it allowed male energy to be directed toward loftier pursuits (Kimmel 1996). A host of manuals were published to help males control their sexual impulses and especially to avoid masturbation. Nineteenth-century physicians and moral reformers had an obsessive concern with the dangers of male masturbation: It was linked with a host of problems, from loss of vitality, dilapidation, and moral depravity to insanity and death. Indeed, in both Europe and America in the nineteenth century, physicians and reformers railed against the physical and moral dangers of masturbation in both women and men.

Most Americans probably do not know that a leader of the crusade against male masturbation was John J. H. Kellogg of Kellogg's Corn Flakes. In fact Kellogg designed the corn flakes as a dietary substance that would reduce sexual impulses in American men! And well before this, Sylvester Graham had concocted the graham cracker for the same purpose. Both Graham and Kellogg wrote books teaching parents how to recognize signs of masturbation in their male children and how to treat it. Michael Kimmel (1966, 130) reviews some of Kellogg's "chilling home remedies," which include "bandaging the genitals, covering the organs with cages ... tying the hands ... circumcision ... [and using] silver sutures placed over the foreskin to prevent erection." As Kimmel (1996, 130) remarks: "Although the extent to which Kellogg's sadistic suggestions were followed by terrified parents is impossible to know, one can only cringe at the possibility that any of them did."

Carroll Smith-Rosenberg (1978) felt that this obsessive concern with male masturbation represented a conservative voice in America, the voice of those who feared that rising individualism and economic changes in the country would bring social disruption and moral chaos. These people focused on young male sexuality as a symbol of all they feared, as indeed many young males were now free of parental authority, and were hanging out in cities, giving cause for concern. Restraining this adolescent sexuality was symbolic of bringing about social order.

Historians now see ideals of white, middle-class American manhood as shifting over time and sometimes incorporating alternative constructions of manhood expressed among other groups. Both Kimmel (1996) and Gail Bederman (1995) see such a shift taking place at the close of the nineteenth century. By this time manhood was being challenged by a number of forces. Economic depressions and the expansion of capitalism were making it harder for middle-class men to achieve economic success. Many came to fear "that they would be failures instead of self-made men" (Bederman 1995). At the same time, these middle-class men were being challenged politically by lower-class males and immigrants, who increasingly fought for their own economic success and a voice in American politics. Another challenge to their privileges came from the women's suffrage movement, the struggle to give women the right to vote. As a result, middle-class men lost faith in the earlier dominant image of manly self-control and self-making, and took on a rougher, more primitive image. Bederman describes this as a shift from "manliness" (a concept referring to male honorable character) to "masculinity" (an idea of virile male power). Both she and Kimmel (1996) discuss middle-class males toughening up their image by adopting some characteristics or behaviors of the working class, such as drinking in saloonlike settings and developing a new interest in sports, especially boxing. (We can see essentially the same process going on today with the current adoption of baseball caps—originally worn by working-class males—among middle-class males. Throughout most times and places, lower classes normally emulate higher ones. The American middle-class male attempt to recapture manhood is an exceptional case of the reverse.)

This shift to a rougher, tougher masculinity was reflected as well in a change in the middle-class male body image. Up to and slightly beyond the Civil War the ideal male physique was "lean and wiry" (Bederman 1995, 15) and the ideal man had a "pale complexion and languid air" (Kimmel 1996, 28). By the end of the nineteenth century the ideal male body was big and muscular. Instead of seeing their manhood in their "inner strength" of self-control, men saw it in their toned bodies. Seeking confidence through their physical selves, they "constructed bodily strength and social authority as identical" (Bederman 1995, 8), a process that has, if anything, increased in recent years.

Bederman shows how, in remaking their manhood, middle-class white men were constructing ideas not only about gender but simultaneously about race and civilization. These latter two concepts became particularly important from the 1880s on, as America, following Western European countries, moved into its period of imperial expansion, annexing Alaska, Hawaii, Puerto Rico, part of Samoa, Guam, and the Philippines. America's empire was minuscule compared to that of England or France, and there were antiimperialists who felt that overseas expansion violated American ideals of independence and self-determination. Nevertheless, America was very much influenced by the nineteenth-century imperial ideology of the Western world, and it was here that ideas about race, civilization, and gender came together in a larger worldview.

In this period, middle-class white men perceived themselves as the vanguards of civilization in opposition to blacks and other races, which they saw as the "savage" other. This conception of race was put into the framework of some nineteenth-century ideas about racial evolution. Current at the time was the idea that all human races advanced through various "stages" of progress, going, for example, from "savagery" through "barbarism" and finally reaching "civilization." But the races advanced through these stages at different rates, with some lagging behind others. White men and women were the most advanced; other races were still lower on the ladder. The mission of the white man was to advance white civilization even more, achieving greater and greater progress and perfection, and along the way benevolently bringing civilization to the lower races.

These white men distinguished themselves from the lower races in sexual terms. The savage other was sexually promiscuous and unrestrained, sometimes a "primal savage rapist" (Bederman 1995, 149). In thus contrasting their own sexual self-control with the rampant sexuality of the lower races, white males kept their sense of self-restraint as integral to their manhood. They also believed that as races advanced, differences between males and females increased. Thus among lower races males and females were similar—women worked outside the home and engaged in "male" tasks— whereas among themselves women were kept and protected in the domestic sphere. Yet at the same time, these men incorporated some of the "primitive masculinity" of the "savages" into their own manhood as they effected their shift from manliness to masculinity. Thus they were keeping their older vision of self-restrained manhood, where civilization and savagery were opposed, while putting muscle into their manhood by incorporating some "primitive masculinity" (Bederman 1995).

Needless to say, the most compelling heroes of fact or fiction for these men would be those who somehow encompassed both self-control and primitive masculinity. Bederman sees that at the turn of the century these ideals were readily found in the figures of President Theodore Roosevelt and Tarzan of the Apes. Roosevelt was, on the one hand, an upper-class male who exuded the Victorian manly values of "strength, altruism, self-restraint, and chastity" (Bederman 1995, 172). At the same time he portrayed himself as a virile frontiersman, and glorified the white man's winning of the West through conquering the "savage" Indians. He single-handedly organized his individualistic regiment of Rough Riders to fight the Spanish–American war, and he went on a manly safari to Africa where he killed dozens of rhinos, elephants, and lions. As for Tarzan, his "perfect masculinity stems from two factors—his white racial supremacy, inherited from his civilized Anglo-Saxon parents, and his savage jungle childhood with the primitive apes" (Bederman 1995, 221). Meanwhile, Jane is "pure, white womanhood," whom Tarzan defends from savage beasts and carries off into the jungle. There, however, his inner civilized nature emerges and he restrains himself from raping Jane. Instead, he allows her to civilize him even more, though, of course, never completely. Tarzan is manly self-control and primitive masculinity all in one, and the tension between these opposing traits is what makes him so appealing.

Another example of the male effort to retain self-control but combine it with primitive masculinity is seen in the American westward expansion. Kimmel (1996) sees this movement as a male strategy to bolster manhood through escape—those who were unsuccessful in the East moved west. There they could affirm their manhood anew by struggling against Indians and wild nature. In doing so they developed a new sort of American spirit that became known as "rugged individualism." A whole new American lore was built around figures such as Davy Crockett and Daniel Boone. In the popular imagination the westward expansion became a thoroughly masculinized tale of adventure, individualism, and violence (Armitage and Jameson 1987). Only recently has this myth been challenged by historians who recognize that many men went west not as lone rangers but in family groups, and that there "were women in them thar hills" (Armitage and Jameson 1987, 3). Elizabeth Jameson (1987) has shown that, contrary to the myth of a passive "sunbonneted helpmate," some women who went west were active in public and political realms.

VICTORIAN WOMEN AND THE CULT OF TRUE WOMANHOOD

Meanwhile, as American men were embracing individualism, middle-class women were interacting with it in quite a different way. As mentioned earlier, proper women at this time embodied the antithesis of individualism in order to assist males in their harsh, competitive, individualistic struggles for success. Ultimately, however, this assigned position demanded of women so many contradictory roles—all of them in contradiction to the dominant theme of individualism reflected in their culture—that the effect was to fragment them. American women began to discombobulate.

Before showing how this happened, a word of caution is in order concerning the topic of Victorian sexuality. Previously, historians saw middle-class people of this period as overwhelmingly sexually repressed or as simply against sex altogether. This view was based primarily on the books and advice manuals written by scores of social reformers, men and women, of the period. Some of this advice literature rants and raves against suspected sexual excesses in society and quite clearly seeks to repress sexuality in any number of ways; other reform writings are more moderate (Lystra 1989). In any case, these sources do tell us a lot about Victorian society, but they are not good guides to what average people of the nineteenth century actually did or felt (Degler 1974). For example, Karen Lystra (1989), using private love letters written between courting couples or married people temporarily separated, has shown that passionate romantic love and eroticism frequently characterized the very personal communication between women and men. These letters express anything but prudery. It is true that these secret letters were carefully guarded and hidden away, and refer to extremely private realms. In any public context, expressions of sexuality were inappropriate. But the private communication between these couples shows an absorbing interest in romantic love and its mysteries. Among the authors of the letters, it is clear that true romantic love, and not just legal marriage, purified sex. Romantic love was expressed as an intimate process of self-revelation. The men and women who left the letters, all married or thinking to become married, were after love, intimacy, and sexual pleasure.

Nevertheless, outside this very private and personal realm, early Victorian culture developed what has come to be called the "Cult of True Womanhood," and it is here that we see some ways in which womanhood fragmented. This cult set a lofty standard for Victorian women that was centered on the feminine virtues of piety, purity, submissiveness, and domesticity (Welter 1966). Thus the cult emphasized a social ideal; it focused on the perfection of women's domestic work and on women's virtue in their roles as wives and mothers.

By the standards of True Womanhood, Victorian middle-class "ladies," as they were called then, were not to work outside the home. Though they were encouraged by physicians and others to literally stay at home to protect their delicate health, in fact they were not confined to the domestic sphere. Many were active in charitable organizations. Middle-class women also went out of the home to visit one another and, toward the end of the century, frequently spent hours shopping in department stores. At least in the North, many became involved in reform movements, fighting against prostitution and for temperance, the abolition of slavery, and, later, women's right to vote. Some fought for an end to the double sexual standard through a "purity crusade" aimed at restricting male sexuality. These women saw their reform movements not as rebelliousness against domesticity, but merely as logical extensions of their virtue to the world outside.

Women did, however, have a primary responsibility to look after the domestic sphere, which was defined as exclusively theirs. Here they were to create a "haven in a heartless world" for their working husbands. Off being individualistic competitors in the capitalist jungle, men needed a haven at home where they could experience human connection rather than competition and the continual tests of their manhood, to say nothing of all the amenities of having a clean house, cooked meals, and someone to take over childrearing. Finally, men needed the civilizing influence of women. A task earlier entrusted to his mother, civilizing a man became an important duty to be continued by his wife.

All of this women could provide on account of their possession of virtue. Women were believed to be innately more virtuous than men. With their superior virtue, women were to make good citizens of their children and tame their husbands. Feminine virtue meant, above all, sexual purity. It was especially important for a wife to use her virtue to curb her husband's lust. That some males themselves sought this civilizing and moderating influence is seen in men's letters to their fiancées: "'Help me fight myself—my worse self that has so long had the mastery,' pleaded one man to his future bride. Another wrote, 'you are the very incarnation of purity to me ... and you shall help to cleanse me'" (D'Emilio and Freedman 1988, 180). Both men and women were to develop sexual restraint, but this was acknowledged as easier for women, whose sexual appetites were believed to be less than those of men. Men were to try to restrain themselves, but their greater natural lust meant that they could not always do so.

There was a pronounced double sexual standard in the Victorian era. It was important for Victorian women to be virgins at marriage but not as important for men. Neither husband nor wife should commit adultery, but this was a serious mishap only for women. Wives were to appear sexually reticent (at least outside their own marital beds). This was, after all, an era in which many men argued for legalized prostitution on the grounds that men needed a sexual outlet but should not be forever pestering their virtuous wives to provide it!

A woman of the cult was not to embrace individualism, which in her would be selfish, but rather was to nobly sacrifice her own petty self-interests for the larger good of her husband and her children. But it was not that simple. We begin to see some cracks in the system that split womanhood into incompatible fragments. One split was between women's minds and their biology, or between their brains and their wombs (Smith-Rosenberg 1985). An idea backed by medical authorities was that if a woman had too much education, or exercised her mental capacities too strenuously, this would damage her reproductive apparatus. This idea was bound up with one we saw earlier, namely the finite and depletable supply of "nervous energy" in humans. A woman's reproductive functions were believed to require a lot of precious energy. From the moment of first menstruation until menopause, women were instructed to be careful, to take a lot of rest, to avoid certain foods and physical activities. The mental activity required in schools (beyond the lower levels) would only deplete women of the energy they needed to keep their reproductive organs in good shape. Too much education, even too much mental exertion on her own, could result in reproductive problems or even barrenness. Not so for men, whose reproductive biology was much simpler and took less energy. For men, education was a proper outlet for stored-up sexual energy that would otherwise be depleted in masturbation. Thus, women were not to indulge too much in the individualistic world of the mind or in intellectual growth and expression on account of their special biology and reproductive role. If they did indulge anyway, they were seen not as good little American individualists increasing their market qualifications (as men would have been seen), but were considered unnatural, selfish, and unwomanly.

Women did gradually pursue higher education, but the way this came about shows one of the contradictions of the Cult of True Womanhood. On the one hand, women were seen as natural nurturers, and motherhood was an exalted role. Good mothers were needed to train their daughters to be virtuous wives and mothers, a relatively easy task, but they were also to train their sons to be manly citizens and strong individualists who could compete in the capitalist market (Coontz 1988). How could they possibly do this if they were uneducated? How could they even be good wives for their educated husbands if they were not more cultivated? On the other hand, how could women be educated without damaging their reproductive organs? The solution was to allow women higher education, but an education geared toward perfecting their roles as wives and mothers. This was the justification used to open the first women's colleges, beginning with Mount Holyoke in 1837 (Rothman 1978).

A second way in which women became fragmented in the Cult of True Womanhood also concerns motherhood, but this time a motherhood in conflict with a woman's sexuality (Stone 1997). Women moral reformers urged considerable sexual restraint in married women and felt that sexual expression in women "represented an elevation of wifehood over motherhood" (Rothman 1978, 84), whereas ideally motherhood should come first. Doctors and women reformers also maintained that too much sex would damage a woman's reproductive capacity or injure future offspring. Some said that marital sexual intercourse should not take place more than once a week; others thought that once a month would be better. Women reformers also opposed birth control, though many of them did advocate what was called "voluntary motherhood," or a woman's right to either accept or refuse sex with her husband in order to herself gain control over when she would be exposed to possible pregnancy (Gordon 1976). Some women were against birth control devices because they felt that sex should be restricted to reproduction. Others held that birth control would only subject women to their husband's carnal desires and encourage irresponsible sex in men (Rothman 1978). Of course, not all women necessarily agreed with the reformers or restricted their sexual intercourse to once a week or month, but they lived in a time when the cultural ideals of the Cult of True Womanhood taught them that female sexuality and good motherhood were at odds. By contrast, male sexuality and good fatherhood were never seen as incompatible.

For all this, some women, not a majority but significant numbers, did occasionally dabble in individualism in covert ways. When they thus expressed individual autonomy and self-assertion, their behavior was often seen as bizarre. We will take a look at two ways in which some women covertly expressed individualism in the nineteenth century: hysteria and shoplifting. Both of these behaviors stirred up gender tensions.

Male physicians in the mid-nineteenth century reported a strange disease they saw particularly in middle-class white women: hysteria. Hysterical women suffered general nervousness and depression; they sometimes started crying for no apparent reason; they complained of great fatigue. Sometimes they displayed a real "fit," which looked something like an epileptic seizure, or they fell into a trance. Sometimes hysterical women clutched their throats or pulled out their hair. Physicians were puzzled by hysteria, but most believed (and this should come as no surprise by this point) that it was caused by a woman's reproductive problems, masturbation, or having too much sex (Smith-Rosenberg 1985). Sometimes those around them suspected they were faking hysteria in order to gain sympathy or get their way. A widely prescribed cure was total bed rest, often for many months. This considerably disrupted the household as the hysterical woman abandoned her many domestic activities: "Household activities were reoriented to answer the hysterical woman's importunate needs. Children were hushed, rooms darkened, entertaining suspended, a devoted nurse recruited" (Smith-Rosenberg 1985, 208).

One thing physicians reported over and over about hysterical Victorian women was their expression of individual autonomy. And this the doctors resented personally; they considered the hysterical woman's assertiveness to be in the way of the doctors' therapy. "Doctors claimed that such women used their symptoms as weapons in asserting autonomy in relation to their physician; their continued illness was a victory. Physicians perceived hysterical women as unusually intractable and self-assertive" (Smith-Rosenberg 1985, 210). These physicians felt they had to break the wills of these women before they could be cured. To this end they used harsh techniques of throwing icy water over them, slapping them with wet towels, or exposing them as frauds in front of family and friends. But once the woman gave in, the doctor turned from an adversary to a supportive, helping figure. He was pleased with his treatment; he "had restored another wayward woman to her family duties" (Smith-Rosenberg 1985, 211).

Another way in which we see an expression of feminine individualism in the middle class is in shoplifting. Women's shoplifting became an issue in the late nineteenth century as America took a great leap forward into consumerism. Many new commodities were now affordable to the middle class, and huge department stores sprang up in urban areas to separate wives from their husbands' cash. It was wives, not husbands, who went to the stores; they became thoroughly female spaces with all sorts of attractions—live music, comfortable lobbies, restaurants, free samples of food and perfume. They displayed their products in the most tantalizing ways to encourage buying.

Department store shopping was seen as not only a female task but an opportunity for "pleasure and personal freedom" (Abelson 1989, 6). Some respectable, middle-class ladies took this thrill a little further, slipping a pin, perfume, or some gloves into the folds of their skirts before paying for their other purchases and calmly exiting from the store. There may have been any number of motives for shoplifting, but its covert individualism is clear: Shoplifters were "exercising power and control" (Abelson 1989, 171).

Catching a woman in the act of shoplifting caused all sorts of problems for store managers, the police, the woman herself, and the broader middle-class society. The problem was the class status of these women. First, no one could understand why a respectable middle-class woman, who could afford to make any number of purchases in the store, would resort to shoplifting. After all, these were virtuous women who understood that filching was wrong. Second, given their class status, they were not easy to prosecute and punish. One would have to deal with their husbands, other kin, and friends who were respectable pillars of communities. The very idea of shoplifting ladies was an affront to middle-class respectability.

A way out of these problems was found with the concept of *kleptomania*. Kleptomania was constructed as a disease peculiar to women on account of some imbalance in their nervous energies. Thus the women themselves were not really to blame, their physiology made them do it. This fit with the excuse most shoplifters themselves gave, that they just couldn't help themselves. Kleptomania became one more example of the relative weakness of Victorian women, a weakness ultimately rooted in their biology. Most important, the idea of kleptomania preserved middle-class respectability. Now lower-class women who took things from stores could be called "thieves," but middle-class women were "kleptomaniacs," a class injustice that did not escape some cynical observers at the time (Abelson 1989). Thus, in the case of shoplifting we see not only a peculiar expression of female individualism, but also a way in which gender and class intersected in the late nineteenth century. Preserving the respectability of the middle class became a paramount concern; to this end middle-class women were purged of responsibility through an acknowledgment of their biologically based inferiority to men.

This viewing of women's behavior in terms of their peculiar biology has continued in the twentieth century. Much as Victorians constructed "hysteria" and "kleptomania" to discuss unruly women, late-twentieth-century society has constructed "premenstrual syndrome" and "menopausal stress" as peculiar feminine "diseases" or causes of women's relative ineptness and emotionality (Tavris 1992; see also Martin 1987).

Whereas the hysteria and shoplifting of individual women may have expressed a veiled discontent with Victorian middle-class society, this society, founded upon male individualism, the Cult of True Womanhood, and an increasingly isolated nuclear family, was openly challenged by a number of utopian movements, many of them religious in nature, especially in the period before the Civil War. These movements presented a variety of stark alternatives to Victorian gender roles and family life. Some advocated complete celibacy for men and women, others believed in free love. Many offered communal childrearing. As we will see, these utopian movements were paralleled by the new religious movements of the late twentieth century.

ALTERNATIVE SEXUALITIES IN THE NINETEENTH CENTURY

Before moving to the twentieth century, a final aspect of nineteenth-century gender that needs to be addressed is relationships between members of the same gender. Nineteenth-century middle-class men and women, sharply segregated into their separate spheres, each developed solidarity and strong bonds with members of their own gender. Women sometimes developed romantic, passionate, intense, and lifelong relationships with other women, relationships that were kept up even after one or both of them married. It was quite acceptable for women not only to hold hands, but to kiss and caress one another. The strength of the passion in these relationships is revealed in the following excerpt from a letter written by Emily Dickinson to a woman friend who later became her sister-in-law:

> Susie, will you indeed come home next Saturday, and be my own again, and kiss me as you used to?… I hope for you so much, and feel so eager for you, feel that I cannot wait, feel that now I must have you—that the expectation once more to see your face again, makes me feel hot and feverish…. (quoted in D'Emilio and Freedman 1988, 126)

Similar passion was sometimes expressed between male friends (D'Emilio and Freedman 1988). Was all of this just a style of expression, or were these relationships homosexual? Certainly by the 1850s there were gay and lesbian subcultures in cities (Kimmel 1996). But most of these passionate friendships among middle-class same-sex individuals were probably not sexual, in our modern sense of the term. D'Emilio and Freedman (1988) emphasize that intense relationships between women were fully tolerated in Victorian society and that the broader society saw them as platonic, even though passionate and even physical. It was only toward the end of the century when, in their view, "the separation of sexuality and reproduction made Americans more conscious of the erotic element of these friendships" (1988, 126) that the relationships came under suspicion and were discouraged. Smith-Rosenberg (1985, 76) suggests that nineteenth-century America permitted a wider range of emotions and sexual feelings between the poles of "committed heterosexuality" and "uncompromising homosexuality" than does the twentieth century.

In order to further cover homosexuality in nineteenth-century America, and, in the next chapter, the twentieth century, it will help to first address the topic of homosexuality in general. In virtually all societies there have been some individuals who have been primarily or exclusively sexually interested in members of their own gender. Such individuals have no desire to change their sexual assignment; they are not men who want to be women or women who want to be men. Thus they are quite different from people who feel at odds with their biological makeup and want to live as members of another gender.

In one society, the Sambia of highland New Guinea, male homosexuality was institutionalized as a part of the initiation of young boys into adulthood (Herdt 1981). Among the Greeks of the fifth century B.C. it was expected that most males would have sexual relationships with other males, in addition to the sexual relationships with females that were necessary to maintain the population.

In societies like the Sambia or ancient Greece no one suggested that male homosexual relationships were intrinsically immoral or held that only certain peculiar kinds of persons indulged in them. There was not much interest in what women were up to sexually with other women in these societies. If they were sexually involved with other women—and the (married) Greek woman poet Sappho certainly was, as her poems tell us—no one found this remarkable. Her lesbian relationships did not threaten her reputation or violate cultural rules as her sexual involvement with a man other than her husband would have done.

In other societies, same-gender sexual relationships have not been as widespread as among the Greeks, nor have they been institutionalized as among the Sambia, but neither have they been the focus of much interest or blame. Among the !Kung of Africa, children often play sexually with members of their own gender (as happens in many societies), but few continue the practice as adults and all marry heterosexually. Some !Kung, however, do continue to interact sexually with members of their own gender as adults. Other !Kung consider the behavior a bit odd, but they are not disturbed by it, nor do they consider it immoral (Lee 1993).

By contrast, societies based on the Judeo-Christian tradition have long held that sexual involvement with one's own gender is immoral, based on Biblical passages that condemn it. But even in these societies, social tolerance of homosexuality has varied by time and place. For example, Kimmel (1996) points out that while male homosexuality was condemned by Victorian society in America, middle-class straight men were not threatened by gay men, with whom they interacted casually, until the end of the century. It was only, according to Kimmel, when middle-class white men were threatened by women, immigrants, and black people moving into the workplace that they turned against and derided gay men, defining real manhood as strictly heterosexual.

Same-gender sexual activity often carried the death penalty in European countries (as it did in England until the middle of the nineteenth century), but prosecution was often lax and always inconsistent. It was also aimed almost exclusively at men. Indeed, an early-nineteenth-century accusation of "sexual indecency" brought against two female teachers in a Scottish school on behalf of one of their female students raised the legal question of whether it was even possible for females to engage in sexual activity with each other (Adam 1987, 5). Even so, "sodomy," as all "unnatural" sexual activity was called in Christian countries, was seen as a sin to which all flesh was heir. That is, it was viewed not as a characteristic of a particular kind of person but as a moral error, like theft, sloth, or gluttony, into which anyone could fall as a result of the sinful nature of humanity.

It was not until 1869 that the term "homosexual" first appeared, in a pamphlet in which Hungarian physician Karl Maria Benekert (writing under the name of Kertbeny) argued for the decriminalization of same-gender sexual activity in Germany. The plea failed, but the term stuck. Along with the term, there developed an idea that "the homosexual" was a distinctive kind of person, at best unhappy and mentally ill and at worst a sinful and potentially treasonous criminal bent on the molestation and seduction of otherwise heterosexual children.

As usual, the focus remained on men throughout the nineteenth century in America and Europe. But, with time, the existence of women who were involved with one another (increasingly referred to as lesbians, after the Greek island of Lesbos, where Sappho had lived) became more generally acknowledged. Outsiders may have been unsure whether there was a sexual component to these relationships, but in any case they were considered by heterosexuals to be less threatening than male homosexual relationships. As part of the continuum of intense female romantic relationships discussed earlier, they were rarely taken seriously, as long as the women continued to appear feminine and carry out their obligation to marry and produce children.

However, as noted earlier, toward the end of the nineteenth century these intense female relationships came under suspicion and drew criticism. Thus, the faculty and students of American women's colleges developed a reputation for "unnatural friendships" that led some families to curtail the higher education of their daughters. A letter written in 1882 describes the crushes or "smashes" of American women college students:

> [They fall] violently in love with one another and suffer ... all the pangs of unrequited attachment [and] desperate jealousy ... they write each other the wildest love letters and send presents.... If the "smash" is mutual, they

monopolize each other and "spoon" [kiss] continually, and sleep together, and lie awake all night talking instead of going to sleep. (quoted in Sahli 1979, 22)

By the end of the nineteenth century, enduring relationships between women, especially educated, elite women, had come to be called "Boston marriages," a term still used in New England. Jane Addams, the Nobel Prize-winning founder of the Chicago settlement house, Hull House, participated in such a relationship with the philanthropist Mary Rozet Smith. Their relationship was such that Addams took pains to ensure that when they stayed together in hotels, they would be assured of a double bed, just as they had at home (Mondimore 1996, 59).

In the next chapter we return to the topic of gay men and lesbians, covering developments in the twentieth century. In this century gay men and lesbians emerge as a politically significant and vocal minority.

SUMMARY AND DISCUSSION

In this chapter we have seen the development and transformations of cultural constructions of gender in America from the colonial era through the Victorian period. In colonial New England, while men and women were regarded as spiritually equal, women were considered physically and mentally inferior to men and rightfully subordinate to them. This subordination was set within an ideology of a necessary and religiously sanctioned hierarchy in all human relationships. Patriarchal male heads of households both socially and legally encompassed wives and children. Only men assumed public leadership roles. Colonial women and men both played a variety of important economic roles. Women, however, did not control important economic resources. Significantly, these colonial women and men lived before the wide separation between domestic and public spheres developed and shaped gender in middle-class American culture.

By the Victorian period of the nineteenth century, this cultural construction of gender was significantly transformed for middle-class white America. With the growth of industrial capitalism we see the emergence of the "domestic sphere" as a nearly exclusively feminine concern and the dominance of males in a separate "public sphere." A woman's place was in the home. Another notion justifying these gendered separate spheres was the idea that women and men have radically different biologies. In the colonial era, women were seen as physically weaker than men, but otherwise biological differences between the genders were not emphasized. In Victorian times, by contrast, women were seen as very largely conditioned by their special and frail reproductive anatomy, which made them suited for domesticity and unsuited for activities in the more threatening public sphere.

Culturally, the world of males became accented by the growing value placed on individualism, itself bolstered by the development of egalitarian democracy. Victorian women, by contrast, were culturally idealized in terms of their virtue, piety, sexual purity, and domesticity. In fact, women were ideally to embrace the opposites of individualism—connection with others, nurturance, and self-sacrifice—in order to provide a haven for individualistic, breadwinning males. Some women, though, expressed a form of individualism in covert ways, for example in hysterical fits and in shoplifting.

Between 1600 and 1900, did middle-class white Americans make any progress toward gender equality, a concept that we raised in Chapter 1? It would seem, at least to us, that neither colonial women nor middle-class Victorian ladies had much in the way of public power, authority, or autonomy as defined earlier, though they undoubtedly exercised all of these in some social contexts. Wives were subordinate to husbands in all periods, perhaps most explicitly so in colonial times. In the colonial period, all relationships were hierarchical, but by the nineteenth century, middle-class men were individually competing on a more equal footing with one another. One could suggest that Victorian women had more autonomy—in the sense of autonomy from men or autonomy within their own separate domestic sphere—than women of earlier times. They also had greater legal autonomy and were soon to gain some political autonomy. As for access to or control over economic resources, women did not fare well relative to men over the three centuries covered in this chapter. Women did, however, make gains in access to education.

At the same time we have suggested that within their "holistic hierarchy," colonial women may have experienced a wholeness, or a feeling that their different dimensions and roles as women were compatible with one another. It is, we suggested, in the nineteenth century, with the growth of individualism and woman's peculiar relationship to it, that American womanhood appeared to fragment into incompatible parts. Apart from this, as we also saw in Chapter 1, it is very difficult to assess a single status of women or men in any society of any period, since the attempt to do so assumes we have some agreed-upon standard by which to measure men's and women's lives. And any such standard would fail to take account of men and women's own views of their situation and the different roles men and women play in a variety of social contexts.

In this chapter we have also encountered cultural ideas about the human body and how these ideas were woven into constructions of gender. Thus in Puritan New England, where the body was construed as Satan's potential route into the soul, women were seen as more vulnerable to Satan on account of their weaker bodies (Reis 1997). We also saw how, over the course of the nineteenth century, the image of the ideal male body shifted from lean to big and muscular (Kimmel 1996; Bederman 1995) as middle-class men faced new threats and remade manhood. (In the next chapter we discuss important shifts in the ideal female body that occurred in the twentieth century). Also relevant to men, nineteenth-century medical theory held that male sexual activity, or sperm loss, depleted a man's "nervous energy," leaving him weakened. Men were to exert control over their sexual impulses, part of a notion of self-control that figured into proper manhood. One achieved manhood through exerting self-control, through becoming "self-made" individualists. There was also the idea that, although men should control their sexual impulses on their own, they really needed pure, virtuous women to help them.

In the nineteenth century what was significant about the female body was its presumed frailty, vulnerability to certain illnesses, and the conflict between women's reproductive organs and their minds. Thus we saw that members of the medical establishment and social reformers believed that too much reading or education would impair women's reproductive health or even result in sterility. This begins, in our view, the process of women being fragmented into incompatible parts. The conflict between women's minds and reproductive organs recedes in the twentieth century, but American womanhood fragments along new dimensions, as we will see in the next chapter.

We also saw in this chapter how religious ideology was interwoven with gender constructions. For the Puritans, women's subordination to men, a lingering notion of woman as the sinful Eve, and ideas that women were more vulnerable to Satan and witchcraft were important in constructing womanhood and shaping relations between men and women. Later, with the Great Awakening, we saw a challenge to the more traditional gender constructions. This movement, though it did not last long, sought to include women in the growing American individualism and to combine spiritual individualism with gender equality. As we will see in the next chapter, this task of combining individualism with gender equality was taken up in the twentieth century in a secular "women's movement."

Finally, this chapter has covered some connections between gender, ethnicity, and class. We saw how the nineteenth-century views of racial evolution figured into the construction of white middle-class manhood and womanhood. We also saw in the discussion of Victorian women's shoplifting how the formulation of "kleptomania," a "disease" afflicting Victorian ladies, worked to preserve ideas of middle-class respectability (Abelson 1989).

DISCUSSION QUESTIONS

1. Early in this chapter we talk about the middle-class, individualist quality of American life. But "middle class" and "individualism" can be slippery terms. Sociologists report, for example, that most Americans consider their own social class to be higher than the class status social scientists would ascribe to them. How would you define "middle class"? What specific characteristics do you think are essential to qualify for middle class status? What about the notion of individualism? What characteristics do you associate with this term? It might be productive to consider what an alternative to individualism might be. Try to describe and name one

or more alternatives. Do you know of any cultures or subcultures that operate through such an alternative?

2. In our discussion of the colonial era, we quote historian Stephanie Coontz as saying "the subordination of women and the dominance of men were based less on ideas about gender than on ideas about the need for hierarchy in all relationships." That is an interesting statement, but it ignores the fact that in all stratified societies (those in which some groups—classes or castes—have higher status ascribed to them than do others), including the United States, it is *women* as a group who are subordinate, and *men* as a group who have dominance. Can you think of a way to resolve Coontz's statement with this fact? (You are not being asked to account for the universal subordination of women as a group in stratified societies, though you might want to consider the problem!) What theoretical perspective are you using in answering this question? You may not be consciously thinking about a theoretical perspective, but your answer will almost certainly fall into some theoretical paradigm or perspective described in Chapter 1.

3. Definitions of adultery vary from culture to culture and from one era to another. So does concern with adultery and with the issue of children born outside of marriage. Why do you think that the colonial definition of adultery was different for men and for women? Perhaps men were making the rules, and it is not surprising that definitions of adultery offered men more latitude than women. But pointing this out only scratches the surface of the issue. What else is going on? What about illegitimate births? Why was the phenomenon of children born to unmarried women of such serious concern in the early days of this country, when it is now increasingly accepted? The power of religion may well be relevant here, but look also at economic and technological issues.

4. The Victorian Cult of True Womanhood was, to a great extent, the social and economic manifestation of the popular notion of woman as the "angel of the hearth." This was a term developed by the English novelist Charles Dickens, who was a most powerful and popular novelist on both sides of the Atlantic throughout the nineteenth century. Certainly the Cult of True Womanhood may be seen as situated in a particular social and economic time and place. But we would argue that the Cult of True Womanhood is in some ways alive and well today. Do you see it in twenty-first century American life? Where? Do you think it fits with today's social and economic realities, or does it seem to be at odds with them? Be specific in your response.

NOTES

1. This is a point made by Simone de Beauvoir (1953), who claimed that Americans lacked a sense of their collective power.
2. This John Cotton was the great-nephew of an earlier John Cotton, a prominent minister in New England.

3. After the first generation of Puritans, the saints dwindled in numbers. This led church leaders to wonder about who should have rights to baptism. In 1622 a Halfway Covenant was enacted that gave the Puritans of later generations the right to be baptized but not to partake of communion or to vote in the church. Later the distinction between full church members and "halfway" members became blurred.

4. A Second Great Awakening peaked about a century after the first one and showed many parallels to it. This one advanced spiritual individualism even more. The First Great Awakening encouraged the seeking of personal salvation, but it did not overthrow the Calvinist doctrine of predestination. The Second Great Awakening did; by the end of this revival the idea that the individual would achieve salvation through his/her actions and religious life was firmly in place in American Protestantism. Both revivals contributed to American denominationalism and the emergence of a plurality of client-oriented Protestant churches.

5. The term "Victorian" comes from Queen Victoria who ruled England from 1837 to 1902. It marks an era generally noted for sexual repression and a sharp split between the male public sphere and the female domestic sphere.

REFERENCES

Abelson, Elaine S. 1989. *When Ladies Go a-Thieving: Middle Class Shoplifters in the Victorian Department Store*. New York: Oxford University Press.

Adam, Barry D. 1987. *The Rise of a Gay and Lesbian Movement*. Boston, MA: Twayne Publishers.

Armitage, Susan, and Elizabeth Jameson. 1987. Editor's introduction. Pp. 3–6 in *The Women's West*, ed. Susan Armitage and Elizabeth Jameson. Norman, OK: University of Oklahoma Press.

Barzini, Luigi. 1983. *The Europeans*. New York: Penguin Books.

Beauvoir, Simone de. 1953. *America Day by Day*. Trans. Patrick Dudley. New York: Grove Press.

Bederman, Gail. 1995. *Manliness & Civilization: A Cultural History of Gender and Race in the United States, 1880–1917*. Chicago, IL: University of Chicago Press.

Coontz, Stephanie. 1988. *The Social Origins of Private Life: A History of American Families 1600–1900*. London: Verso.

Cott, Nancy F. 1976. "Eighteenth Century Family and Social Life Revealed in the Massachusetts Divorce Records." *Journal of Social History* 10 (1): 20–43.

Deetz, James. 1969. "The Reality of the Pilgrim Fathers." *Natural History* 78 (9): 32–45.

Deetz, James. 1996. *In Small Things Forgotten: An Archaeology of Early American Life*. New York: Doubleday.

Degler, Carl N. 1974. "What Ought to Be and What Was: Women's Sexuality in the Nineteenth Century." *American Historical Review* 79:1467–1490.

Degler, Carl N. 1980. *At Odds: Women and the Family in America from the Revolution to the Present*. Oxford, Eng.: Oxford University Press.

D'Emilio, John, and Estelle B. Freedman. 1988. *Intimate Matters: A History of Sexuality in America*. New York: Harper & Row.

Demos, John Putnam. 1982. *Entertaining Satan: Witchcraft and the Culture of Early New England*. New York: Oxford University Press.

Demos, John Putnam. 1987. "Husbands and Wives." Pp. 9–22 in *Our American Sisters: Women in American Life and Thought*, ed. Jean E. Friedman, William G. Shade, and Mary Jane Capozzoli. Lexington, MA: D. C. Heath and Company.

Dumont, Louis. 1970. *Homo Hierarchicus: An Essay on the Caste System*. Trans. Mark Sainsbury. Chicago, IL: University of Chicago Press.

Dunn, Mary Maples. 1979. "Women of Light." Pp. 114–136 in *Women of America: A History*, ed. Carol Ruth Berkin and Mary Beth Norton. Boston, MA: Houghton Mifflin.

Friedman, Jean E., William G. Shade, and Mary Jane Capozzoli. 1987. "Colonial Women." Pp. 2–8 in *Our American Sisters: Women in American Life and Thought*, ed. Jean E. Friedman, William G. Shade, and Mary Jane Capozzoli. Lexington, MA: D. C. Heath and Company.

Gordon, Linda. 1976. *Woman's Body, Woman's Right: A Social History of Birth Control in America*. New York: Grossman Publishers.

Greven, Philip J. 1977. *The Protestant Temperament: Patterns of Child-Rearing, Religious Experience, and the Self in Early America*. New York: Alfred A. Knopf.

Herdt, Gilbert H. 1981. *Guardians of the Flute: Idioms of Masculinity*. New York: McGraw-Hill.

Hunt, Morton. 1994. *The Natural History of Love*. New York: Anchor Books, Doubleday.

Jameson, Elizabeth. 1987. "Women as Workers, Women as Civilizers: True Womanhood in the American West." Pp. 145–164 in *The Women's West*, ed. Susan Armitage and Elizabeth Jameson. Norman, OK: University of Oklahoma Press.

Juster, Susan. 1994. *Disorderly Women: Sexual Politics & Evangelicalism in Revolutionary New England*. Ithaca, NY: Cornell University Press.

Kamensky, Jane. 1995. *The Colonial Mosaic: American Women 1600–1760*. New York: Oxford University Press.

Karlsen, Carol F. 1987. *The Devil in the Shape of a Woman: Witchcraft in Colonial New England*. New York: W. W. Norton and Company.

Kimmel, Michael S. 1996. *Manhood in America: A Cultural History*. New York: Free Press.

Lee, Richard B. 1993. *The Dobe Ju/'hoansi*. Fort Worth, TX: Harcourt Brace College Publishers.

Lerner, Gerda. 1987. "The Lady and the Mill Girl: Changes in the Status of Women in the Age of Jackson." Pp. 125–137 in *Our American Sisters: Women in American Life and Thought*, ed. Jean E. Friedman, William G. Shade, and Mary Jane Capozzoli. Lexington, MA: D. C. Heath and Company.

Lystra, Karen. 1989. *Searching the Heart: Women, Men and Romantic Love in Nineteenth-Century America*. New York: Oxford University Press.

Martin, Emily. 1987. *The Woman in the Body: A Cultural Analysis of Reproduction*. Boston, MA: Beacon Press.

Mintz, Steven, and Susan Kellogg. 1988. *Domestic Revolutions: A Social History of Family Life*. New York: Free Press.

Mondimore, Francis Mark. 1996. *A Natural History of Homosexuality*. Baltimore, MD: John Hopkins University Press.

Norton, Mary Beth. 1979. "The Myth of the Golden Age." Pp. 37–47 in *Women of America: A History*, ed. Carol Ruth Berkin and Mary Beth Norton. Boston, MA: Houghton Mifflin.

Procter-Smith, Marjorie. 1993. "Blessed Mother Ann, Holy Mother Wisdom: Gender and Divinity in Shaker Life and Belief." Pp. 373–380 in *Gender in Cross-Cultural*

Perspective, ed. Caroline B. Brettell and Carolyn F. Sargent. Englewood Cliffs, NJ: Prentice Hall.

Reis, Elizabeth. 1997. *Damned Women: Sinners and Witches in Puritan New England.* Ithaca, NY: Cornell University Press.

Rothman, Sheila M. 1978. *Woman's Proper Place: A History of Changing Ideas and Practices, 1870 to the Present.* New York: Basic Books.

Ryan, Mary P. 1975. *Womanhood in America: From Colonial Times to the Present.* New York: New Viewpoints.

Sahli, Nancy. 1979. "Smashing." *Chrysalis* 8:22.

Salmon, Marylynn. 1979. "Equality or Submersion? Feme Covert Status in Early Pennsylvania." Pp. 92–113 in *Women of America: A History*, ed. Carol Ruth Berkin and Mary Beth Norton. Boston, MA: Houghton Mifflin.

Smith-Rosenberg, Carroll. 1978. "Sex as Symbol in Victorian Purity: An Ethnohistorical Analysis of Jacksonian America." Pp. 212–247 in *Turning Points: Historical and Sociological Essays on the Family*, ed. John Demos and Sarane Spence Boocock. Chicago, IL: University of Chicago Press.

Smith-Rosenberg, Carroll. 1985. *Disorderly Conduct: Visions of Gender in Victorian America.* New York: Alfred A. Knopf.

Stone, Linda. 1997. *Kinship and Gender: An Introduction.* Boulder, CO: Westview Press.

Tocqueville, Alexis de. 1898. *Democracy in America.* Vol. 2. Trans. Henry Reeve. New York: The Century Co.

Tavris, Carol. 1992. *The Mismeasure of Woman.* New York: Simon & Schuster.

Ulrich, Laurel Thatcher. 1980. "A Friendly Neighbor: Social Dimensions of Daily Work in Northern Colonial New England." *Feminist Studies* 6 (2): 392–405.

Welter, Barbara. 1966. "The Cult of True Womanhood, 1820–1860." *American Quarterly* 18:151–174.

CHAPTER 3

THE TWENTIETH CENTURY

The twentieth century saw a number of changes relevant to gender. For women, some political participation was achieved with the right to vote in 1920. Two other trends begun in the nineteenth century accelerated: women's participation in higher education and an increase of women in the workforce. Women in higher education showed a steady rise over the century until, by the late 1980s, half of all college graduates were women. Women working outside the home also increased until, in the 1990s, women came to constitute nearly half of the workforce (Goldin 1990, vii). This increase has steadily included more married women and women with small children. As early as 1960, one in three married women was working outside the home (Mintz and Kellogg 1988, 199).

Many changes relevant to gender were related to the broader economic, technological, and political developments that, since the Civil War, had transformed the country from a small-scale, largely rural agrarian economy to an urban, industrial capitalist world power. By 1920 the majority of Americans lived in cities. By 1925 use of the automobile was widespread, more than half of all American homes had electric power, and most had indoor plumbing. Women could now buy, rather than produce or make, canned goods, bread, and soap. Servants were becoming expensive and scarce, but in the opening decades of the century housework was beginning to be transformed by a vast number of new products: electric irons, refrigerators, vacuum cleaners, washing machines, sewing machines, percolators, and toasters, to name a few (Cowan 1987). Although these devices reduced housewives' workloads for some tasks, rising standards of household cleanliness and new expectations for the quality of cooked meals kept homemaking a time-consuming job (Margolis 1984). In this context, middle-class housewives also took on new roles as managers of family consumption, a consumption that was crucial to the expansion of the U.S. economy of this period. Broader economic forces thus created a new economic function—buying and using new consumer items for the family—for housewives: "What better and more appropriate role for the middle-class housewife who had lost many of her traditional domestic functions?" (Margolis 1984, 147).

All of these changes were, of course, a part of a larger and more far-reaching phenomenon in twentieth-century America: the development of a "consumer culture," most prevalent among the middle class. The consumer culture means not just that Americans became materialistic or acquisitive, nor that advertising came to bombard us through the media, nor that Americans came to value a higher "standard of living." It refers to far more subtle and complex ways in which an ideology of consumer capitalism, or an ethic of "market values," came to penetrate nearly all facets of life. Richard Fox and T. J. Jackson Lears (1983, xii) write that in the American consumer culture, "Individuals have been invited to seek commodities as keys to personal welfare, and even to conceive of their own selves as commodities." Thus we not only identify our self-worth with the status symbols we buy (clothing, cars, and so on) but we now try to "sell ourselves" or "market" our own images as we go through the trials of life.

Indeed, the consumer culture has so penetrated American life that even our most intimate, personal relationships have been affected. Thus, whereas in the nineteenth century romantic partners spoke of love as mutual self-revelation, many people now "… evaluate relationships by weighing their costs against the extent to which they satisfy one's needs" (Illouz 1997, 194). Relationships must be "monitored"; where individual needs are not satisfied people are to "negotiate," (Illouz 1997) and relationships should be terminated when they cease to "grow."

The developing consumer culture also effected subtle shifts in American individualism, which are important both in this chapter and in Chapter 6, where we discuss student culture. Values of self-reliance and achievement in the public sphere were retained, but in the twentieth century, individualism additionally came to be expressed as "freedom of choice." Anthropologist William Beeman (1986, 59) writes that "There are few things all Americans can agree on. Near the top of the list, along with mother and apple pie, lies 'freedom of choice.'" It is almost as though, by merely offering Americans a smorgasbord of breakfast cereals, lipsticks, or shaving cream (or for that matter, health insurance plans or university majors), they will feel automatically that they are in control and expressing their individuality. Possibly "freedom of choice" developed as an expression of American individualism because of its broad-based appeal. Obviously, not everyone can become a self-reliant success in the public sphere, whereas anyone can exercise choice in a smorgasbord of consumer goods.

Beeman points out that advertisers, ever alert to all subtleties of American culture, came to directly exploit "choice" in their strategies to sell their goods. Make Americans feel that choice is imperative and that they are really choosing ("choosy mothers choose Jif" peanut butter is one example he gives), and you will have brought about "a symbolic action that allows Americans to assert their commitment to individualism" (Beeman 1986, 54).[1] If we sense something deceptive and manipulative in this process, and if we realize that millions of Americans actually buy products controlled by a few corporations, it suggests that consumer capitalism encourages an illusory individualism. But however expressed, American individualism did, in the twentieth century, come to be an issue for women as well as men, as we will see in this chapter.

Another significant change in the twentieth century was the development of a distinct youth culture. In the nineteenth century Americans had been, in many contexts, separated by gender, but in the twentieth century they were more often segregated by age (Bailey 1988). For example, young persons mingled together in gender-mixed, age-graded school classes. Advertisers also saw that they could directly target youth, who could then very effectively coerce their parents into buying products for them (Coontz 1992). In the process, advertisers helped construct a plethora of images and commodities around which youth could identify. A separate youth culture was also promoted by middle-class parents who became increasingly permissive and indulgent toward children. British anthropologist Geoffrey Gorer (1948) held that Americans sought not obedience but love from their children, and so became afraid to discipline them for fear that the children would withdraw their love. Left to their own devices, youth modified gender relationships on their own; the changes were then transmitted to subsequent generations, who made yet other modifications. Youths were now an active force in cultural change.

RUGGED MEN AND NEW WOMEN

For twentieth-century middle-class men, generally we see further movement toward a more "rugged" individualism and a more masculinized image of ideal manhood. Some of this image was lived through fantasy. For example, in the 1950s, popular television shows like *Gunsmoke* and *Bonanza* idealized manhood as rugged "wild West" individualism (Dubbert 1979). *Superman* was an urban counterpart. The heroes of these shows, along with film stars such as Alan Ladd and John Wayne, encompassed manhood both as rugged individualism and as honor and self-control, much as Roosevelt and Tarzan had at the turn of the century.

In both the later nineteenth century and the twentieth century, the home was so much a woman's sphere that some men felt uncomfortable within it. "How could man return to home without feeling like a wimp?" (Kimmel 1996, 158). Kimmel sees that one solution was to carve out a special male space within this sphere: "like the den or the study in the nineteenth century or the

basement, the workshop, the garage or even the backyard barbecue pit today"
(1996, 158). Another concern for men was that since women were so dominant in childrearing, young boys were becoming too soft. Organizations such
as the Boy Scouts of America (founded in 1910) were established to masculinize the experience and training of young males. Boy Scouts went on
rugged camping trips where they were to learn discipline and manly survival
skills. Later, after World War II, many people felt that fathers should take a
more active role in raising male children to help masculinize them and to
combat growing problems such as juvenile delinquency (Kimmel 1996).

  While twentieth-century men advanced a masculine individualism,
twentieth-century women were moving from covert to overt expressions of
individualism. This brought changes to women's lives and reformulations of
their roles. However, as we shall see, the overall effect of the twentieth century on women was neither liberation nor gender equality but a change in
the nature and meaning of their fragmentation.

  In the opening decades of the twentieth century, new and challenging
types of middle-class women were actively embracing individualism. There
were various manifestations of what came to be called the New Woman. One
variant of the New Woman, who emerged in the latter part of the nineteenth
century, was an unintended consequence of the opening of higher education to women. As we saw, the early women's colleges were to help make
women better wives and mothers. But in the colleges women discovered both
a new world apart from their patriarchical families and new possibilities for
their own achievements and self-definition. New Women used their education to pursue their own careers. Some taught in the women's colleges after
graduation (Smith-Rosenberg 1985). Some were vocal feminists who fought
for women's suffrage and other women's causes. Many continued the reform
work of an earlier generation of middle-class women. Some, for example,
established or participated in settlement houses in urban slums. These were
community centers set up for the poor, and within them the reformers sought
to better understand poverty. Here reform women, along with men reformers, sought to bring education, health care, new values, and new hope to the
poverty stricken.[2] By 1910 there were more than four hundred settlement
houses in the country. These reform women developed a "sisterhood" among
themselves, with a strong sense of solidarity. Some of these women had lifelong passionate relationships with each other.

  New Women at the turn of the century might look very familiar to late-
twentieth-century Americans. Yet in two respects they were quite different
from most educated career women and/or feminists of today. For one thing,
New Women did not challenge the notion of innate sexual differences. Like
men of their time, they believed that men and women are fundamentally
different and that the differences are rooted in biology. They did not seek
the right to vote because they saw themselves as similar to men but because they saw themselves as different, bringing a special feminine virtue

and humanitarian caring to the political realm (Conway 1987). Similarly, as had reform-minded Victorian ladies before them, they saw their reform work as an extension of their superior virtue as women.

Second, most of these New Women did not marry or have children. And this brings up one aspect of their fragmentation: New Women could have their education and their careers, but usually only at the expense of marriage and reproduction. Many men and other women saw them as unnatural and unwomanly. Some men even went so far as to categorize them as an "intermediate sex," and "by the 1920s, charges of lesbianism had become a common way to discredit women professionals, reformers and educators" (Smith-Rosenberg 1985, 281).

American author Henry James, who coined the term "New Woman," made them leading characters in his novels. Here they are both exciting and yet ultimately wrong and out of place. New Women in his fiction are strong characters who lead adventuresome lives. But, because of their unnatural choice of autonomy and individualism over marriage and motherhood, they always come to some bad end (Smith-Rosenberg 1985).

Another variant of the New Woman was the "flapper," a figure associated with the Roaring Twenties. Originally an upper-class rebellious youth who had discovered urban fun, the flapper filtered down to the middle class. Typically she was a young, unmarried woman living and possibly working in the city. The flapper challenged gender patterns in an entirely new way: She was sexually assertive. She put on makeup, shortened her skirts, and bobbed her hair; she smoked, drank, and danced in public. She went to parties and other places of amusement with men. Most of all, she insisted upon her sexual autonomy and freedom. She sought (and failed) to end the double sexual standard, not by reforming men as had nineteenth-century "purity crusaders," but by adopting male sexual freedoms. Needless to say, while many of her male peers found the flapper exciting and refreshing, more conservative members of society found her utterly outrageous and despicable.

Relatively few women were true New Women, but these women were at the vanguard of broader long-term changes. Thus, while not striking out to pursue careers, increasing numbers of young women of subsequent generations followed New Women in pursuing higher education. One long-term change the flapper initiated was a shift in dress styles and ideal body images for American women. Gone were the painful undergarments and yards of cloth of the Victorian ladies. Gone, too, were the ideals of women's full hips and breasts of the earlier period, now replaced with an ideal slim, "boyish" figure. Some have interpreted the new body image as a rejection of gender distinctions (Smith-Rosenberg 1985), while others have emphasized that "the androgynous flapper was in fact a monument to heterosexuality" (Friedman, Shade, and Capozzoli 1987, 417). Whatever her messages, the flapper was a symbol of the loosening of sexual restrictions on women. Many surveys undertaken in the early twentieth century showed that in fact there had been an increase in female premarital and extramarital sex between 1890 and 1920 (Mintz and Kellogg 1988). But what is more important than change in actual behavior is that sexuality was now being openly and publicly expressed. Sexual expression had moved from the strictly private to the public sphere.

THE COMPANIONATE FAMILY

In the early twentieth century, very much as today, many Americans were seriously concerned with the fate of the family for many reasons. First, the fertility rate, already lowered in the nineteenth century, continued to decline. It was particularly low for the white middle class, leading President Theodore Roosevelt in 1903 to bemoan the "race suicide" of this leading segment of society. Second, divorce rates were rising. Third, many people were deeply afraid of the collapse of sexual order and decency that the flapper represented. And finally, many people were disturbed by the fact that so many women were working outside the home instead of staying in their proper domestic sphere, holding the family together (Mintz and Kellogg 1988).

There were many efforts to save the family, for example by stiffening divorce laws, opposing birth control, or enacting state laws against certain styles of dress and forms of dance. Like the New Right movement today, this was an attempt to turn the clock back to an earlier tradition. But none of these efforts seemed to work. An alternative strategy eventually adopted was the promotion of a new "companionate family." Family historians Steven Mintz and Susan Kellogg describe this new family form:

> Instead of idealizing the family as a sacred refuge in a corrupt world, a small but influential group of psychologists, educators, and legal scholars gave shape to a new conception of a "companionate family" in which husbands and wives would be "friends and lovers" and parents and children would be "pals." Convinced that the "old-style" family based on sexual repression, patriarchal authority, and hierarchical organization, was "unsatisfactorily adjusted to twentieth century conditions," these "experts" on the family sought to facilitate the transition to a new kind of family better suited to "modern society and industrial conditions." (Minz and Kellogg 1988, 113)

This transition to the companionate family marks a rather interesting shift in the fragmentation of middle-class women. In Victorian times the Cult of True Womanhood mandated that a woman could not be simultaneously a good mother, or even a good civilizing wife, and a sexually expressive person. A virtuous woman was to publicly downplay sexuality and emphasize motherhood. Now, in the companionate family, it was the reverse: A woman was supposed to be sexually attractive to her husband and to express herself sexually, not just in the strict privacy of the innermost sanctum of the bedroom, but more openly in society. As sexuality was emphasized, motherhood was downplayed; indeed it was feared that motherhood could threaten the new-found "friends and lovers" relationship between husband and wife. Motherhood was still important but it was not to interfere with the new romantic and sexual husband–wife bond. This change of attitude was seen in the ideas about birth control. Nineteenth-century reform women opposed it because it would encourage male lust and irresponsible sex. Now birth control was openly supported by middle-class women as a way to keep pregnancy, childbirth, and children from dampening marital sexual love. Thus we see that whereas values had reversed, the idea of an incompatibility between motherhood and female sexuality remained. The different dimensions of womanhood were still fragmented.

In the 1920s and 1930s many middle-class women embraced the companionate family. Though many went to college and some worked before marriage, the majority stopped working when they married and became domestic companionate wives in the home. That this was an increasingly lonely, isolated, and otherwise unrewarding experience for many women is usually associated with the period after World War II, as popularized by Betty Friedan (1963) in her book, *The Feminine Mystique*. Ruth Cowan, however, has demonstrated that in fact this state of affairs began in the period between the wars and was merely renewed after it. "Whatever it was that trapped educated American women in their kitchens, babbling at babies and worrying about color combinations for the bathroom, the trap was set in the roaring 20s, not the quiet 50s" (Cowen 1987, 447).

World War II brought brief changes for both men and women. Needless to say, the war bolstered a sense of strong, virile American manhood and gave many opportunities for individual men to decisively prove their manhood (Kimmel 1996). For women, the war brought new, productive roles. With so many men off to war, women were needed to temporarily fill their jobs. Far from being condemned as unwomanly feminist upstarts, these women were applauded for helping out in a crisis. Posters of a young woman actively working in construction, "Rosie the Riveter," were circulated in praise of women for their war effort. But once the war was over, many women left their jobs or were pushed out of them.

AMERICAN DATING

The transition to the companionate family was accompanied by a transition to a new type of courtship: dating. American dating began in the 1920s, was somewhat interrupted during World War II, and then resumed after the war in a different form. In the 1920s it replaced an earlier form of middle-class courtship known as "calling." In calling, a woman or her mother invited a particular gentleman to call on the woman at her home. There he was taken to the family parlor, where he could visit with the woman. Usually other family members would be present, but if the relationship proceeded toward engagement, the couple would gradually be allowed some privacy in the parlor. If the man lost interest in the woman he ceased to call, and if she lost interest in him, he would be told that she was ill or absent on his subsequent calls (Bailey 1988).

Notice that in the calling system, the courtship was initiated by the woman who extended the invitation to call and that it took place on the woman's "turf" in the private sphere of her home. Beth Bailey (1988) shows how the transformation from calling to dating in the 1920s changed all of this. First, in dating, the man took the initiative by asking the woman for a date. Second, in dating, the couple went out to the male public sphere, to the man's "turf," to some public place of amusement or refreshment arranged by him. And third, the man paid for everything. The date was completely based on his money, just as marriage would be.

Thus, although women had won the vote by 1920, they had lost control over courtship. With dating, a woman was out there in the public sphere completely dependent on her male escort and his money. Until the 1960s there was a rather strict code of etiquette surrounding dating, whereby the man was to guide and protect the woman by, for example, opening doors and pulling out chairs for her and ordering for her in restaurants. As Bailey (1988, 112) writes, "Such protection and mastery, incidentally, robbed women of their autonomy and their power of speech."

The connection between dating and male money carried additional gender messages. That a man should pay for everything was insisted upon by all. Even if the woman needed to make a financial contribution due to some unfortunate miscalculation, it was appropriate for her to give the money to the man, who would then make the payment in public. What a man could pay for was a measure of his status and worth as a provider; at the same time it was a statement of the woman's worth as a date (Bailey 1988).

The rooting of courtship in male money and in consumerism also set up an ideology of the date as a commercial exchange. Men were paying, but what exactly were they buying? Female companionship? A good time? Possibly, but there was always an uncomfortable undercurrent of "sexual favors" lurking in the background. The reliance on male money made for an imbalance in the system, justifying a subtle and unspoken idea that there was really only one way a woman could even out the exchange. It is interesting that in the nineteenth century, long before it acquired its current meaning, the word "date" was used to indicate the event of buying a prostitute's services (Bailey 1988, 22).

Once it got going, American youth turned dating into a frenzy of ritualized status seeking that could only have seemed bizarre to an outsider. This was especially true in the earlier pre-World War II form, which Bailey (1988, 26) calls the period of "the rating-dating system." The point of dating, for males and females, was to be popular: "You had to rate in order to date, to date in order to rate" (Bailey 1988, 30). Beginning on college campuses but filtering down into high school and into the broader society generally, among youth, having a date was a mark of success; not having a date was a failure (Gorer 1948).

In the prewar period, dating was fiercely competitive and emphasized an ideal of dating many different people. The more dates a person had with different people, the greater the public demonstration of popularity. Bailey (1988, 30) found the following refrain from a female high school student in 1943 in the popular magazine, *Senior Scholastic*:

Going Steady with one date
Is okay, if that's all you rate.

She continues with a description of this competitive promiscuous dating:

In the 1930s and 1940s, this competition was enacted most visibly on the dance floor. There, success was a dizzying popularity that kept girls whirling from escort to escort. An etiquette book for college girls (1936) told girls to strive to be "once arounders," to never be left with the same partner for more than one turn around the dance floor. (Bailey 1988, 31)

The interpersonal relationships between boys and girls or men and women on a date was not necessarily important. What was important was the public demonstration of popularity (Mead 1949). This public presentation of self became so important that some women in college dorms without a date on Saturday night would turn out their room lights so that others would not know they were home dateless. The agonies of "wallflowers," the trauma for females never asked out, the pain for males whose requests for dates were refused, and the embarrassment to a female of "getting stuck" (dancing with only one male and not having other males "cut in" on him to dance with her) are sad legends of the prewar period (Bailey 1988).

Of course, even in this system of dating, young people could occasionally have a good time, enjoy a meaningful conversation, get to know an interesting person, or even fall madly in love; certainly all of this did sometimes happen. But as a whole, the system was so entrenched in a status-seeking popularity contest that these other potential rewards were overshadowed. It is in terms of money spent and popularity of participants that the people themselves talked about dating. Survivors of American dating often look back with a mixture of bemused nostalgia and utter embarrassment—embarrassment over their own social clumsiness or embarrassment over the fact that they enthusiastically engaged in something so inherently shallow.

One eyewitness outside observer of the American prewar style of dating, Geoffrey Gorer (1948), felt that the popularity males and females sought was not so much with the opposite sex as with one's same-sex peers, with whom the details of dates were often discussed at length. He also observed a very particular verbal style in dating; the man gave out "lines" that the woman would then "parry," or, if she were socially unskilled, would "fall for." He was describing a kind of back-and-forth exchange of one-line sarcasms. This type of dating discourse continued after the war. It seems to suggest some underlying tension or hostility between the sexes played out in dating. Postwar films—for example *Pillow Talk* starring Doris Day and Rock Hudson—reeked of this type of sarcastic bantering between the sexes, a discourse that seemed to haunt male–female romantic relationships through courtship and into marriage. Simone de Beauvoir (1953, 290) during her visit to America in the early 1950s also noticed a "mutual mistrust" between men and women, and observed: "The thing I noticed immediately in America was that men and women seldom like one another" (1953, 289).

American prewar dating was often a frenzied, competitive, materialistic, impersonal, individualistic struggle to continually demonstrate popularity among peers. One might have thought that a world war would have had a sobering effect on this frivolity, but that was not the case. Frantic dating resumed after the war, though the form of dating took a new turn. After the war the "rating-dating system" was replaced with "going steady" (Bailey 1988). Here, the male gave a female some symbol (such as a class ring) to show that they were officially boyfriend and girlfriend. For as long as this relationship lasted, they were not to date other people. Each was a guaranteed date for the other at school functions. This relaxed the competitiveness of prewar dating, but the goal was the same: popularity. Simply by acquiring a steady boyfriend or girlfriend, one gained peer recognition.

The average age of marriage dropped after the war and so did the age of dating and going steady, filtering down to the early teens. Going steady was a prominent feature of postwar high school life. These relationships could be more intense, romantic, and personal than the promiscuous prewar dating, but only in rare cases did they end in marriage. No one really expected them to last, even though official boyfriends and girlfriends spent a great deal of time in one another's homes and often became close friends of each others' families. "Going steady" was easily terminated (though "breaking up was hard to do"), with new unions formed. It was almost as though postwar young people were preparing themselves for what in fact many would later face: serial monogamy.

Bailey, who calls going steady "play marriage," suggests that postwar youth sought temporary social security instead of fierce competition. "The Bomb, the Cold War, the certainty of military service … perpetuated that classic wartime desire for something stable in an unstable world" (Bailey 1988, 49). Also they were emulating those slightly older than themselves who were now marrying younger, at age nineteen or twenty, and who were themselves seeking something stable in an unstable world.

By the postwar period and extending to the 1960s, the ideal female body underwent a change away from the boyish flapper and back to full breasts and hips. Indeed, American males came to measure and evaluate females by the size of their breasts. This caused considerable anxiety in flat-chested women. "Not an insurmountable problem, however. American women imitated the ideal; they went about the task of making nature over with a little help from the garment industry. In its 1951 catalogue, Sears offered twenty-two kinds of falsies..." (Bailey 1988, 74). However it wasn't just women who were depersonalized in the dating system; the same system "transformed men into no more than wallets" (Bailey 1988, 67), the thickness of which women used to evaluate men.

Both before and after the war, in both high schools and colleges, the American cultural celebration of dating was expressed in the formal dance, or prom (see Figure 3.1). This dance event became so important that a girl's first prom was like a ritual rite of passage into adulthood (Bailey 1988). Of course, one had to have a date for a prom, and in this context more than any other the quality of the date was a symbol of social success. The most successful of all became prom queens and kings. For proms, people dressed formally; women and girls (or their parents) spent a great deal of money on their formals. Men and boys, of course, spent money on the prom itself and any after-prom entertainment. They bought the mandatory corsage, whose cost became a symbol of their and their date's worth. "These flowers were not private gifts—cut flowers for the woman's dressing table—but public symbols. They said, for the man, 'See what I can afford,' and for the woman, 'See how much I'm worth'" (Bailey 1988, 65).

FIGURE 3.1
High school semi-formal, 1961. (*Linda Stone*)

The goal of dating, both pre- and postwar, was not sexual gratification, although sexual activity might take place. Logically, some sexual activity would be more likely as greater privacy was attained through use of the automobile and as parents were increasingly permissive toward their children. From the 1920s on, though, dating in the context of loosened sexual mores placed a special burden on women: An ideology quickly developed that placed responsibility for setting the sexual boundaries largely on them (Bailey 1988). Possibly this was a carryover from the nineteenth-century idea that women possess superior virtue. Or perhaps people reasoned that since women can get pregnant, they had more at stake in the consequences of sexual activity. Also, the double sexual standard of the nineteenth century lived on (as it does to this day), so that a woman had her "reputation" to consider. In any case, it was up to the woman to set the sexual boundaries and if anything went wrong, it was her fault. From this it was easy to conclude, for example, that if a woman was raped, she must have encouraged it, however unwittingly (Bailey 1988).

Father Knows Best

While all this dating and going steady was going on among youth in the postwar years, companionate marriage was also resumed and revived. This period after the war, from the late 1940s through the early 1960s, marks what some see as the Golden Age of the middle-class American family. In its romanticized version this family lived in the suburbs and consisted of a husband, wife, and a couple of children. The couple owned its own home. The husband was a successful breadwinner who went out to work; the wife was an attractive and happy homemaker who baked brownies for her children and those of the neighbors, all of whom were very polite and well-behaved. Current television reruns of *Leave It To Beaver* and *Father Knows Best* are graphic illustrations of the ideal (see Figure 3.2).

Coontz (1992) has pointed out that this Golden Age family is a mythologized American past. It is true that postwar prosperity allowed many couples to pursue "the American Dream"—to move to the suburbs, buy their own homes, and raise a few children, with a breadwinning husband and a nonworking wife. In the 1950s about two-thirds of all married-couple families had husbands in the labor force and wives at home; today less than one-fifth of all married-couple families take this form (Costello and Krimgold 1996, 52). Today fewer than 10 percent of all families resemble the "Leave It to Beaver" form, with a working father, a full-time homemaking mother, and dependent children (Coontz 1992, 23).

But hidden away in many of those suburban homes of the 1950s were drinking problems, bickering spouses, abusive relationships, and bored wives. In addition, the Golden Age family didn't last for long. By the mid-sixties it

FIGURE 3.2
The Companionate Family: A housewife and children greet the breadwinner with joy. (*Photo by Willinger/Getty Images, Inc.*)

had become nearly impossible for such a family to survive on one income, leading many middle-class married women into the workforce. What is important about the Golden Age family is that it represents what many contemporary Americans nostalgically seek to revive. As we will explore in Chapter 6, many people, concerned and frustrated with the breakdown of the American family, seek to return to this "tradition." Yet this is no longer an economically realistic option, and for many Americans it never was.

That it was, and for many still is, a glorified cultural ideal is important. Middle-class Americans loved watching Golden Age families on television sitcoms and soap operas. Anthropologist Susan Bean (1976) analyzed how daytime soap operas in the 1960s and 1970s, watched mainly by women, expressed a continual fascination with the ideal American nuclear family. To be complete, this family had to consist of a husband and wife in love with each other and had to include these people's own biological children, an expression of that love. Over and over again, the soap opera subplots of the period started out with this ideal family. Then something would happen to disrupt this perfection—the wife or husband could not have children, or suddenly the husband would fall out of love with the wife or vice versa, or suddenly the husband would find (what the audience knew all along) that his children were not biologically his. This unit would accordingly crumble apart, but then, over time, sometimes over many years, a new perfect unit would reemerge, only to be torn down again, and so on. It was as though viewers were fascinated with confronting all the potential threats to the perfect but fragile American family, while watching it reemerge whole and perfect again.

GENDER CRISES

It was in the 1960s that we began to see signs of some middle-class women's discontent with the role of full-time wife and mother in suburbia. Many women came to feel that they lived through their husbands or children with no independent identity of their own.[3] One of the best novels to describe a suburban housewife's frustration was Marilyn French's *The Women's Room*. French (1977, 49) describes a typical day in the early married life of Mira, her central character:

> She shopped, and cleaned the apartment, and cooked, and took the laundry to the laundromat (little dreaming that after the baby was born this would become one of her great pleasures—the chance to get out of the house alone, or at least accompanied only by a great white silent uncrying laundry bag). She ironed sheets and Norm's shirts and read the recipe columns of the newspapers searching for an interesting or different way to serve inexpensive foods. The thing she most notably did not do was think.

Later Mira and Norm move to the suburbs where they raise two boys. French (1977, 145) gives a view of her daily morning hours in this period:

> [Norm] gave her the chores for the day—suits to be cleaned, shoes to be mended, some business at the bank, a telephone call to the insurance agent about the dent in his car. Then he left as she woke the children and prepared their eggs ... then she drove them the mile to the school bus stop ... then she returned to the house.... The greasy frying pan sat on the stove, the spattered coffee pot behind it. Dirty dishes lay on the kitchen table. The four beds were unmade and there was soiled underwear lying about. There was dust in the living and dining rooms, the family room held used soda glasses and potato chips from the night before. What bothered her was not that the tasks that had to be done were exerting.... It was that she felt that the three others lived their lives and she went around after them cleaning up their mess.

Gradually Mira becomes more and more depressed, she takes to drinking brandy alone in the dark at night, and eventually her husband leaves her for another woman.

In the 1960s a number of interrelated forces—more women in the workplace, a concern over frustrations in the role of nonworking wife, and a renewed questioning of the double sexual standard—brought about a new middle-class woman's movement. Probably the greatest factor behind this women's movement was the sharp and steady increase of women in the workforce beginning in the 1950s. This increase was prompted by inflation, which meant that two incomes per family were increasingly needed to maintain a middle-class standard of living. In addition there were more openings for "female" labor in the U.S. economy (i.e., more jobs for secretaries, clerks, and retail workers) (Margolis 1984). A new awareness of gender inequality and concerns for the dissatisfactions of suburban housewifery were thus stirred up by the fact that sizable numbers of middle-class women had already left the home for work, work that was moreover largely part-time, temporary, lower paying, and less prestigious than men's work.

While the 1920s had seen individual "flappers" challenge more traditional sexual mores, this 1960s organized women's movement explicitly raised issues of "sexual liberation" for women, or the demand for acceptable sexual expression equal to that of men. The nineteenth century had seen a woman's suffrage movement, but the 1960s women's movement was much broader, calling for gender equality in all realms of life. And in contrast to nineteenth-century thinking, the new women's movement denied innate differences between men and women. Women could and should be allowed to do whatever men were doing. One thing this movement tried and failed to do was unite women across classes and ethnic groups (Rothman 1978). It remained a white, middle-class movement.

This movement raised a fundamental issue that returns us to the fragmentation of the American woman. The 1960s movement was, above all, a cry for autonomy. Sheila Rothman (1978, 231) refers to it as a movement promoting the "woman as person," a woman who is autonomous, competent, and fully able to define herself. This autonomy was most often expressed as, and associated with, a woman's right to pursue a career outside the home. It was an explicit demand for women's right to pursue happiness, to embrace American individualism in the public sphere. Simultaneously, women wanted all of their dimensions of womanhood—their sexuality, fertility (motherhood), and autonomous persons (careers)—to be seen as perfectly compatible, as compatible as the equivalent dimensions of manhood are for men. The movement was a demand for wholeness, a demand which so far has not been met.

Gradually most people came to accept that a wife may work outside the home, but now some people feel that a mother should not. To understand why this is so, it is helpful to return to nineteenth-century middle-class ideas about the family and women. In the last chapter, we saw that nineteenth-century women were to hold the family together as a refuge from the world of male individualism. They could do this, the thinking went, not as autonomous persons but as women. It was their special nature as women (i.e., virtuous, nurturing, selfless, domestic beings) that made them natural caretakers and maintainers of the family. Thus the well-being and indeed the survival of the family depended on the denial of female autonomy, the denial of "woman as person."

In the twentieth century, the cry for female autonomy was seen by many as a direct threat to the institution of the American family and all it provided in the way of warm, human sentiments to counterbalance the impersonal, individualistic world outside. What gains for female autonomy were made were gradual and piecemeal; they were resisted and are still being resisted. Women themselves were long reluctant to argue for their own autonomy; as we saw, they advocated their right to vote not because women are persons, equivalent to men, but because they are women and thus possess special virtue (Degler 1980).

Today no one would suggest that women should be allowed to vote because they are women; it has been accepted that as far as voting goes, women are persons, just like men. In a similar way, women as unmarried persons or persons yet to have children are today acceptable as autonomous beings, permissible in the workforce. But many feel that to grant autonomy to women as mothers is going too far; motherhood, if no longer womanhood altogether, is, in this view, the last bastion of the American family, the last hope for preserving that selfless core of nurturing that we all need. If women's autonomy overtakes motherhood, we're doomed; the American family and all that it stands for will vanish. For this reason, historian Carl Degler sees the granting of full autonomy and personhood to women as at odds with the values of the American family: "The central values of the modern family stand in opposition to these that underlie women's emancipation" (1980, 471). Degler points out that it is a woman's role as childrearer that most fundamentally conflicts with female individualism: "An assumption of the modern family has always been that women are the primary childrearers. As a result there has been a primary tension, if not conflict, between the individualistic interests of women and those of the family" (1980, 463).

The 1960s women's movement, then, stirred up an issue that is at the heart of current debates on gender, namely, the relationship between motherhood and extradomestic work. Many people, women and men, resisted or contested the 1960s movement precisely because they saw motherhood and autonomous personhood as incompatible. By this time no one had any problem with female sexuality and motherhood fitting together, which had been the problem behind the fragmentation of the nineteenth-century woman. But now the fault line fell between motherhood and autonomous personhood as expressed in extradomestic work.

This whole issue of careers versus motherhood came to divide American women in the 1970s and 1980s. Bitterness and resentment strained relationships between women in middle-class suburbia where, by the early 1980s, often as many as half of the women worked outside the home. Some of those who stayed at home resented the women who worked outside. Journalist

Nancy Rubin records the following comment from a suburban woman who chose to stay at home:

> But the working women look down their noses at us, and meanwhile there we are, picking up the pieces for them, being the unofficial neighborhood baby-sitters or the ones who give time to the community activities. Don't bother me, they say, don't ask me to do things in the community, because I'm holy—I'm working. (Rubin 1982, 132)

Another woman made the following complaint:

> You can't even go to a cocktail party anymore without someone asking you what you do. It makes me sick. And if you say, "Well, I'm just a wife and mother" ... they look at you funny. Why can't they accept you as a human being? Why do you have to be something all the time? (Rubin 1982, 142–143)

Some women who made these complaints accused feminists of causing all the trouble, of devaluing motherhood or pressuring women to feel that they all have to be something. Feminists retorted that they never denied any woman's (or for that matter any man's) right to stay at home with her children. What they wanted was gender-equal opportunity to work outside the home or pursue a career. They also questioned why it is the mother and not the father who is given total responsibility for rearing children. They rejected the notion that just because women undergo pregnancy and birth that they must be the ones to assume full-time child care and housework. In place of the question, "Why do you have to be something all the time?" feminists asked, "Why is it that women, and not men, can only be one thing at a time?"

Meanwhile, working suburban women resented others' accusations that they were selfish or bad mothers. They struggled to "balance" the demands of work and home and often felt considerable guilt that they were depriving their children of proper care (Rubin 1982).

A lot of this tension between women continues today. American women today do not have to choose between a career and marriage, as most New Women did in the nineteenth century, but they are still being pressured to choose between careers and motherhood. Of course, many women do have both, but others continue to consider them selfish or think they are neglecting their children. Alternatively, those who choose full-time motherhood are still sometimes accused by others of doing nothing with themselves or being unwisely dependent financially on men.

While women have been agonizing over the incompatibility of their fragmented parts, motherhood and careers, middle-class men have expressed problems of their own in the late twentieth century. Some have identified a new "masculinity crisis," fueled by the demands of the women's movement, the gay rights movement, charges of sexual harassment, the encroachment of women and ethnic minorities into the workplace, and so on. There has been a variety of responses to this, ranging all the way from advocating a return to Golden Age "tradition," as seen most recently with the Promise Keepers (a loose organization of Christian men who promise to protect family values), to advocating that men become actively pro-feminist. Perhaps the most interesting response of all has been the 1990s "men's movements," which seek to recapture manhood through weekend retreats. Here men go off together to face wild nature, bond together in Indian sweat lodges, and offer each other pop psychological therapy and solace. Spearheading these movements has been the book *Iron John* (1990) by Robert Bly. While claiming that his work is not antifeminist, Bly argues that males need to recreate manhood in their own space. Like his nineteenth-century counterparts, he claims that men suffer from absent fathers and feminization by mothers.

BODIES

As in every culture, treatments of the human body resound with gender messages in American society. In Chapter 1 we drew attention to the body rituals of the Nacirema and noted there how dissatisfaction with the body, for both men and women, has been a pervasive theme in American middle-class culture. In Chapter 2 we discussed nineteenth-century perceptions of women's bodies as frail and vulnerable, with special threats to their reproductive biology from strenuous physical or mental activity.

Over the twentieth century American society saw some new body developments. As noted, the ideal female shape went from plump and voluminous to thin and androgynous in the 1920s. In the 1950s it was fuller and plumper again but by the 1970s the super thin ideal had emerged. Over the same period male muscularity came into vogue. In the late twentieth and early twenty-first centuries it appears that women are spending more time on bodily improvement than ever before. Women are now so focused on physical self-modification that it depletes both their time and their energy from other interests as well as leaving them with perpetual feelings of inadequacy (Bordo 1997). Of course Madison Avenue has capitalized on American women's obsession with the body and so has perpetuated and strengthened the ideal. These days there is no limit to what magazines and TV commercials encourage women to do:

> A woman's skin must be soft, supple, hairless, and smooth: ideally it should betray no sign of wear, experience, age or deep thought. Hair must be removed not only from the face but from large surfaces of the body as well … accomplished by shaving, buffing with fine sandpaper, or foul-smelling depilatories.… The removal of facial hair can be more specialized. Eyebrows are plucked out by the roots with a tweezer. Hot wax is sometimes poured onto the mustache and then ripped away when it cools. The woman who

wants a more permanent result may try electrolysis. This involves the killing of a hair root by the passage of an electric current down a needle which has been inserted into its base. The procedure is painful and expensive. (Bartky 1997, 131)

And this is just body and facial hair! For American women there is much more to attend to with regular skin and hair care, clothes and makeup, continual dieting, tummy tucks, face lifts, and breast alterations.

We can also see gender inscribed in male and female body language. Studies have shown that women smile more than men. In many contexts, American women position their bodies in a more restrained way, keeping to smaller spaces, while men spread out, look more relaxed, and take more space. Men stride along while walking, with arms loose and dangling, whereas women take smaller steps and hold their arms to their bodies (Bartky 1997).

Medical discourse about human bodies is also replete with subtle gender messages. For example, Emily Martin (1997) has shown how scientific textbooks covering human reproduction reflect and reaffirm gender stereotypes. Thus female menstruation is depicted as a "failure" and female egg production as "wasteful." By contrast the texts marvel at the sheer volume of male spermatogenesis and in general describe male reproductive physiology in laudatory, positive language. Martin (1987) also showed how twentieth-century medical discourse and hospital birth practices developed a metaphor of the woman's body as "like a machine" that works (labors) to make a "product." But in the process of giving birth, the woman is made to feel that the master of this machine (and the real manager of the whole "production" process) is not the woman herself but the doctor. In the experience of hospital birth, the mother herself emerges as somewhat secondary, passive, dehumanized, and split into separate parts. Martin saw, then, that American middle-class women's feeling of fragmentation and lack of autonomy is fostered by the medical treatment of their bodies. Also interesting is Martin's finding that middle-class women are likely to have internalized the view of their bodies projected in medical discourse, whereas women from working-class backgrounds are more likely to reject and resist these images of the female body.

Continuing in this line of work, Robbie Davis-Floyd (1992) analyzed childbirth in American hospitals as a "rite of passage." In all societies, some significant transitions in the life cycle—such as birth, puberty, marriage, death—are surrounded with rituals through which core cultural values are symbolically expressed and transmitted to or reinforced for participants. In this way ritualized rites of passage become powerful agents of socialization. Analyzing hospital births as ritualized rites of passage, Davis-Floyd showed how hospital procedures express the "technocratic model" underlying American cultural ideology. The technocratic model is a dominant cultural ideology or worldview that places high value on science and technology and those institutions and people who control them. This dominant technocratic worldview also becomes a framework for understanding other social processes. Thus Davis-Floyd found that in the hospital, birth follows a model of "assembly-line production of goods" where "a woman's reproductive tract is treated like a birthing machine by skilled technicians working under semiflexible timetables to meet production and quality-control demands" (1992, 55). Or as one doctor reported to her:

> We shave 'em, we prep 'em, we hook 'em up to the IV and administer sedation. We deliver the baby, it goes to the nursery and the mother goes to her room. There's no room for niceties around here. We just move 'em right on through. It's hard not to see it like an assembly line (fourth-year resident). (Davis-Floyd 1992, 55)

Davis-Floyd takes us on an often chilling ride through hospital birthing rituals—from the shaving of the woman's pubic hair, the administering of an enema, her intravenous feeding, episiotomy (enlarging of the vaginal opening), the strapping on of an external fetal monitor, labor, and finally to ritual treatments of the newborn. The medical rationale for these procedures is often questionable. At every step of the way, Davis-Floyd spells out the messages of the rituals. One message that comes out loud and clear is that the woman's body is a defective machine, inadequate on its own to give birth. These birth rituals

> transform the birthing woman into a mother in the full sense of the word— that is, into a woman who has internalized the core values of American society: one who believes in science, relies on technology, recognizes her inferiority (either consciously or unconsciously), and so at some level accepts the principle of patriarchy. (1992, 152–153)

Thus the ritual experience of giving birth in an American hospital is for women a lesson in their own inferiority.

For all that we hear of American women's anorexia, their pressures to attain an ideal body, and the negative cultural evaluations of their various life processes such as menopause, it is clear that it is not just women who suffer body problems in America. For men, a distinctive body issue with social, psychological, and cultural implications is impotence. One study conducted in the Boston area showed that about 40 percent of men over age forty suffered some degree of erectile dysfunction and seventy percent of men age 70 did so (Goldstein 2000). Given the aging of the global population, these researchers estimate that in twenty-five years, over 330 million men worldwide will suffer from impotence. On the bright side of science and technology, medical research is uncovering the role of the brain in sexual dysfunctions for both men and women, leading to more effective treatment (Goldstein 2000). But as with female "body problems," male impotence is tied up with cultural constructions of gender. Specifically, impotence becomes a particularly stressing problem in contexts where, as in the United States, masculinity is so strongly constructed in terms of male sexual performance (Tiefer 1992).

New Religious Movements

However imperfect it may always have been, the American family is under greater stress than ever in the early twenty-first century. The rising rates of divorce (now at 50 percent); poor, single mothers; alienated, uncontrollable, and drug-dependent youth; child abuse and wife-beating are all of great concern to many people. As in the 1920s, family "breakdown" is being discussed and debated, with many searching for a return to "tradition." Others, either discontent with "mainstream" gender roles and family options, or themselves suffering from family breakdown or abuse within the family, are turning to New Religious Movements (NRMs), sometimes referred to as cults (Palmer 1994). A few of these, like the Rajneesh Movement, draw their largest membership from the middle class; most draw members across class lines.

These NRMs offer a bewildering variety of alternative gender systems and familial arrangements. Although these represent radical alternatives, Palmer sees them as, in many ways, caricatures of gender arrangements or ideologies within the broader society. Some, for example the International Society for Krishna Consciousness, emphasize chastity for both men and women and insist on the subordination of wives to husbands. This group, a kind of caricature of more traditional American gender roles, attracts more men than women. At the same time, many women members "voiced a disappointment about their mothers who had chosen to join the workforce instead of being homemakers, and they expressed a deep satisfaction in choosing to stay home with their children" (Palmer 1994, 38). This NRM, like many others, offers a particular spiritual solution to social change and the problems these changes bring to the family.

A very different gender arrangement is offered by the Rajneesh Movement (this is the group that settled for a while in a commune in Antelope, Oregon). In this movement women are believed to be more spiritually evolved than men and they take active leadership roles within the movement. Among Rajneesh followers, sexuality is seen as a path to higher spiritual consciousness (the "cosmic orgasm"). Free love is encouraged and the formation of exclusive sexual relationships is frowned upon. This group attracts more women than men. Palmer sees it as characterizing the lifestyle of many childless professional women who become involved in a succession of short-term love relationships. But in the Rajneesh movement, these women not only find spiritual justification for a lifestyle, but also communal solidarity, a new sense of family in place of the loneliness of their previous lives.

A very interesting group is the Raelians (headquartered in Canada). Raelians believe that humans were placed on earth by space aliens who created human DNA in their labs. Most humans will destroy themselves through nuclear warfare, but a select few will, with the help of the aliens, become immortal through cloning and will relocate on new planets. The leader of the Raelians claims to have had contact with these aliens and to have visited their spaceships. Raelians believe that Jesus Christ, Mohammed, Buddha, and Joseph Smith were previous prophets in touch with the aliens. The Virgin Mary was taken to the alien space labs and impregnated there, then returned to earth. Unlike the Rajneesh followers, who see women as superior to men, Raelians preach complete gender equality. Free love is encouraged, as are homosexual relationships. With regard to cloning, this group is very serious. Indeed the Raelians have founded a company, Clonaid, with plans for human cloning. One couple has offered the company $500,000 to clone their dead infant and a number of surrogate mothers have been recruited to carry other cloned embryos (*Science* 289, 29 September 2000: 2271).

Interestingly, all the NRMs covered in Susan Palmer's (1994) study reject American dating altogether. Sometimes parents arrange marriages of their children (as in Krishna Consciousness) or the spiritual leader arranges unions (as among the followers of Reverend Moon) or the group rejects both dating and marriage, as with the Raelians and the Rajneesh Movement.

With respect to the fragmentation of the American woman, one interesting feature of all of the NRMs in Palmer's study is that they emphasize only one or at most two dimensions of womanhood. Thus the Krishna Consciousness group emphasizes wifehood and motherhood; it also encourages female modesty, downplays sexuality, and encourages the restriction of sexuality to procreation. When a man decides to enter his last stage of life (the sannyasa), he abandons his wife and children and becomes a celibate devotee of Lord Krishna. His wife becomes a "widow." She can never see her husband again or remarry. The Raelians as well as the Rajneesh followers encourage free expression of sexuality but denounce marriage and motherhood. The Rajneesh followers consider motherhood and marriage oppressive to women. Raelians reject marriage because it turns men and women into each other's property. They do not denounce reproduction altogether but say it should be delayed at least until one is spiritually very advanced.

It is as though, frustrated in their fragmentation, women join these NRMs to find peace in at least one dimension of their American womanhood. Palmer herself (1994, 213) sees that these women may be trying to escape the "triple burden" of American women—the conflicting demands of being wife, mother, and worker. We suggest, however, that this attempt reflects the larger issue of how American culture has fragmented and continues to fragment women in the first place.

GAY MEN AND LESBIANS

While middle-class women were coping with the fragmentation of "woman-hood," the twentieth century also saw another group, gay men and les-bians, grapple with their own distinctive issues of sexual and self-identity. We saw in the last chapter that nineteenth-century America had constructed a religious view of homosexuality as sin. In the twentieth century, this con-struction melded into the perspective of the medical establishment that ho-mosexuals were "sick" as well. Homosexuality came to be officially listed in the Diagnostic and Statistical Manual of the American Psychiatric Associa-tion as a "mental disorder," amenable to psychiatric treatment. This is par-ticularly remarkable since Sigmund Freud, the founder of psychiatry, believed that homosexuality was neither an illness nor a treatable "condi-tion." Freud's perspective, however, had been forgotten until the *American Journal of Psychiatry* published a copy of Freud's 1935 "Letter to an Ameri-can Mother" in 1951. In the letter Freud attempted to assuage a mother's distress over her son's homosexuality by saying the following:

> Homosexuality is assuredly no advantage, but it is nothing to be ashamed of, no vice, no degradation, it cannot be classified as an illness.... Many highly respectable individuals in ancient and modern times have been homosexu-als, several of the greatest men among them (Plato, Michelangelo, Leonar-do da Vinci, etc.). It is a great injustice to persecute homosexuality as a crime and cruelty too....
>
> By asking me if I can help, you mean, I suppose, if I can abolish homo-sexuality and make normal heterosexuality take its place. The answer is, in a general way, we cannot promise to achieve it....

It is not surprising that Freud's letter failed to change the minds of the psychiatric community, which had already resisted the massive empirical study of Alfred Kinsey and his colleagues, published in 1948. Officially titled *Sexual Behavior in the Human Male,* and informally referred to as the "Kinsey Report," it caused a popular furor because of its straightforward, nonjudg-mental presentation of a great variety of male sexual activity, including same-gender sex. Kinsey demonstrated, on the basis of interviews with a wide range of men, that at some time in their lives nearly 40 percent of all Amer-ican men had engaged in same-gender sex (Kinsey et al. 1948, 664), and that roughly 10 percent of all males had more or less exclusively engaged in same-gender sex for at least three years between the ages of sixteen and fifty-five (Kinsey et al. 1948, 651). A companion volume on women's sex-ual experiences appeared five years later, presenting the finding that by the age of forty, 19 percent of the women interviewed had had intentional sex-ual experience with other women (Kinsey et al. 1953, 453). Kinsey stated strongly that same-gender sexual behavior was merely part of the repertoire of human sexual activity, neither pathological nor uncommon, and certainly not something that should be prosecuted as criminal.

Despite Kinsey's report, it would take another twelve years before the medical establishment would begin to move away from its position that homosexuality was evidence of "severe emotional disturbance," usually caused by such parental failure as an absent or distant father or a smothering, "close-binding" mother. Since homosexuals were "sick," anguished parents frequently tried to "cure" homosexual children by sending them to psychiatrists who believed they could turn them into heterosexuals, or who would commit them to mental hospitals.

Educational institutions, when they believed they had evidence of a homosexual student, usually removed the student so as not to contaminate the others. John D'Emilio reports an event that occurred at an "elite college in the Northeast" in the 1960s, in which two women students were observed engaging in sexual activity with each other by male students across the street, who kept their telescope trained on the windows of the women's dormitory.[4] When the college administration learned of the event, the two women were disciplined, but nothing happened to the men (D'Emilio 1992, 149).

Perhaps more terrifying to homosexuals than these kinds of incidents was the political campaign that developed in the United States after World War II under the direction of Senator Joseph McCarthy. McCarthy is best known for his hysterical persecution of Communists and suspected Communists, but along with the witch-hunt for political traitors went a parallel hunt for sexual traitors. Barry Adam describes the postwar perspective that

> associated maleness with toughness and effectiveness, in opposition to supposedly female weakness and failure [so that] male homosexuality symbolized the betrayal of manhood—the feminine enemy within men. (Adam 1987, 58)

Homosexuals were widely labeled as "destroyers of society" and traitors, and were hounded from public life by numerous commissions, committees, policies, and individuals at all government levels. In March of 1950 the chairman of the Republican National Committee announced his conviction that "Perhaps as dangerous as the actual Communists are the sexual perverts who have infiltrated our Government in recent years" (Adam 1987, 58). Just as it was not necessary to be a proven Communist to have one's life ruined by the witch-hunts, it was not necessary to be a demonstrated homosexual, either. Communist sympathies and homosexual tendencies were enough, and what this meant in practice was that people were denounced by disgruntled employees, employers, students, teachers, neighbors, and business competitors—in short, anyone who might hold a grudge.

Thousands of gay men and lesbians lost their jobs, not only in government, but in private industry as well. The government informed employers of their employees' suspected homosexuality, bars that catered to homosexual men and women were chronically raided, and police officers systematically entrapped gay men by posing as gay men themselves, and offering themselves for a sexual encounter. Equally frightening was the violence directed against homosexuals (usually men) by heterosexuals. When a gay man was murdered in Miami in 1954, local newspapers urged that "homosexuals be punished for tempting 'normals' to commit such deeds" (Taylor 1982, 9, quoted in Adam 1987, 59). Though antihomosexual hysteria died down after the decline of the McCarthy era, few gay men or lesbians felt comfortable acknowledging their homosexuality to "straight" (heterosexual) people. For most gay men and lesbians in the 1950s and 1960s, life was lived wholly or partially "in the closet."

Nonetheless, over the course of the twentieth century, gay men and lesbians have felt increasingly committed to an identity as homosexuals. In 1950, several gay men founded a small secret society in Los Angeles with the aim of educating members of the gay community about their civil rights and enhancing their identity as legitimate in itself. The Mattachine Society (named after masked entertainers in the courts of medieval Europe) gained prominence after its involvement in a court case in which charges were dropped against the defendant, one of the founders of the Mattachine Society, who had been entrapped by a police officer in a case of sexual solicitation (Mondimore 1996, 235–236).

Shortly thereafter, the lesbian group, the Daughters of Bilitis, was founded in San Francisco. Established in 1955, the Daughters of Bilitis was initially intended primarily as a social alternative to lesbian bars, which were in perpetual danger of being raided. With the publication of its newsletter, *The Ladder*, it rapidly became more than merely social, following in the path of the more politically conceived Mattachine Society (Martin and Lyon 1972, 121).

Gay and lesbian activism took a new turn with the Stonewall riots. On Friday night, June 27, 1969, the New York City police raided a gay bar in Greenwich Village (a neighborhood in New York with a high gay and lesbian population) called the Stonewall Inn. Instead of responding passively to the routine raid, as the police had expected, many of the bar's patrons fought back, initially in support of a lesbian who was struggling with her police captors. These instigators were soon joined both in spirit and in person by gay men and women of all backgrounds and personal styles. By the end of the weekend, the Stonewall Inn had been burnt out and the area around it destroyed. But the news stories and photographs of gay men and lesbians violently confronting police harassment had transformed the tentative efforts of associations like the Mattachine Society and the Daughters of Bilitis into a powerful gay and lesbian rights movement.

Life after Stonewall has been marked by an increasing unwillingness on the part of self-identified gay men and lesbians to allow themselves, their lives, and their possibilities to be defined by the straight majority. One of the earliest victories of the gay rights movement was the removal of homosexuality from the category of "mental disorders" in the Diagnostic and Statistical Manual of the American Psychiatric Association. This caused a serious rift within the membership, some of whom were so committed to the notion of homosexuality as pathology that they demanded a plebiscite on the question. For homosexuals, important issues still to be resolved include such civil rights as marriage, employment, military service, and the extension of medical and insurance benefits to homosexual domestic partners.

The progress of gay rights seemed assured, despite opposition, in the 1970s. There was substantially less police harassment of gay individuals and such gay institutions as bars, clubs, and bathhouses. Gay political figures were elected to public office at the local, state, and federal levels. Liberal corporations and localities established policies and passed laws to protect gay employees and citizens. However, when it became obvious in the early 1980s that there was a sexually transmitted fatal illness that disproportionately afflicted gay men, some conservative heterosexuals interpreted it as a scourge sent by God to punish homosexuals for their homosexuality. Others were inclined to believe that gay men had brought this scourge upon themselves (by too much sex), though it became evident that AIDS (Acquired Immunodeficiency Syndrome) is transmitted in ways other than sexually, and that huge numbers of heterosexuals suffer from it in the United States. In other parts of the world, AIDS primarily afflicts heterosexuals.

As a result of the AIDS scare, violence against gay men began to increase in some areas, as did grassroots campaigns in some states and cities to enact legislation that would allow discrimination against homosexuals in employment and housing. Some of this legislation was soundly defeated, but other campaigns have been successful. AIDS has, however, served as a powerful organizing force for gay men in the 1980s and 1990s. Anger at the devastation of AIDS has driven many gay men into activism in support of those living with HIV (Human Immunodeficiency Virus) or full-blown AIDS. Out of the tragedy of AIDS has come a purpose, a unity, and a commitment to a personal and group identity that would probably not have been forged by a less searing flame.

The question heterosexuals most frequently ask about homosexuals is "Why are they that way?" That question has not yet been conclusively answered. Exploration of the cause of same-gender sexual attraction is a controversial undertaking in the gay and lesbian community itself. Though many homosexuals encourage research into the question, others say that it is fundamentally heterosexist in orientation. No one, they say, questions the origin of heterosexual interest; why, then, the focus on homosexual interest?

A growing number of studies point to a biological basis for homosexuality. Some studies point to differences in the neuroanatomy of the brains of gay men and, to a lesser extent, lesbians (LeVay 1993). Others point to the fact that identical twins manifest a much higher than random rate of both having a homosexual orientation if one does (roughly 50 percent, see Bailey and Pillard 1991; Bailey et al. 1993). Another series of studies demonstrated that, at least in some families, male (but not female) homosexuality could be associated with a specific location on a specific chromosome (Hamer et al. 1993). Despite their inconclusive nature at this date, studies like these suggest that however complex the etiology of same-gender sexual attraction turns out to be, a biological component is likely to be involved for many if not all individuals.

While biologists, geneticists, psychiatrists, and psychologists continue their research, gay men and lesbians themselves tell remarkably consistent stories about awakening to their homosexuality. Virtually all feel that the notion of sexual "choice" is a misnomer. Though they may have felt compelled to deny it at first to themselves and/or others, same-gender sexual interest was as spontaneous and as natural for them as cross-gender interest is for heterosexuals.

For most gay men and lesbians the process of "coming out" to friends and family is an important milestone in their self-identity and self-acceptance. It is, of course, an event whose contemplation is fraught with fear and tension. Given the negative view much of American society has of homosexuals, many people fear that their families or their friends will reject them outright, and this does happen. Several of the gay men Kath Weston interviewed were beaten by male relatives after they came out, on the grounds that they were an "embarrassment to the family" (Weston 1991, 51). The father of another told his son, "You're homosexual. You're diseased, and I don't want you back in the family" (Weston 1991, 64). One lesbian said of her mother, "To her it was just this social embarrassment, and she doesn't want to deal with it … if I'm willing to be quiet and pretend I'm not who I am, then she's willing to accept me.… I haven't spoken to her in about three years" (Weston 1991, 63).

On the other hand, many parents reacted with love and acceptance when their gay or lesbian children came out to them. Some had known about it for many years, like the mother who told her son, "Look. You lived with Jorge for fourteen years. We knew you were gay" (Weston 1991, 66). Others responded much like the Irish-American mother of a gay son and a daughter who had married a black man—not acceptable in their working-class white community: "When Sharon married William, I realized that I can't control you kids. That each one of you is gonna find your love wherever you can, and I can't control that. And I accept that. And I still love you" (Weston 1991, 69).

For all the acceptance of their families and their straight friends, many gay men and lesbians feel that their lovers or life partners (men are more likely to use the former term and women the latter) are not accepted as fully as a heterosexual spouse would be. Further, gay men and lesbians often feel that they are expected by the heterosexual majority, even by their straight friends, not to talk about their domestic, romantic, and sexual lives, nor to show any physical affection toward their partners. This amounts to an informal "don't ask, don't tell" policy. It is as though these heterosexuals, having accepted the fact of a friend's or relative's homosexuality, are psychologically too exhausted to contemplate a larger world in which gender-based roles and relationships fail to conform to traditional, heterosexual stereotypes. Or, as Sonny Bono is reported to have said about his opposition to legalized gay marriage, "I'm not a bigot, I just can't handle it" (*Newsweek*, 19 January 1998:47).

Heterosexuals tend to believe that in homosexual relationships there is a strong, "masculine" partner and a weak, "feminine" partner, and that these individuals pursue gender-stereotypical tasks within the relationship. In fact, this is not the case. Gender-stereotypical activity is a characteristic of heterosexual relationships, and in fact it usually intensifies in two stages: first after marriage and second after the birth of the first child (Green et al. 1996, 217). But it is not a characteristic of most homosexual relationships, whatever the personal style (clothing, hairstyle, demeanor) of the partners. Though some lesbians adopt a "butch" (masculine) or "femme" (feminine) appearance or persona, in fact, gay and lesbian couples exhibit substantially more flexibility and egalitarianism than straight couples. This is particularly true for lesbian couples. The ability to construct such balanced relationships has for many lesbians "meant a way to escape this society's constraining gender expectations" (Laird 1996, 105).

There are differences between gay male and lesbian relationships beyond the greater egalitarianism of lesbian couples, and most of them have to do with sex. In the early days of a relationship, men are likely to have sex more frequently than women. As the relationship matures, men may have sex with each other less and less frequently, though women's rate of sexual contact diminishes much less dramatically. Some gay men turn to other sexual partners while maintaining a committed relationship, a pattern that is uncommon with lesbians. Finally, the relations of power in many gay relationships may turn upon money and differential emotional investment: Whoever has access to greater wealth and less psychological need to maintain the relationship is more likely to control the terms of the relationship. This is a pattern not usually seen in lesbian partnerships, but it is quite common in heterosexual marriage. The greatest difference is that in heterosexual marriage the power variable is likely to be gender linked (Green et al. 1996).

SUMMARY AND DISCUSSION

We have seen in this chapter and the previous one that a tension between the various dimensions of womanhood—sexuality, motherhood, and personhood—is an old theme that runs throughout the history of the American middle class. As with the contemporary New Religious Movements, various eras have emphasized one or two roles or aspects for women while submerging or denying others. Thus in the nineteenth century motherhood was glorified but sexuality downplayed; in the twentieth century motherhood was no longer at odds with sexual expression, but it came into conflict with female "personhood," autonomy, or women's expression of individualism. The result has been a continual fragmentation of the American woman of the dominant culture.

As the century opened, men continued a quest for a more masculine individualism that had begun the century before. Women, however, began a whole new relationship with American individualism: They began to embrace it for themselves. In the first half of the century this movement was implicit in the increasing numbers of women entering higher education and the workforce; by the 1960s, middle-class white women were explicitly demanding autonomy and recognition of their personhood.

In the early twentieth century we saw the development of the companionate family, which, in direct contrast to nineteenth-century idealizations, encouraged the expression of female sexuality as a boost to marriage and the new "friends and lovers" (Mintz and Kellogg 1988, 113) relationship between husband and wife. Though disturbed by World War II, the companionate family resumed as an ideal in the 1950s. In this period, sometimes seen as a Golden Age of the American family, an ideal "Father Knows Best" type of family was constructed. This prosperous, homeowning family consisted of a breadwinning male and a nonworking wife who was an attractive companion to her husband and a full-time mother to her dependent children. For a variety of economic reasons, this model of the American family did not last long, and it came to be criticized by a new women's liberation movement that saw it as stifling to women and as a denial of their autonomy. This women's movement has left in its wake a male gender crisis, being dealt with through a variety of men's movements beginning in the late twentieth century.

The middle-class women's movement stirred up a central issue in American culture that continues as a source of debate and controversy. This issue concerns relationships between gender and reproduction. For more than two centuries, mainstream middle-class American culture constructed woman's place as in the home, away from the outside world of work, individualism, and personal autonomy. Gradually women ventured out, but this was only socially acceptable at certain points or within particular positions of their life cycle. It became acceptable for middle-class, unmarried women to work outside the home; later it became acceptable for childless wives to work. But today, for many people, it is not quite acceptable for mothers to work outside the home, particularly full-time or when they have very young children to raise. In the late twentieth century, motherhood emerged as the last dimension of womanhood to be denied autonomy and individualism. Some have seen the cultural construction of American motherhood as the last bastion of the American family (Degler 1988). If mothers, not just women but mothers, can embrace individualism just as fathers do, what will be left to hold the family together as a place of nurture and human connection, needed by all but lacking in the world outside the home?

In this chapter we also took a look at twentieth-century middle-class youth culture. This group, now active in its own cultural constructions, developed the distinctive phenomenon of American dating, which influenced gender relationships in the broader society. Dating transformed the previous nineteenth-century method of courtship, moving it into the male public sphere and under male control. Dating also became enmeshed in the American "consumer culture." What a man spent on and for a date became a public measure of his worth as well as that of his female companion. We also saw that dating moved from a frenzied, competitive, promiscuous prewar form to the "going steady" version after World War II, where it appeared as an emulation of real marriage, even following a pattern of serial monogamy.

This chapter also discussed female and male "body problems" that developed over the twentieth century. We traced the changes in ideal body types and the stresses placed on men and especially women to attain these ideals, often at great risk to their health. For both women and men body problems are inseparable from cultural constructions of gender.

Finally, in this chapter we looked at gay men and lesbian women, who in the twentieth century became an important and vocal minority. We saw that in this century the dominant culture constructed homosexual relationships through a medical model that defined homosexuals as "sick" and "abnormal." In the late twentieth century, AIDS was a further setback. But through their own political activism, gay men and lesbians have insisted that their voices be heard and injustices toward them addressed. We also saw how gay men and lesbians have challenged traditional gender roles, though this is not often known or understood by the broader heterosexual society. Most notably, gay and lesbian couples show greater equality and flexibility in their roles than do most heterosexual couples.

DISCUSSION QUESTIONS

1. One of the amazing phenomena of the twentieth century is the great speed with which American women took to higher education. At the beginning of the twenty-first century, there are now more women than men enrolled in higher education. And by now, nearly as many women as men are in the paid workforce. Yet women still earn substantially less than men, despite the widespread American belief that a good education will result in a good job. What do you think is the reason for the disparity? We will explore these issues again in the last chapter of this book, but it is useful for students to consider these issues now, before they have any specialized information on the subject.

One other interesting and related exercise is to chart the educational attainments of your ancestors, both male and female, as far back as you have information. Don't forget to include yourself. What do you find out? If you are like most Americans, you find a pretty steady increase in education through the generations. Why do you think this occurred?

2. Provide a brief account of the dating practices of the modern Nacirema, in the style of Horace Miner (cited in Chapter 1). In your account, include the perspectives of those who engage in dating as well as your own perspective as an outside observer. And remember that in addition to a description of dating practices, you should include a discussion of the motivations and purposes behind dating.

3. Many of our students appear to subscribe to the myth of the Golden Age of the American family, as they have seen it portrayed in television sitcoms like *Father Knows Best* and *Leave It to Beaver*. Yet, as we point out in this chapter, there were cracks in the shiny veneer of the American family in the two decades following World War II, despite unparalleled prosperity and technological advances. What were the causes of some of these cracks, and how did they manifest themselves? The women's movement of the late sixties and early seventies was probably the single biggest response to problems in the American family, but what about men? Were they, too, experiencing difficulties? If so, what were they, and why are men's problems so little discussed, when whole courses and departments are devoted to the discussion of women's issues?

4. In all societies known to anthropologists, some of the population prefer sex with members of their own gender. In some societies these sexual interests do not provoke much attention; in others they are considered natural for some or most individuals; and in still others, they are considered immoral or "sick." The United States has such a large and diverse population that all of these viewpoints are probably represented today. Still, it is probably safe to say that the most widespread American perspective is that homosexual activity is either wrong or the result of some emotional disturbance. Why do you think this is true? If you cite the influence of religion, you certainly have a point, but you have not worked through the problem completely. In the first place, many Americans who are not religious still find homosexual activity wrong in some way. In the second place, Christianity condemns many kinds of human behavior that are far more prevalent than sexual interest in one's own gender, yet we do not hear of uncharitable people or liars or those who fail to honor their parents being subject to hazing, violence, or torture. So the causes of the widespread American resistance to homosexuality must have some other components as well. What do you think some of them might be?

NOTES

1. Beeman (1986) feels that American advertisers actually play upon two contradictory impulses of the American people—individualism, on the one hand, and the desire to conform on the other.

2. The settlement houses reflected the noble ideas of reformers, but they were not without class tensions. Some slum dwellers resented being told by middle-class reformers how to live, and some reformers were paternalistic. In the end, divisions of class undermined this reform movement (Rothman 1978).

3. Much more was going on with women in the postwar period, even among white middle-class women, than the "frustrated suburban housewife" syndrome. Many middle-class women of this time were active in the civil rights movement and assumed other public leadership roles (see the collected articles in Meyerowitz 1994). In addition, some full-time wife-mothers were perfectly happy in their dependent domestic roles.

4. This example is striking, not only because it demonstrates the devastating power of the mental illness model of homosexuality, but because it is almost certainly a case that occurred when one of us (McKee) was a student at the "elite college in the Northeast," and the students were her classmates. Information reached the administration by way of a college telephone operator who had listened in on one of the male students as he reported his evening's viewing to a woman friend. The "offending" students were immediately suspended on medical grounds, lest they taint other students or the reputation of the college. Ironically, the same college is now prominent in lesbian studies.

REFERENCES

Adam, Barry D. 1987. *The Rise of the Gay and Lesbian Movement*. Boston, MA: Twayne Publishers.

Bailey, Beth L. 1988. *From Front Porch to Back Seat: Courtship in Twentieth Century America*. Baltimore, MD: The John Hopkins University Press.

Bailey, J. Michael, and Richard C. Pillard. 1991. "A Genetic Study of Male Sexual Orientation." *Archives of General Psychiatry* 48:1089–1096.

Bailey, J. Michael, Richard C. Pillard, Michael C. Neale, and Yvonne Agyei. 1993. "Heritable Factors Influence Sexual Orientation in Women." *Archives of General Psychiatry* 50:217–223.

Bartky, Sandra Lee. 1997. "Foucault, Femininity and the Modernization of Patriarchal Power." Pp. 129–153 in *Writing on the Body: Female Embodiment and Feminist Theory*, ed. Katie Conboy, Nadia Medina, and Sarah Stanbury. New York: Columbia University Press.

Bean, Susan S. 1976. "Soap Operas: Sagas of American Kinship." Pp. 80–98 in *The American Dimension*, ed. W. Arens and Susan P. Montague. Port Washington, NY: Alfred Publishing Company.

Beauvoir, Simone de. 1953. *America Day by Day*. Trans. Patrick Dudley. New York: Grove Press.

Beeman, William O. 1986. "Freedom to Choose: Symbols and Values in American Advertising." Pp. 52–65 in *Symbolizing America*, ed. Hervé Varenne. Omaha, NE: University of Nebraska Press.

Bordo, Susan. 1997. "The Body and the Reproduction of Femininity." Pp. 90–110 in *Writing on the Body: Female Embodiment and Feminist Theory*, ed. Katie Conboy, Nadia Medina, and Sarah Stanbury. New York: Columbia University Press.

Conway, Jill. 1987. "Women Reformers and American Culture, 1870–1930." Pp. 399–413 in *Our American Sisters: Women in American Life and Thought*, ed. Jean E. Friedman, William G. Shade, and Mary Jane Capozzoli. Lexington, MA: D. C. Heath and Company.

Coontz, Stephanie. 1992. *The Way We Never Were: American Families and the Nostalgia Trap*. New York: Basic Books.

Costello, Cynthia, and Barbara Kivimae Krimgold, eds. 1996. *The American Woman, 1996–1997*. New York: W. W. Norton and Co.

Cowan, Ruth Schwartz. 1987. "Two Washes in the Morning and a Bridge Party at Night: The American Housewife between the Wars." Pp. 447–468 in *Our American Sisters: Women in American Life and Thought*, ed. Jean E. Friedman, William G. Shade, and Mary Jane Capozzoli. Lexington, MA: D. C. Heath and Company.

Davis-Floyd, Robbie E. 1992. *Birth as an American Rite of Passage*. Berkeley, CA: University of California Press.

Degler, Carl N. 1988. *At Odds: Women and the Family in America from the Revolution to the Present*. Oxford, Eng.: Oxford University Press.

D'Emilio, John. 1992. *Making Trouble: Essays on Gay History, Politics, and the University*. New York: Routledge.

Dubbert, Joe L. 1979. *A Man's Place: Masculinity in Transition*. Englewood Cliffs, NJ: Prentice Hall.

Fox, Richard Wightman, and T. J. Jackson Lears. 1983. Introduction. Pp. ix–xvii in *The Culture of Consumption: Critical Essays in American History, 1880–1980*, ed. Richard Wightman Fox, and T. J. Jackson Lears. New York: Pantheon Books.

French, Marilyn. 1977. *The Women's Room*. New York: Summit Books.

Friedan, Betty. 1963. *The Feminine Mystique*. New York: Norton.

Friedman, Jean E., William G. Shade, and Mary Jane Capozzoli. 1987. "The Illusion of Equality." Pp. 415–425 in *Our American Sisters: Women in American Life and Thought*, ed. Jean E. Friedman, William G. Shade, and Mary Jane Capozzoli. Lexington, MA: D. C. Heath and Company.

Goldin, Claudia. 1990. *Understanding the Gender Gap: An Economic History of American Women*. New York: Oxford University Press.

Goldstein, Irwin. 2000. "Male Sexual Circuitry." *Scientific American* 283 (2): 70–75.

Gorer, Geoffrey. 1948. *The American People: A Study in National Character*. New York: W. W. Norton.

Green, Robert-Jay, Michael Bettinger, and Ellie Zacks. 1996. "Are Lesbian Couples Fused and Gay Male Couples Disengendered? Questioning Gender Straightjackets." Pp. 185–230 in *Lesbians and Gays in Couples and Families*, ed. Joan Laird and Robert-Jay Green. San Francisco, CA: Jossey-Bass.

Hamer, Dean, Stella Hu, Victor Magnuson, Nan Hu, and Angela Pattatucci. 1993. "A Linkage between DNA Markers on the X Chromosomes and Male Sexual Orientations." *Science* 261:321–327.

Illouz, Eva. 1997. *Consuming the Romantic Utopia: Love and the Cultural Contradictions of Capitalism*. Berkeley, CA: University of California Press.

Kimmel, Michael S. 1996. *Manhood in America: A Cultural History*. New York: Free Press.

Kinsey, Alfred C., Wardell B. Pomeroy, and Clyde E. Martin. 1948. *Sexual Behavior in the Human Male*. Philadelphia, PA: W. B. Saunders Company.

Kinsey, Alfred C., Wardell B. Pomeroy, Clyde E. Martin, and Paul H. Gebhard. 1953. *Sexual Behavior in the Human Female*. Philadelphia, PA: W. B. Saunders Company.

Laird, Joan. 1996. "Invisible Ties: Lesbians and Their Families of Origin." Pp. 89–122 in *Lesbians and Gays in Couples and Families*, ed. Joan Laird and Robert-Jay Green. San Francisco, CA: Jossey-Bass.

LeVay, Simon. 1993. *The Sexual Brain*. Cambridge, MA: MIT Press.

Margolis, Maxine L. 1984. *Mothers and Such: Views of American Women and Why They Changed*. Berkeley, CA: University of California Press.

Martin, Del, and Phyllis Lyon. 1972. *Lesbian/Woman*. San Francisco, CA: Glide Publications.

Martin, Emily. 1987. *The Woman in the Body*. Boston, MA: Beacon Press.

Martin, Emily. 1997. "The Egg and the Sperm: How Science Has Constructed a Romance Based on Stereotypical Women's Roles." Pp. 85–98 in *Situated Lives: Gender and Culture in Everyday Life*, ed. Louise Lamphere, Helena Ragoné, and Patricia Zavella. New York: Routledge.

Mead, Margaret. 1949. *Male and Female: A Study of the Sexes in a Changing World*. New York: William Morrow & Company.

Mintz, Steven, and Susan Kellogg. 1988. *Domestic Revolutions: A Social History of Family Life*. New York: Free Press.

Meyerowitz, Joanne, ed. 1994. *Not June Cleaver: Women and Gender in Postwar America, 1945–1960*. Philadelphia, PA: Temple University Press.

Mondimore, Francis Mark. 1996. *A Natural History of Homosexuality*. Baltimore, MD: John Hopkins University Press.

Palmer, Susan Jean. 1994. *Moon Sisters, Krishna Mothers, Rajneesh Lovers: Women's Roles in New Religions*. New York: Syracuse University Press.

Rothman, Shiela M. 1978. *Woman's Proper Place: A History of Changing Ideas and Practices, 1870 to the Present*. New York: Basic Books.

Rubin, Nancy. 1982. *The New Suburban Woman: Beyond Myth and Motherhood*. New York: Coward, McCann, and Geoghegan.

Smith-Rosenberg, Carroll. 1985. *Disorderly Conduct: Visions of Gender in Victorian America*. New York: Alfred Knopf.

Taylor, Clark. 1982. "Folk Taxonomy and Justice in Dade County, Florida, 1954." *American Research Group on Homosexuality Newsletter* 4 (1–2): 9.

Tiefer, Leonore. 1992. "In Pursuit of the Perfect Penis: The Medicalization of Male Sexuality." Pp. 450–456 in *Men's Lives*, 2nd ed., ed. Michael S. Kimmel and Michael A. Messner. New York: Macmillan.

Weston, Kath. 1991. *Families We Choose: Lesbians, Gays, Kinship*. New York: Columbia University Press.

CHAPTER 4

ETHNIC MINORITIES: NATIVE AMERICANS AND AFRICAN AMERICANS

All Americans have been affected by the cultural constructions of gender discussed in the preceding chapters. But not all Americans are of European or solely European heritage, and so it is also important to examine the forces that have shaped the distinctive evolution of gender roles and values among members of ethnic minorities. Our ethnic heritage plays a powerful part in the way we all participate in twenty-first century American culture. This chapter examines the distinctive gender patterns of two American ethnic minorities: Native Americans and African Americans.[1] We also discuss the ways in which the patterns of these minority groups have been affected by the dominant Euro-American culture. The two groups share in common the fact that their encounters with the dominant white group (which meant conquest in one case and slavery in the other) were involuntary. They were also the first ethnic groups perceived as minorities in the United States. The next chapter explores Latinos and Asian Americans, ethnic minorities who voluntarily migrated to the United States, and who became numerous somewhat later. Both chapters draw out a theme mentioned in Chapter 1: the intersections of gender, ethnicity, and class.

INDIAN PEOPLES: THE INDIGENOUS AMERICANS

Most Americans can remember sitting in elementary school learning about the Pilgrims, who fled their repressive monarchist European homelands looking for religious and political freedom. When they arrived in the New World, there were the "friendly" Indians, eager to help them get along in their newly commandeered territory. There were noble warriors and Indian "princesses," and everyone sat down together to eat turkey. Only somewhere along the way things fell apart. The noble warriors turned into bloodthirsty savages, and the "princesses" turned into "squaws."

The seeds for this transformation were, of course, present at the very first encounter. The Pilgrims were not looking for anything like "freedom," except for themselves. They wanted to be allowed to practice their own religion, but they were as intolerant of others' practices as the Europeans in their own homelands had been of theirs. This intolerance was passed along from one generation to the next, through the Pilgrims, the founding fathers, and the pioneers, who became the settlers on the western frontiers. Generation after generation of European immigrants and their descendants encountered native peoples whose lives they altered drastically, and whose cultures were forever changed as a result.

It is beyond the scope of this book to provide detailed descriptions of the enormously varied cultures that prevailed in what is now the United States before the arrival of Europeans. There is no such thing as "Indian culture"; rather, there are many separate Native American cultures (Klein and Ackerman 1995). We can, however, point to some general cultural patterns, focusing on those that have to do with gender roles and values, that distinguished most precontact native groups from European immigrants. And we can describe the distinctive patterns derived from them that are present today in the lives of many Indian people.

We begin with a discussion of Native American gender constructions in terms of marriage and the family, sexuality, and relationships of production. We will look at how gender relationships in these areas were affected and modified by contact with Europeans.

MARRIAGE AND THE FAMILY

Virtually all Indian groups permitted polygyny, the marriage of one man to more than one woman at a time. As in most polygynous societies in the world, most marriages were monogamous, but rich, senior, and influential men often had several wives. Divorce was possible in nearly all native societies, and it could usually be initiated by either the husband or the wife. There was seldom any opprobrium attached to divorce, and divorced persons usually married again.

Some native peoples were organized patrilineally. That is, they calculated their membership in descent groups (patrilineages) through the male line only. Other Indian societies were organized matrilineally, in matrilineages whose members calculated their membership through the female line only. Many matrilineal peoples also practiced matrilocality, whereby a newly married couple moved in with the bride's family. And then there were those peoples who had no lineages at all, but who formed kin groups through both male and female links. Further, many native peoples, especially those who were nomadic or seminomadic, lived in groups of varying composition, sometimes traveling with extended family members and at other times leaving children with grandparents or aunts and uncles.

By contrast, European immigrants came from societies where polygyny was not permitted, divorce either forbidden or difficult to obtain, and kinship was narrowed down to a small, restricted set of relatives. To these Europeans patrilineal descent, or descent through the male line, sounded vaguely familiar and acceptable, but the idea of matrilineal descent and matrilocality seemed not only foreign to them but also "unnatural." Large, complex kin groups, too, were beyond the ken of most Europeans. In their dealings with Indians, Europeans relied on their own model of what a family should be in assessing Indian ways of life. As we shall soon see, this reliance brought cross-cultural misunderstandings and, ultimately, altered relationships between men and women in Native American groups as Europeans became politically dominant.

SEXUALITY

The sexual practices of native peoples varied widely, from restrictive to permissive. The constant factor was that Europeans usually misunderstood the sexual practices of the peoples with whom they came into contact. As we have seen, the earliest European immigrants had no aversion to marital sexual activity, but they maintained an ideal model of sexual behavior, freely adapted from the medieval ideal, in which thoroughly covered women evinced no overt interest in sex but were pursued by men who did. By contrast, Indian women's bodies were often wholly or partly visible, which alone was enough to convince many Europeans that they were lascivious. This impression was intensified by the gender practices of groups such as the Ute, in which women sometimes initiated sexual activity (Osburn 1995, 158), or by the willingness of men in others, like Virginia's Algonquians, to share their women with visitors. Indeed, a contemporary account of Captain John Smith's encounter with thirty young, naked Algonquian women who tried vainly to seduce him (Tyler 1907, quoted in Brown 1955, 34) gives an early and vivid account of the European reaction to what they saw as the unconstrained sexual nature of the New World "savages."

In the Europeans' condemnation of the laxity surrounding premarital sex among some Indians, and in their view of Indian women as sexually aggressive, we see an important link between gender construction and ethnic relations. It was not just that Europeans had a negative reaction to Indian practices; it was that Europeans used their contact with the Indians and their perception of Indian "savagery" to assert their own gender practices as superior (D'Emilio and Freedman 1988). Their vision of the sexually aggressive Indian woman was used to highlight a contrast with their own superior "passionless" white women.

A final distinctive feature of Indian sexuality was the institution of the *berdache* (see Figure 4.1 on page 100), a French word of Persian origin, in which males who preferred to live as females took on the names, clothing,

Figure 4.1

A Native American (Zuni) berdache. (*Smithsonian Institution/Office of Imaging, Printing, and Photographic Services*)

and daily pursuits of women, often marrying polygynously as one of several wives of powerful men (Williams 1986). This practice existed in several societies (Blumenfeld and Raymond 1993, 49), and was complemented in some groups by the less-frequent option for women to live as men. Though parents were not always happy if a child decided to take on life as the other gender, it was not considered in any way immoral, and parents did not try to interfere with a child who had made up his or her mind, since to do so would be to frustrate the child's true nature. In many groups, transgendered (or "twin spirit") individuals were greatly respected as shamans (healers) and for their unusual energy and originality.

Naturally, everyone in the community would be aware of a twin spirit's change of gender identity, though it was generally considered bad manners to refer to it. Europeans were not, however, always aware of the anatomical nature of berdaches whom they met. When they did recognize a transgendered individual, their reactions ranged from amused to (more commonly) horrified. For Europeans the berdache was more evidence of the depraved sexuality of native peoples.

RELATIONSHIPS OF PRODUCTION

A great deal has been written about gender in relation to specific spheres of activity of American Indians. Many authors line up behind Michelle Rosaldo (1974) and her earlier contention, discussed in Chapter 1, that women everywhere have operated primarily in the private, or domestic, sphere, while men's work has taken place in the public sphere, which accounts for the higher evaluation of men and male activities. Other authors follow Eleanor Leacock (1981), who argued that the division into distinctly public and private spheres was for Native Americans an artifact of European contact, and that in many cases Native American women lost power and status in the process of colonization. Some anthropologists have reported cases where Native American women have been able to regain their former power and status, such as among the Tlingit (Klein 1995) and Southern Paiute (Knack 1995). Lillian Ackerman (1995) discusses how Plateau women have maintained gender equality throughout different historical periods, although in different ways. Today, Plateau women and men have equal access to domestic, political, economic, and religious spheres whereas they had different but complementary access in traditional times.

Although there was variation in Native American gender patterns, Europeans were often struck and disturbed by the economic and social power of Native American women and by Native American divisions of labor by sex. Though no matriarchies (communities governed by women) existed in the Americas any more than they had ever existed in the Old World, Europeans sometimes felt as though Indian women controlled economic and even social life. Part of this was due to the fact that in groups like the Iroquois (matrilineal and matrilocal), women nominated the men who made policy decisions for the group and determined the fate of war captives, even joining in the ritual torture. Indeed, the well-known fable of Pocahontas probably derives from a similar function of women among the Algonquians (Kupperman 1988, 151, 156).

But more of the Europeans' puzzlement came from the fact that the Indian women were not economically dependent on men. True, European women worked in colonial times, but, as we saw in Chapter 2, they rarely owned or controlled the means of production (land, standing crops, domestic animals) or the result of production (harvested foods or the income they generated), which was nearly always in the hands of men. By contrast, Indian women very often owned or controlled the means and the result of production of important plant foods. These foods, whether from wild plants or cultivated cornfields, provided up to three-quarters of the calories consumed. Men mostly fished and hunted game, which to Indians were important subsistence tasks. In the Europeans' view, however, male hunting and fishing were interpreted as indolent recreation, while the sight of women and children planting, weeding, and harvesting ran counter to their notion of appropriate women's work.

Native women not only produced and distributed corn, beans, squash, and other foods in groups that practiced horticulture, but they also considered the lands that they worked to be under their control. Thus, when whites had arranged to move horticultural groups from their traditional territory, they were often surprised by resistance from large numbers of women, even when the removal had been negotiated with Indian men. European government officials tried to deal exclusively with native men, who sometimes overreached their authority in ignoring the traditional realm of women's control.

In 1831 a group of Sauk women, faced with relocation in the midst of the growing season, arrived to talk with Major General Edmund Gaines, the U.S. government's chief negotiator, at Rock Island in the Mississippi River. The women were introduced by the chief male negotiator, Black Hawk, who presented the women's objections to moving from the fields they had so long tended, which were now full of standing corn. The leader of the women then spoke, saying "that she had a right to know of any bargains, and never having heard of the sale of the lands she had come with her women to say that they had never consented to such a measure" (Whitney 1973, quoted in Murphy 1995, 73). Gaines replied that "the president did not send him here to make treaties with the women" (Jackson 1955, 112).

It was not only cornfields and their corn in which Indian women had a proprietary interest. Native women everywhere produced manufactured items, from basketry to leather goods to the famous Navajo rugs, which they disposed of themselves, increasingly entering into trading arrangements with European travelers and settlers.

In their negotiations with Indians, Europeans not only bypassed women's rights in land, but they also ignored the way native peoples transmitted property over the generations. Previously among the Choctaw, for example, women controlled the land and transmitted this control matrilineally to their daughters. Clara Sue Kidwell (1995) describes the lowering in status of Choctaw women as Europeans shifted the land women had controlled into male hands and so dissolved the descent lines that had originally passed through women.

Katherine M. B. Osburn's account (1995) of changes in Ute land tenure as a result of the Dawes Act is another illustration of the conflict between native and European principles of kinship and property ownership. The Dawes Act went into effect in 1887. Its goal was to integrate Indian peoples into mainstream American life by turning them into small farmers on government-designated "allotments." These allotments were granted ideally to the male head of the household. Married women did not receive allotments of their own, though they were considered co-owners of their husbands' land and could inherit it upon their husbands' death.

These land allotments posed no immediate difficulty for married Ute women. But if these women divorced, as was fairly common in Ute society, their claim upon the land they had been jointly allotted with their husbands had no legal standing. Osburn examined the attempts of these divorcees to claim land or other property based on the allotments they had shared with their ex-husbands. She shows that the white officials who tried to assist them considered the divorcees' claims to be based on their status as former dependent wives, whom their ex-husbands had a continuing obligation to support. The women themselves, however, claimed property either because of their subsistence activities when married or because of their positions as mothers of an ex-husband's children. They had clearly not at this point adopted the Euro-American notion of female economic dependency. Indeed, Ute women's claims for property were based on their perceptions of continuing independence, while Euro-American intervention, even though on their behalf, was based on a perception of natural female dependence.

In the Dawes Act we see how powerfully gender patterns among Native Americans became shaped by their interactions with the conquering European immigrants. What the Dawes Act did was to make Ute women, whose pre-contact economic position with respect to men was largely egalitarian, almost completely economically dependent upon men. On the other hand, through contact with Europeans, women's spheres of operation, their subsistence and other activities, were less likely to be disrupted than men's. Men's aboriginal occupations of hunting and sometimes warfare were repressed by Europeans in favor of the "civilized" occupation of farming, which Indian men considered women's work. This left many men without clear or comfortable roles to play in their societies.

TRADITION AND CHANGE

The contemporary picture of gender variables among American Indian peoples is complex. In part this complexity has to do with cultural variation within the Indian population as a whole, as well as the length of time specific groups have been in contact with Europeans and the conditions of that contact. For example, the experiences of the Connecticut Pequot, owners of the phenomenally successful Foxwoods gambling casino, are radically different from the experiences of the destitute Oregon Paiute band. And the large population of matrilineal, matrilocal sheepherding Navajos of Arizona manifests quite a different perspective from that of a small, formerly foraging group like the Achomawi of north central California.

Another aspect of the complexity of contemporary Indian approaches to gender has to do with assimilation of native peoples into the dominant Euro-American cultural norms. Though this process has profoundly affected all Indian groups, white Americans are often unaware of the lasting and powerful influence of traditional culture in the lives of most Indian people. Miranda Warburton (1997, personal communication), an anthropologist employed by the Navajo Nation, points to the power of Navajo gender assumptions and kin ties as providing a basis for many contemporary Navajo activities. Two examples may illustrate the persistence of this aspect of aboriginal culture in Native American culture generally. First, the Navajo tradition of berdache, no longer practiced in its original form, has given way to a widespread acceptance by many (though certainly not all) Navajo of male homosexuality. This is true not only on an individual basis but is reflected in an annual Navajo gay dance festival, marked by extensive cross-dressing and the participation of many non-Navajos.

A second example concerns the practice of bride-price (payment of goods from the groom's family to the bride's family at marriage). Bride-price remains a dimension of contemporary Navajo marriage and tends to discourage divorce, even when one or both spouses are unhappy with their relationship. One Navajo man who had strongly considered divorce told an Anglo friend that he had been unable to go through with it, not only because of a community sentiment against divorce, but because many members of his family had contributed to the bride-price for his marriage. These contributions were now mingled in stock holdings of his family and his in-laws, and divorce would mean a complicated disentanglement of these joint holdings. "I couldn't do that to my family," he said.

Despite the undeniable pervasiveness of Euro-American institutions in the lives of modern Navajo, the single most powerful organizational force remains the ties of kinship (see Figure 4.2). Introductions between Navajo, whether formal or informal, whether at a professional meeting or a *kinaalda* (girl's puberty ritual), invariably involve the exchange of clan affiliations and the search for common kin. Navajo, like other Indian people, participate in

FIGURE 4.2
Navaho family. (*Alan Band Associates/Canadian National Film Board*)

a world dominated by Euro-Americans, but the Navajo have retained their allegiance to the extended family, and have resisted the Euro-American cultivation of individualism.

Issues of tradition and change in gender are complicated by the pervasiveness of poverty in the lives of Native Americans, the poorest ethnic group in the United States. This situation points out some complex intersections among gender, ethnicity, and class, intersections that are often difficult to unravel. It is sometimes difficult to assess the extent to which Indian variation from the white majority norm is due to the maintenance of aboriginal patterns, or whether the primary cause of this variation is adaptation to poverty. A large number of Indian households, for example, are headed by women. To what extent might this be attributed to native traditions of female independence and ease of divorce, and to what extent is it promoted by modern male unemployment, commonly seen among poor Americans of all ethnic groups?

At the same time, increasing numbers of Indian women are now earning associate's and bachelor's degrees and taking up relatively (or absolutely) well-paid jobs as nurses, dental assistants, teachers, social service professionals, and even tribal administrators, positions originally restricted to men. Meanwhile, the educational achievements of men now often lag behind those of women, and men are less likely to find well-paid employment.

To what should these Indian women's educational and occupational achievements be attributed? One plausible explanation combines elements of tradition with the impact of European contact and the economic context of modern America, pointing out that in many native groups, women had substantially greater autonomy than European women. In many native groups before contact, women were considered "neither inferior nor superior to men, [but] merely different. Both sexes [were] valued for the contributions they make to society. They [were] cooperative rather than competitive" (Powers 1986, 6).[2] In addition to this traditional factor, we saw that with European contact, women's aboriginal activities were less disrupted than men's. And finally, a modern factor that may lie behind Indian women's achievements is that women frequently have the burden of child support, which drives them to acquire more education in order to compete for better jobs in the increasingly credentialed world of the United States.

Some Native Americans who have moved off reservations and are adapting to life and work within white-dominated institutions feel torn between their own Indian cultural values and those of the dominant white culture. Recently one of our Native American students, whom we will call Alisa, a single mother of a young son, found herself in difficult economic circumstances and far from family members. In order to continue her education while living in housing that she felt was inadequate for her son, Alisa took him to live on the reservation with her mother, giving her mother temporary guardianship. With reference to Euro-American values, Alisa expressed a profound sense of failure because she had been unable to remain the sole caretaker and support of her son. At the same time she was able to activate traditional solutions for solving personal and economic difficulties.

Alisa's experience reflects the conflicting values of the dominant Euro-American culture and the values of Native American culture. The former stresses co-residence among nuclear family members and individual success, and it judges divergence from that pattern as weakness and failure. The latter allows flexibility of residence and household composition and reliance on extended family members as components of a traditional and expected way of handling the complexities of life.

One new gender issue confronting Native Americans is feminism; Indian women are often reluctant to espouse feminist causes for at least three reasons. First, most feminist activists are urban, educated white women with little awareness of the lives of Native Americans. The corporate glass ceiling that is so distressing to mainstream white feminists, for example, is largely irrelevant to Indian women, especially those on reservations, where any kind of employment for men or women is hard to find. Thus self-identified feminists and feminist groups seem alien and alienating to all but the most educated or assimilated native women. Second, many Indian women feel that, though they would like to see improvement in their status or opportunities, overt espousal of feminist goals and rhetoric would be disloyal to their husbands and brothers, fathers and sons. This is particularly true since women are acutely aware that it is Native American men who have been most severely damaged by Euro-American contact and institutions. Third, the Indian tradition of women's solidarity and competence in their own sphere of operations has created a sense of confidence and security that may make Euro-American feminism irrelevant for many.

Marla Powers argues that, at least for the Oglala, women maintain the fiction, to which many men also subscribe as reality, that men are superior to women. Women uphold men's roles as chiefs and leaders and stress that the Oglala's survival will depend on men's negotiations with the federal government. But, behind this fiction,

> empirically it is the women who are more stable as workers, educators, students, and professionals, and there is a current increase in the participation of women, not only in the work force, where they have always felt comfortable, but in the ranks of leadership: as superintendents of reservations, district and community leaders, judges, and contenders for the presidency of the Oglala Sioux Tribe. The reality is that men increasingly defer to women. (Powers 1986, 204)

The experience of Native Americans shows many ways in which gender is not only interwoven with culture, but also intersects with broader political and class relationships. First, there is the effect of traditional cultural patterns. Though there was (and remains) considerable diversity, most native cultures were characterized by the following features:

1. Separate but complementary spheres of operation for men and for women, allowing for solidarity and a sense of competence for both genders
2. Involvement of women in primary subsistence activities, rather than just the domestic sphere, as became common for middle-class and elite Euro-American women
3. A focus on the importance of the larger family group (extending even to the clan or ethnic group) rather than, as has been true for Euro-Americans, on the individual

Though many years of association with Euro-Americans have resulted in varying degrees of assimilation, the effects of aboriginal cultural patterns are still strong and continue to have a powerful influence on the gender roles and values of Indian people today.

A second force intersecting with Native American culture is Euro-American contact itself. Its most significant result in the sphere of gender was probably the destruction of nearly the entire range of aboriginal male activities, leaving many Indian males without a traditional gender role or the means by which to adopt a Euro-American one. Not only has this affected men but it has moved women, whose domestic roles were not seriously interfered with, into formerly male roles and activities they had not traditionally occupied. At the same time, contact brought about a loss of control over land for some women, as among the Choctaw and Ute.

Poverty and class relationships are a third element intersecting with Native American culture in the lives of Indian people. Poverty is inextricably linked to the effects of Euro-American contact and is allied with such features of postcontact life as lack of employment opportunities, poor education, and poor medical care. The result is an increasing number of female-headed households, as men retreat from family responsibilities that unemployment and alienation prevent them from meeting. This process also results in an increasing proportion of women pursuing secondary and higher education and relatively well-paid employment.

AFRICAN AMERICANS: UNWILLING IMMIGRANTS

There is an enormous amount of literature on black American gender and family life, but there is still substantial disagreement about how best to interpret it. One of the fundamental debates concerns the extent to which traditional patterns of African culture are reflected in the kinship relations and gender roles of today's African Americans. As with Native Americans, the issue is complicated by the widespread poverty of many African Americans, to which distinctive subcultural patterns may be an adaptation.

There is, of course, also the overwhelming fact of slavery, which forces us to ask the inevitable question: How did slavery influence the ways of life of African Americans? Sociologist E. Franklin Frazier argued in 1939 that African cultural influence was wholly negated by the experience of slavery, which so destroyed memories of Africa on the one hand, and so interfered with the normal workings of authority within black families on the other hand, that African American families after slavery had no choice but to remake themselves in the image of white families if they wanted to thrive and prosper.

More recent scholars have pointed to some structural similarities African American families have shared with their West African ancestral societies through the days of slavery into the present. Niara Sudarkasa (1997), for example, points to the similarities between traditional West African family compounds and the extended families among enslaved African Americans. These similarities included many nonnuclear kin as "family," few women, whether married or not, wishing to be childless throughout their lives, and what she calls "core adults" who were sometimes more important than those whom Euro-Americans would identify as the "heads" of households.

The African heritage of the American slaves left a mark on the language, the legends, the music, and the food of every place they were settled. Though it is now difficult to connect contemporary African American family organization to three-hundred-year-old African patterns, as we shall see, it is reasonable to contend that several slender though sturdy threads may join the two. At the same time the present form of African American culture is in many ways the result of New World solutions to New World problems.

SLAVERY

For the impact of slavery on African American gender roles and family forms, the best guide is historian Herbert G. Gutman's (1976) superbly detailed study of slavery and its aftermath between 1750 and 1925. This work is partly based on detailed handwritten plantation registers of slave births, marriages, sales, and deaths.

Gutman begins by demolishing the myth of the slave household in which husbands and fathers were primarily absent, so that "normal" relations of respect, authority, and control within slave households were also absent. Certainly it is true that the authority of a slave father within his own household was severely limited by the power of a slave owner. But Gutman notes that in Virginia at the end of the Civil War, more than 75 percent of black households contained either a husband or father. Indeed, Gutman points to many examples of enduring families that persisted under slavery, and even of husband-wife ties that transcended sale and forced remarriage.

There were also so-called "broad" marriages, permitted by only some slave owners. In these marriages the husband and wife lived on different plantations, the children remaining with the wife, while the husband visited as often as he was allowed. Even runaway husbands (the majority of runaway slaves were young men) often put themselves in considerable danger to try to regain their wives. One such young man, who had become a steamship steward, wrote the following in a letter:

> I must see my wife ... if not I will die.... You have never suffered from being absent from a wife as I have.... I am determined to see her, if I die the next moment. I can say I was once happy, but never will be again, until I see her; because what is freedom to me, when I know that my wife is in slavery. (Still 1968, quoted in Gutman 1976, 265–266)

Many escaped slaves ran not to free states but to locations where parents, children, and spouses were held. That more slaves did not run away was due not only to the risks of apprehension, but also to the fact that most slaves preferred slavery to separation from their families (Gutman 1976, 267 et seq.). The strength of these slave families and the persistence of the relationships within them are remarkable, especially considering that black families had no standing under the law.

Marriage ceremonies were sometimes performed by black preachers, sometimes by white, and sometimes by a layperson or group of friends; but none of them had any legal standing. Most owners allowed slaves to make and break their own marriages unless the relationships were disruptive or the owner specifically wanted to capitalize on the fertility of a newly acquired female slave and therefore forced her to take a husband of the owner's choice. In some communities, however, the white slave-owning class clung to the fiction that slaves had no families of their own, and slaves were prohibited from referring to their own siblings as "sister" or "brother" (Gutman 1976, 217).

In considering the West African heritage of African American slaves, it is essential to realize

> the sheer importance of kinship in structuring interpersonal relations and in defining an individual's place in his society ... and the importance to each individual of the resulting lines of kinsmen, living or dead, stretching backward and forward through time.... The aggregate of newly-arrived slaves, though they had been torn from their own local kinship networks, would have continued to view kinship as the normal idiom of social relations. (Mintz and Price 1974, quoted in Gutman 1976, 196–197)

Gutman (1976, 223) demonstrates that, through time, the original West African patterns of kinship were transformed into a complex web of inter- and intragenerational kin linkages that also gave rise to notions of quasi-kin and nonkin obligations. These linkages and their resulting obligations were encoded and reinforced by a system of slave etiquette according to which children were taught to address and refer to older slaves, whether actually related to them or not, as "Aunt" and "Uncle." While part of the genesis of this system was the white prohibition of the use of "Mr." and "Mrs." for African Americans (precisely to deny respect relations among slaves), more of it reflected the importance of slave kin relationships (see Figure 4.3).

It is well known that many slave owners fathered children with some of their slaves. Sometimes these relationships were consensual (to the extent that anything involving the consent of a slave may be said to be consensual), and sometimes they were not, though forcible sex with a slave could not legally be considered rape. Whoever their fathers might be, the children of slave women were slaves themselves. As such, they were important capital, and slave owners frequently reviewed the growth of their human capital with some satisfaction. There was considerable irony in this view, since slave owners also considered extramarital pregnancy, including premarital pregnancy, to be one of the many marks of African depravity. In a legal sense, of course, the term "premarital" was irrelevant when it referred to slaves. In a moral or religious sense, however, it was meaningful both to owners and to the slaves themselves.

That white male slave owners had free sexual access to their black female slaves points out some deep and disturbing connections among gender, sexuality, race, and class. For one thing, denying black women control over their own sexual beings was itself a statement of their low status in terms of

FIGURE 4.3
A Louisiana slave household. (*Courtesy of The New-York Historical Society, New York City; photo by Barnard Charleston*)

both gender and race. The sexual abuse of black women also propped up the slave owners' construction of white women as "pure." Male owners' sexual access to female slaves created deep bitterness in black women and between black women and the white wives of the southern planters (Whites 1992). Yet the relatively leisured lives of white women of the slave-owning class, and their view of themselves as "refined," was made possible by slavery itself.

The study of immediately postbellum Virginia cited earlier demonstrates that the incidence of very young unmarried women (ages fifteen to nineteen) with children was only 3 percent in the former slave population (Gutman 1976, 11). Gutman points out that though young slave women often became pregnant before they were married, they usually married the father of their child either before it was born or afterwards, sometimes after a second child had been born. Mary Chesnut, the slave-owning white woman whose letters and diaries provide an excellent picture of the South during the Civil War, summed up the slave marital situation with acuity and perhaps irony: "Negro women ... are married, and after marriage behave as well as other people" (quoted in Gutman 1976, 68). In spite of the disruptions of slavery "the two-parent household was the characteristic black arrangement at all times" (Gutman 1976, 118). Even when matricentric slave households on some plantations became more numerous (though still a minority), Gutman cautions against the interpretation that this was a carry-over from West African matricentric households in extended polygynous families. The pattern was not a common one in earlier generations of slave families, when African patterns would most likely have been reflected. The pattern appeared after 1840, and only in some locations for more than a small minority of families. Thus the appearance of matricentric households is most likely explained as a local adaptation to a specific phenomenon (such as an unstable male population due to frequent sales on a particular plantation). Its formal similarity to West African family structure is thus the result of parallel development rather than cultural transmission.

EMANCIPATION, GENDER, AND WORK

After emancipation, the children of African American parents ceased to represent wealth to white plantation owners, and the destruction and dislocation of the war had left numerous orphans and abandoned children throughout the South. Care was provided for these children by destitute ex-slaves who were their aunts, cousins, grandparents, or sometimes only friends of their deceased parents. In time, these individual efforts began to take the form of African American community provisions for public education and welfare for widows and orphans. This care of the poor by the poor demonstrates the phenomenal strength of the African American kin network, extended to include even those with no formal claims of blood or marriage (Stack 1970). It shows "how adaptive kin obligations ... [were] transformed by the slaves themselves into larger social and communal obligations" (Gutman 1976, 229).

With emancipation came a dramatic renegotiation of the relations of employment. A pervasive idea that kept the system of slavery afloat was that white women were too refined and delicate for heavy physical labor, particularly any labor outside the home. When slavery ended, plantation owners were infuriated to find that their former slaves had adopted the ideas about gender and work held by the dominant class. Gutman quotes planters from Virginia and Louisiana in the early days of emancipation: "The women ... say that they never mean to do any more outdoor work, that white men support their wives, and they mean that their husbands shall support them" (1976, 167–168). From another, "The female laborers are almost invariably idle—[they] do not go to the field but desire to play the lady and be supported by their husbands 'like the white folks do.'" And a Georgia plantation owner complained that "Planters ... hiring twenty hands, have to support on an average twenty-five to thirty negro women and children in idleness, as the freedmen will not permit their wives and children to work in the fields."

The view of whites that a gendered division of labor into public and private spheres should apply only to their own race thus survived the slavery that (at least in the Southeast) supported it. One might argue that in the popular call to put welfare mothers (widely perceived to be African American) into the workforce, this view persists into the present.

In fact, through keeping the wages paid to male field hands low, white planters in the postbellum South ensured that most African American women would have to work outside their households, if not in the fields then in the kitchens, laundries, and parlors of white houses. From 1900 to 1930, for example, a higher proportion of African American women worked for pay than women of any other ethnic group: nearly 40 percent of married women in 1920, which was five times the rate of whites (Amott and Matthaei 1996, 164). As bell hooks, a black female theoretician (who spells her name with lowercase letters), points out, "until it was accepted that most women, black or white, would be in the capitalist work force, many black women bitterly resented the circumstances that forced them to work" (1981, 83).

Even so, this economic necessity had far-reaching implications for women in African American society, some of them positive, according to the values of many women in contemporary U.S. society. Because so many black families were two-earner households, they were characterized by more egalitarian gender roles. Thus, black women were much less likely to be "passive and subordinate," like the white women whose family structure was characterized as "a patriarchy sustained by the economic dependence of the female" (Staples 1997, 269). As we have seen, middle-class Euro-Americans in the late nineteenth and twentieth centuries have regarded mothering and working as incompatible roles. Black women (like the Native American women discussed in the preceding section), however, have traditionally combined the two and transmitted the notion to succeeding generations that childrearing need not conflict with a woman's other roles, nor must it necessarily produce economic dependency of women (Carothers 1990, 233–234).

Today African Americans are no longer limited to menial occupations, though compared to whites they continue to be disproportionately represented in poorly paid fields, to have higher unemployment rates, more trouble in finding full-time work, and, among women, a greater likelihood of dependent children to support on their own (Amott and Matthaei 1996, 189). The long history of African American women's work outside the household, however, continues to have an effect on their relative occupational success. Though white women earn roughly 62 percent of white male salaries, black women earn 84 percent of black male salaries. True, the salaries of black men are lower than those of white men, but the comparisons with women's salaries is still remarkable. The lesser gender disparity within the black population is certainly due to the fact that more African American women than men graduate from college each year. In 1997 there were nearly 1,500,000 more African American women than men in college (Staples 1997, 271).

Interestingly, college-educated black women have higher median incomes than college-educated white women—possibly because of the different use to which women put those degrees. Even in the late twentieth century, white women were more likely to be influenced by the nineteenth-century ideal of "true womanhood," according to which they are expected to devote themselves to their families exclusively rather than work as well, even if they are educated (see Chapter 6 for an exploration of this idea among contemporary U.S. college students). African American women, by contrast, come from a tradition in which most women worked away from home, and in which the idea of combining a job and motherhood was routinely accepted. Figures from 1993, for example, indicate that 79 percent of all married black mothers worked versus only 59 percent of married mothers of all races (Glick 1997, 132).

Initially, virtually all African American women worked at physically demanding, low status, and poorly paid jobs, but there was one occupation that came to offer an alternative to labor as a field hand, factory worker, or domestic servant—that of teaching in the segregated schools. While their sons were needed at home on the farm, many black families worked to send their daughters to college so that they could fill this white-collar job. Not only did school teachers receive a better salary than was paid to most other black women, but even more important, teaching in these schools put them out of the reach of sexually predatory white male supervisors and employers.

The heritage of white male sexual violence against black women had its origin in slavery, but it continued almost unabated after emancipation. Black women seldom complained officially about white offenders, and when they did, few courts were willing to hear the complaints and even fewer judges and juries were willing to call for substantial penalties against offenders. Black men who defended their wives or daughters or retaliated against their attackers were often brutally beaten, tortured, or killed. Though black women were now legal persons, as they had not been during slavery, and their rape was now a legal offense against them, as it had not been during slavery, old habits and old views died hard—and some are still dying.

Especially in the South, whites, both male and female, thought of black women as in some way more sexual than white women, and certainly devoid of the finely tuned sensibilities white women were believed to have. Just as we saw earlier with the white construction of the "sexual" Native American woman, this image of the "sexual" black woman was used to construct white women as contrastingly pure and passionless. This perspective fostered a pervasive climate of sexual abuse of black women by white men (Amott and Matthaei 1996, 164). Well into the twentieth century, southern white supervisors of agricultural labor selected sexual partners from among the girls and young women who worked for them.

Rosa Lee, an African American woman born into poverty in Washington, D.C., in 1936, passed on to a journalist, Leon Dash (1996), stories her mother had told her about her life as a field hand in the South. Though women on plantation crews tried to protect their daughters from the overseer, in the end they acquiesced to his sexual predation; to have done otherwise would have meant blackballing from any agricultural work within the county, and thus certain destitution. An additional feature of Rosa Lee's narrative concerns her half-sister, whom she never met, and of whose existence she learned from her mother's sister only late in life, her mother having concealed the story until her death. Lee's mother gave birth to a daughter as a result of her forced sexual encounter with the field boss. But as the infant grew older, it became clear that she was so fair-skinned and European featured that she appeared white, rather than black. Because of this, the baby's father demanded his child and took her away. Neither her mother nor anyone else in the local African American community ever saw her or heard of her again, and no one ever spoke of her again to her mother, though everyone was well aware of the child's seizure by her father. This same kind of event, Rosa Lee's aunt told her, had happened several other times in their rural southern county. In the family stories of Rosa Lee, then, we see the continuation of the intersection of gender, sexuality, race, and class that were generated during slavery.

THE AFRICAN AMERICAN FAMILY

Aside from the issue of slavery, no aspect of African American life has compelled so much attention as the structure of the African American family. Observers from every imaginable discipline have offered their views on the black family, frequently in strident harangue. The popular argument can be reduced to something like this: Black families are in trouble because so many of them are headed by women, and that is why so many black children do poorly in school and end up on welfare.

This argument has been in existence for many years, but it gained coherence and popularity when it was articulated by Daniel Patrick Moynihan in 1965 in his study, *The Negro Family: The Case for National Action*, written for the Office of Policy Planning and Research of the federal Department of Labor. Senator Moynihan, a political scientist by training, was a liberal Democrat, as were Presidents Kennedy and Johnson, under whose aegis the so-called *Moynihan Report* was prepared. It was Moynihan's intention that the information contained in his report should be used by government agencies to improve the lives of African Americans. In the more than thirty years since the publication of the *Moynihan Report*, its findings with respect to black families have been questioned primarily by African Americans and some academic social scientists. Most of Euro-American society and popular culture have accepted the report's findings largely at face value, whether or not they are aware of their source or have ever heard of Senator Moynihan.

The *Moynihan Report* includes the identification of severe unemployment as a major force in the distress of African Americans. However, its most memorable focus was on what it referred to as "the weakness of the family structure" that was "at the center of the tangle of pathology" in the "disorganized and matrifocal family life in which so many Negro youths come of age." As a specific solution for young African American men, Moynihan suggested that "the armed forces are a dramatic and desperately needed change; a world away from women, a world run by strong men of unquestioned authority"; but he also called for a "national effort ... to strengthen the Negro family" (*Moynihan Report*, cited in its entirety in Rainwater 1967, 1–48). A curious feature of the *Moynihan Report*, made even more curious by the passage of time, is the following quotation from Chapter 4, "The Tangle of Pathology":

> There is, presumably, no special reason why a society in which males are dominant in family relationships is to be preferred to a matriarchal arrangement. However, it is clearly a disadvantage for a minority group to be operating on one principle, while the great majority of the population, and the one with the most advantage to begin with, is operating on another.... Ours is a society that presumes male leadership in private and public affairs. The arrangements of society facilitate such leadership and reward it. (Rainwater 1967, 29)

Certainly the shape of the African American family in the 1960s had begun to change. Looking for a solution to black poverty, many white observers pointed not to complex features of the relationship of African Americans to the economy and dominant culture, but to the distinctive form of the black family. Blaming the black family was easier, and it fulfilled ethnocentric inclinations that rarely lurk too far under the surface. The correct family, they felt, was composed of a coresident husband and wife and their young children. Any family pattern that diverged from the mainstream norm was considered not merely different (let alone adaptive to ineluctable circumstances), but potentially "pathological," particularly if it was reflected in increasing numbers of cases, and particularly if it reflected a shift in the gender base of family authority. The specific "pathological" feature of the African American family was the increasing absence of a male household head, which convinced white (though interestingly, not black) observers that young black men lacked appropriate role models. Basically, too much authority in the hands of women was ruining the race.

As mentioned earlier, there was and is a general assumption that the institution of slavery destroyed the African American family. A related assumption held that slavery fostered the birth of large numbers of infants by different fathers to unmarried women. As we have seen, Gutman's painstaking research has demonstrated that none of these phenomena was common. The structure of the African American family as it presented itself to white awareness in the 1960s had not been delivered in this form directly from the hand of slavery. At slavery's end, black and white families reflected nearly the same proportions of two-parent families. Even by 1925, after the great northern migration of African Americans had begun, black and white families, whether in the North or the South, were little different as to the presence of a male household head (Gutman 1976, 461–475). Indeed, even in 1960 (shortly before the appearance of the *Moynihan Report*), as seen in Table 4.1, if incomes are held constant, figures for black and white families in which males were present tell us that family structure was a function as much of income and urban versus rural locale as it was of race.

TABLE 4.1   MALE-PRESENT BLACK AND WHITE FAMILIES (1960)

	BLACK FAMILIES	WHITE FAMILIES
All families	79%	94%
Rural families	86	96
Urban families	77	93
FAMILIES UNDER $3,000		
All families	64%	78%
Rural families	82	88
Urban families	53	6
FAMILIES OVER $3,000		
All families	93%	97%
Rural families	95	98
Urban families	92	96

Source: From *The Black Family in Slavery and Freedom, 1750–1925* by Herbert G. Gutman, copyright © 1976 by Herbert G. Gutman. Used by permission of Pantheon Books, a division of Random House, Inc.

It is, of course, undeniable that the horrors of slavery had lasting psychological effects on the descendants of slaves. But the changing shape of African American families was due to something quite different. Between the end of the Great Depression and 1970, more than 4,000,000 blacks (along with 16 million whites) left the countryside for the city. In 1940, 50 percent of black Americans were rural residents; thirty years later all but 20 percent lived in cities (Gutman 1976, 466). As had happened a hundred years earlier in England, and as is continuing to happen in third-world countries, new agricultural machines and methods increasingly put rural workers not only out of work, but also out of their homes, and cut them off from the subsistence gardens they had traditionally grown. As they flooded into the cities, whether in the South or the North, they found that their agricultural skills were unsuitable for all but the most poorly paid occupations, and that, except during World War II and to a lesser extent the Korean War, there were not enough even of these jobs to absorb them. At roughly 22 percent, black unemployment was three times as high as white unemployment in 1966, the year after the *Moynihan Report* was issued; in ghetto areas one in three African Americans was unemployed (Gutman 1976, 467–468).

State and federal governments responded with increased relief for the new victims of agricultural reorganization. The most important of these relief programs was the federal Aid to Families with Dependent Children (AFDC), which is what people usually mean when they talk about "welfare." AFDC was intended to assist households of widowed and abandoned women, but the entitlement was specifically derived from their children. The assumption was that every man was responsible for his own support, but that women encumbered by children were less so; children, however, were part of the larger community's responsibility if their parents were destitute. With very few exceptions, any household with an able-bodied adult male present was ineligible for support. Until 1968 AFDC eligibility was also affected by the so-called "man in the house rule," according to which a woman's sexual partner, if he spent the night in her dwelling (and if welfare authorities found out), could make her ineligible for benefits. More recently AFDC authorities have increasingly ruled that a woman's consort has an obligation to support her child (even when the child is not his) if he is living with the woman and her child, though this is not required by most state laws (Hemmons 1996, 147).

Clearly all of the foregoing have had a chilling effect not only on the persistence of the African American nuclear family, but on the institution of marriage itself within the African American community. Even the shape of the extended family has been affected. With unemployment so intense and widespread, fewer black men have been willing to commit themselves to marriage. The chance that they can support a family is very low, and the chance of failure is very high. For their part, young black women, though they may want to become mothers, may have no interest in marrying the fathers of their children. These young men can contribute little of economic value to the household, and marriage to them would end eligibility for AFDC. It is not that a public assistance check is itself the motivation for pregnancy, but it can certainly act against a decision to marry in the case of many poor young couples. AFDC has also reshaped extended African American families—"disaggregated" them in the words of Sudarkasa (1975, 27). Until the 1950s or early 1960s, very young women with one or more children would be likely to move in with a mother, grandmother, or aunt. But AFDC policy in the past thirty-five years has encouraged the establishment of new, independent, female-headed households for these young women.

On the other hand, Sudarkasa and other students of the black family point to family bonds along lines much less well-developed in white families.

> Black families are not necessarily centered around conjugal unions, which are the sine qua non of the nuclear family.... That black families exhibit considerable stability over time and space is evidenced by the enduring linkages and bonds of mutual obligation found among networks of consanguineal kin. (Sudarkasa 1975, 238)

This also means that the failure of a conjugal relationship may have a less injurious effect on the individuals involved (including children), since they are to some degree buffered by their strong relationships with other significant kin.

One final word on black woman-headed households comes from Barbara Omolade, an African American historian:

> ... Black single mothers and their families have something to offer us all. By daily demonstrating that they can survive and succeed without marriage, that they may even be better off without it, they challenge the basic patriarchal ideal.... In a society where men are taught to dominate and women to follow, we all have a lot to overcome in learning to build relationships, with each other and with our children, based on love and justice. For many Black single mothers, this is what the struggle is about. (Omolade 1986, quoted in Amott and Matthaei 1996, 186)

Female-headed, single-parent African American households have increased dramatically since 1960, as Table 4.2 indicates. This picture is fleshed out by Paul Glick (1997, 121–123), who notes that between 1970 and 1990 the percentage of births of black infants to single mothers went from 35 percent to 67 percent (compared to a shift from 6 percent to 28 percent for infants of all races).

Another perspective on the black family, as seen in Tables 4.3 and 4.4, indicates that African Americans postpone marriage for longer than the rest of the population, that many do not marry at all, and that these proportions are increasing.

TABLE 4.2　FEMALE-HEADED AFRICAN AMERICAN HOUSEHOLDS

YEAR	PERCENTAGE
1960	22
1970	33
1980	49
1990	57

Source: Based on Sudarkasa 1997:23.

TABLE 4.3　NEVER MARRIED ADULTS, AGES 20 TO 29

	1970	1992
All races, men	39%	63%
All races, women	25	49
Black men	44	76
Black women	34	70

Source: Based on Glick 1997:12.

TABLE 4.4　UNMARRIED ADULTS OF ALL AGES (1995)

Single black women	61.9%
Single white women	40.9
Never-married black women	38.7
Never-married white women	20.8
Single black men	58.8
Single white men	39.2
Never-married black men	44.8
Never-married white men	28.0

Source: Based on Hemmons 1996:188.

The situation is bleak for black women who wish to marry. For those in the lower classes (and this includes a large part of the African American population) there are few men to choose from if employment is a criterion. According to Staples and Johnson (1993, 235), "46 percent of Black males between the ages of 16 and 62 are not active participants in the American labor force." For educated women the prospect of marriage is equally grim. Part of this is due to the fact that there are twice as many college-educated black women as men; Staples (1997, 271) argues that "The greater a woman's educational level and income, the less desirable she is to many Black males. Whereas a male's success adds to his desirability as a mate, it detracts from a woman's." Thus, he and Johnson contend, the pool of prospective spouses is ten times as great for middle-class black men as it is for middle-class black women (Staples and Johnson 1993, 117).

With regard to cultural constructions of physical attractiveness, in the African American community generally, a wider range of body sizes and types is considered attractive, or at least acceptable, than in the white community. As we saw in Chapter 3, middle-class white women feel such extreme pressure to conform to a rigid aesthetic standard for physical appearance, including overall slenderness, small hips, and large (but not too large), firm breasts, that many diet constantly, and some become bulimic or anorexic.

Black women may be less subject to such standards. Nonetheless, as one moves up the social and economic scale, conventions of appearance for black women begin to approach those for white women (Dull and West 1997; Hall 1997). One black girl, whose body form had never before come under family discussion, was pressured to diet and slim down as her father's business became more successful and he spent more time with higher-status associates, some of them white (Thompson 1997, 191). In these kinds of cases class identifications can override cultural traditions in the construction of ideas of feminine beauty.

Despite the pervasive poverty of African American women and the difficulty many of them have in finding suitable marriage partners, at least one study of school children found that black girls had greater self-confidence than did either white or Latina girls (American Association of University Women 1991). This may come from a perspective that views male and female behaviors as more generally comparable in the black community (Lewis 1975, 230), and it very likely results from the high proportion of households headed by competent black women whose lives combine work and extended family involvement, as well as childrearing.

The relationship of African Americans to the feminist movement has a long history. Black women were generally unwelcome in the nineteenth-century women's reform movement. Though most early white women reformists supported abolition, temperance, and women's education, as black women also did, many rejected the participation of black women in their associations either out of fear that it would compromise the success of their objectives or simply out of the pure racist objection that it would make black women appear to be, in the words of the Fall River, Massachusetts, Female Anti-Slavery Society, "on an equality with ourselves" (Amott and Matthaei 1996, 152–153). In this case we see a head-on collision between the two systems of inequality, with the one governing race superseding the one governing gender. The much-quoted speech attributed to the former slave Sojourner Truth was delivered at an 1851 women's rights convention in Akron, Ohio, to which she had not been invited, and at which she was not welcome:

> Look at my arm. I have ploughed and planted and gathered into barns, and no man could head me—and aren't I a woman? I could work as much and eat as much as any man—when I could get it—and bear the lash as well!

And aren't I a woman? I have borne thirteen children and seen most of 'em sold in slavery, and when I cried out with my mother's grief, none but Jesus heard me—and aren't I a woman? (Davis 1982, 53–55, quoted in Amott and Matthaei 1996, 153)

Some black nationalist movements, including most prominently the Nation of Islam, promote the subordination of women, arguing that the improvement of life for African Americans as a group will not be possible until the authority of black men ceases to be compromised by black women. Though this is primarily a position articulated by men, at least one woman (Shaharazad Ali 1989) has added her voice to the call for a return to the subordination of women. A few African American women are willing to tolerate a subordinate position if it seems to them that their family lives are improved by it overall.

But far more African American women reject the notion of female subordination, though, like many Native American women, some feel that feminism is basically a white issue. Author bell hooks says that though she originally wanted to join with white feminists in resisting and eliminating male domination, she and her colleagues

were disappointed and disillusioned when we discovered that white women in the [feminist] movement had little knowledge of or concern for the problems of lower class and poor women or the particular problems of non-white women from all classes.... [They were] primarily concerned with gaining entrance into the capitalist patriarchal power structure. (hooks 1981, 188)

To conclude the discussion of the black experience, we can see that gender among African Americans owes everything and nothing to slavery. Though the distinctive configuration of the African American family is due neither to slavery nor to African cultural origins, it is certainly the result of slavery's legacy: unemployment and poverty, fostered by continued, pervasive racism. This is a world in which lower-class black men find few opportunities to fulfill a male role, either according to traditional patterns (agricultural or wage labor) or more modern patterns (skilled or professional occupations requiring substantial education). Finding these realms closed to them, large numbers of young black men turn elsewhere for rewards, opting out of the formal economy and out of roles as husbands and fathers.

But black women, though often husbandless, are not often willing to be childless. They establish families with an alternate structure, compared to the (white) culturally mandated (though decreasingly common) nuclear family composed of wife, husband, and their young children. Instead, many African American households have no resident husband, but may include many of the mother's family members, especially her mother, brothers, sisters, and sisters' children. Additionally, family members and close friends who do not live in a household may play important roles in African American families of choice.

As they have for centuries, African American women continue to combine work and motherhood, a pattern that has only recently become common for white women. And as they have for at least a century, many African American women strive for improvement in issues of specific interest to them: better education and child care for their children, better employment conditions and benefits for themselves, better housing, employment, and legal protection for their whole community.

SUMMARY AND DISCUSSION

In this chapter we have seen that gender in America is embedded in a complex web of historical encounters between groups, and continues to be entangled with cultural tradition, class interactions, and interethnic relationships. It was noted that the dominant white group formulated its own gender and family patterns as superior in contrast to what it constructed as Indian and black "savagery" and "sexuality." We also saw that the white conquest of Native Americans rearranged land tenure and work roles in ways that profoundly altered traditional gender patterns in these groups. Slavery dealt a devastating blow to black families, but the African American family proved resilient, and strong kin ties remain a significant aspect of the black community. We noted how the intersection among gender, sexuality, race, and class that was generated through slavery persisted after emancipation. And we saw that inequities of race and gender collided in the white women reformist's rejection of black women's participation in their cause in the nineteenth century.

From this chapter we can also see that while the experience of Native Americans and African Americans has differed with respect to particular gender relationships, on a more general level the two groups mirror one another. From the destruction of the male gender role and its resulting alienation, to the importance of extended family groups, to the forced prominence of women in the world of work and community affairs, to ambivalence toward (or rejection of) organized feminism, the two groups share remarkable similarities. Despite their manifestly different origins as ethnic minorities in the United States, they share characteristics in gender roles and values that largely represent a common adaptation to the unemployment and poverty that have been fostered by the racism of the dominant population over the past century and a half.

DISCUSSION QUESTIONS

1. Though popular books and articles sometimes allude to matriarchal societies, especially among Native American peoples, none has ever been proven to have existed. What characteristics of many Indian cultures led Euro-Americans to believe they were matriarchies? The U.S. government

set up reservations and other bureaucratic institutions intended to serve as conduits for Native American participation in Euro-American society, albeit from a very subordinate position. What aspects of Native American gender roles were ignored, misunderstood, or changed in this process? What have been the long-term results of this failure to understand and respect traditional Native American gender roles?

2. The institution of berdache falls into the category of *gynomimesis*, or simulation of women, which is known in many societies in the world. For Native American groups in which berdache existed, the whole society was well aware that the individual berdache was a biological male by origin who was living as a female. How does the practice of berdache illustrate the difference between sex and gender?

    In modern Euro-American society the practice nearest to berdache is transsexualism, in which a person born as a member of one sex undergoes surgery and continual hormone therapy so that she or he may live as a member of the other sex. Or is it other gender? Which is it? Aside from modern medical technology, what makes transsexualism culturally different from berdache?

3. Before Emancipation, the rape of a slave was a legal impossibility since slaves were by legal definition property rather than persons. This denial of legal personhood is one dimension of race/gender stereotypes that have been maintained even into the twenty-first century concerning African American sexuality. Consider some of these stereotypes and trace their roots from slavery into the present century. Do you think such racist stereotypes are diminishing? Why or why not?

4. For many years the structure of the African American family has been of concern to social scientists and government policymakers because of the increasing proportion of households headed by divorced and never-married women. Why should this family configuration be a source for concern? Is it anything more than a matter of personal choice? Initially, social scientists believed that the relatively low rates of marriage among African Americans might be the result of a tradition developed under slavery, when slave marriages had no legal legitimacy. But research indicates that slaves clung tenaciously to their marriages through all means open to them, so we must look elsewhere for an explanation of the unmarried African American mother. What do you suggest as some of the elements in such an explanation? In fact, today households of all ethnic groups are increasingly headed by unmarried or never-married women. Why do you think this is the case?

NOTES

1. Ethnic terminology presents a particular problem to those outside the group in question. For example, many of those whom outsiders call Native Americans usually refer to themselves as Indian people. Americans with African ancestry identify themselves both as black and as African American. And Spanish-speaking Americans identify themselves by a variety of terms, including Hispanic and

Latino as umbrella identifiers, and by more specific terms indicating the country of origin of their ancestors, such as Mexican American or Chicano for those of Mexican heritage. Often ethnic terminology takes on substantial political significance. In this book we have tried to use a wide range of terminology, with the intention of including as many perspectives as possible and alienating as few people as possible.

2. The contention that gender roles in precontact Native American life were primarily complementary rather than, like Euro-American gender roles, primarily unequal, warns us against over-generalizing from the experience of our own culture. On the other hand, such practices as carefully guarding the chastity of unmarried girls (but not boys) and harsh penalties, including gang rape and mutilation (often cutting off the tip of the nose) for adulterous wives (but not husbands), indicates that at least in some Native American groups male superiority was certainly a fact of life.

REFERENCES

Ackerman, Lillian A. 1995. "Gender Status in the Plateau." Pp. 75–100 in *Women and Power in Native North America*, ed. Laura F. Klein and Lillian A. Ackerman. Norman, OK: University of Oklahoma Press,

Ali, Shahrazad. 1989. *The Blackman's Guide to Understanding the Blackwoman*. Philadelphia, PA: Civilized Publications.

American Association of University Women. 1991. *Shortchanging Girls, Shortchanging America*. Washington, D.C.

Amott, Teresa, and Julie Matthaei. 1996. *Race, Gender, and Work: A Multi-Cultural Economic History of Women in the United States*. Boston, MA: South End Press.

Billingsley, Andrew. 1992. *Climbing Jacob's Ladder: The Enduring Legacy of African American Families*. New York: Simon & Schuster.

Blumenfeld, Warren J., and Diane Raymond. 1993. *Looking at Gay and Lesbian Life*. Boston, MA: Beacon Press.

Brown, Kathleen M. 1995. "The Anglo-Algonquian Gender Frontier." Pp. 26–48 in *Negotiators of Change: Historical Perspectives on Native American Women*, ed. Nancy Shoemaker. New York: Routledge.

Dash, Leon. 1996. *Rosa Lee: A Mother and Her Family in Urban America*. New York: Basic Books.

Davis, Marianna W. 1982. *Contributions of Black Women to America*. Columbia, SC: Kenday Press.

D'Emilio, John, and Estelle B. Freedman. 1988. *Intimate Matters: A History of Sexuality in America*. New York: Harper & Row.

Dull, Diana, and Candace West. 1997. "Accounting for Cosmetic Surgery: The Accomplishment of Gender." Pp. 90–107 in *Race, Class and Gender in a Diverse Society*, ed. Diane Kendall. Boston, MA: Allyn and Bacon.

Frazier, E. Franklin. 1939. *The Negro Family in the United States*. Chicago, IL: University of Chicago Press.

Glick, Paul C. 1997. "Demographic Picture of African American Families." Pp. 118–139 in *Black Families*, ed. Henrietta Pipes McAdoo. Thousand Oaks, CA: Sage Publications.

Gutman, Herbert G. 1976. *The Black Family in Slavery and Freedom, 1750–1925*. New York: Pantheon Books.

Hall, Ronald E. 1997. "The Color Complex: The Bleaching Syndrome." Pp. 39–47 in *Race, Class and Gender in a Diverse Society*, ed. Diane Kendall. Boston, MA: Allyn and Bacon.

Hemmons, Willa Mae. 1996. *Black Women in the New World Order: Social Justice and the African American Female*. Westport, CT: Praeger Publishers.

hooks, bell. 1981. *Ain't I a Woman: Black Women and Feminism*. Boston, MA: South End Press.

Jackson, Donald, ed. 1955. *Black Hawk, An Autobiography*. Urbana, IL: University of Illinois Press.

Jorgensen, Joseph G. 1984. "Indians and the Metropolis." Pp. 67–113 in *The American Indian in Urban Society*, ed. Jack O. Waddell and O. Michael Watson. Lanham, MD: University Press of America.

Klein, Laura F. 1995. "Rank and Gender in Tlingit Society." Pp. 28–45 in *Women and Power in Native North America*, ed. Laura F. Klein and Lillian A. Ackerman. Norman, OK: University of Oklahoma Press.

Klein, Laura F., and Lillian A. Ackerman. 1995. Introduction. Pp. 3–16 in *Women and Power in Native North America*, ed. Laura F. Klein and Lillian A. Ackerman. Norman, OK: University of Oklahoma Press.

Knack, Martha C. 1995. "The Dynamics of Southern Paiute Women's Roles." Pp. 146–158 in *Women and Power in Native North America*, ed. Laura F. Klein and Lillian A. Ackerman. Norman, OK: University of Oklahoma Press.

Kupperman, Karen Ordahl. 1988. *Captain John Smith: A Select Edition of His Writings*. Chapel Hill, NC: University of North Carolina Press.

Leacock, Eleanor Burke. 1981. "Women's Status in Egalitarian Society: Implications for Social Evolution." Pp. 133–182 in *Myths of Male Dominance: Collected Articles on Women Cross-Culturally*, ed. Eleanor Burke Leacock. New York: Monthly Review Press.

Lewis, Diane K. 1975. "The Black Family: Socialization and Sex Roles." *Phylon* 36:221–237.

Mintz, Sidney W., and Richard Price. 1974. An Anthropological Approach to the Study of Afro-American History. Unpublished ms.

Moynihan, Daniel Patrick. 1967. "The Negro Family: The Case for National Action" [*The Moynihan Report*]. Pp. 39–124 in *The Moynihan Report and the Politics of Controversy*, ed. Lee Rainwater and William L. Yancey. Cambridge, MA: MIT Press.

Murphy, Lucy Eldersveld. 1995. "Autonomy and the Economic Roles of Indian Women of the Fox-Wisconsin Riverway Region, 1763–1832." Pp. 72–89 in *Negotiators of Change: Historical Perspectives on Native American Women*, ed. Nancy Shoemaker. New York: Routledge.

Omolade, Barbara. 1986. "It's a Family Affair: The Real Lives of Black Single Mothers," *Village Voice*, 15 July 1986.

Oritz, Vilma. 1994. "Women of Color: A Demographic Overview." Pp. 13–42 in *Women of Color in U.S. Society*, ed. Maxine Baca Zinn and Bonnie Thorton Dill. Philadelphia, PA: Temple University Press.

Osburn, Katherine M. B. 1995. "'Dear Friend and Ex-Husband:' Marriage, Divorce, and Women's Property Rights on the Southern Ute Reservation, 1787–1930." Pp. 157–175 in *Negotiators of Change: Historical Perspectives on Native American Women*, ed. Nancy Shoemaker. New York: Routledge.

Powers, Marla N. 1986. *Oglala Women: Myth, Ritual and Reality*. Chicago, IL: University of Chicago Press.

Rainwater, Lee, and William L. Yancey, eds. 1967. *The Moynihan Report and the Politics of Controversy*. Cambridge, MA: MIT Press.

Rosaldo, Michelle Zimbalist. 1974. "Women, Culture and Society: A Theoretical Overview." Pp. 16–42 in *Women, Culture and Society*, ed. Michelle Zimbalist Rosaldo and Louise Lamphere. Stanford, CA: Stanford University Press.

Stack, Carol B. 1970. *All Our Kin: Strategies for Survival in a Black Community*. New York: Harper & Row.

Staples, Robert. 1997. "An Overview of Race and Marital Status." Pp. 269–272 in *Black Families*, ed. Henrietta Pipes McAdoo. Thousand Oaks, CA: Sage Publications.

Staples, Robert, and Leanor Boulin Johnson. 1993. *Black Families at the Crossroads: Challenges and Prospects*. San Francisco, CA: Jossey-Bass.

Still, William. [1872] 1968. *The Underground Railroad*. New York: Arno Press.

Sudarkasa, Niara. 1975. "An Exposition on the Value Premises Underlying Black Family Studies." *Journal of the National Medical Association* 67:235–239.

Sudarkasa, Niara. 1997. "African American Families and Family Values." Pp. 9–40 in *Black Families*, ed. Henrietta Pipes McAdoo. Thousand Oaks, CA: Sage Publications.

Thompson, Becky W. 1997. "Childhood Lessons: Culture." Pp. 187–202 in *Race, Class and Gender in a Diverse Society*, ed. Diane Elizabeth Kendall. Boston, MA: Allyn and Bacon.

Tyler, Lyon Gardiner, ed. 1907. *Narratives of Early Virginia 1606–1625*. New York: Charles Scribner.

Whites, Lee Ann. 1992. "The Civil War as a Crisis in Gender." Pp. 3–21 in *Divided Houses: Gender and the Civil War*, ed. Catherine Clinton and Nina Silber. New York: Oxford University Press.

Whitney, Ellen M., ed. 1973. *The Black Hawk War, 1831–1832*. Springfield, IL: State Historical Library.

Williams, Walter L. 1986. *The Spirit and the Flesh: Sexual Diversity in American Indian Culture*. Boston, MA: Beacon Press.

CHAPTER 5

ETHNIC MINORITIES: LATINOS AND ASIAN AMERICANS

This chapter looks at gender among Hispanic Americans and Asian Americans. These groups became significant minorities in America later than did Native Americans and African Americans. Unlike the groups of the last chapter, they were neither conquered nor enslaved; their migrations to the United States were voluntary. As we shall see, however, their adaptation has not been easy. Their migration history continues to reveal the many collisions of gender, ethnicity, and social class in America.

LATINOS: NEIGHBORS AND IMMIGRANTS

Most Latinos in the United States today are voluntary immigrants or the descendants of voluntary immigrants. Some, however, are descended from Mexican citizens who were living on the huge tract of northern Mexico that was sold to the United States in 1848 for the sum of $15,000,000. This forced transaction, which was part of the Treaty of Guadalupe Hidalgo that ended a war between Mexico and the United States, included what became the states of California, Nevada, Colorado, Arizona, New Mexico, and Texas, along with portions of what are now Utah and Wyoming. Inhabitants of the territory, both tribal Native Americans and largely mixed-race people who participated in Mexican culture as farmers and ranchers, were guaranteed protection of their property, culture, and language. These promises were rarely kept, especially where they conflicted with the interests of the newly arriving Anglo-American population.

Any discussion of gender among Hispanic Americans (many of whom prefer to be called Latinos) is complicated by the great diversity within this group. More than half of U.S. Hispanics are of Mexican heritage (roughly 70 percent of those born in this country), and the other half are divided among

Puerto Ricans (all of whom are U.S. citizens) and other Caribbean Hispanics, including Cuban Americans and immigrants from Central and South America. Thus the group reflects many distinctive national cultures. Latinos are also ethnically diverse, including individuals who identify with European, African, and Native American roots—sometimes all three. They come from a wide range of social classes, educational levels, and income groups, with the largest group in the middle class being the Cubans. In contrast, for example, to Mexican American adults, more than half of whom have not completed high school, 58 percent of Cuban (and Cuban American) adults have twelve years or more of education (Fernández Kelly 1990, 185). Thus, unlike the majority of Latinos in the United States, Cuban Americans, especially those who arrived before the so called "Marielitos" in the huge boatlift of 1980, tend to fill middle- and upper-middle-class social ranks as professionals and entrepreneurs (Fernández Kelly 1990, 186).

This diversity is not lost on Latinos, who seldom feel a sense of unity with those whose national ancestry is different from their own. In fieldwork with impoverished Mexican American residents of the Texas border area, one of the authors (McKee) often heard derogatory remarks made about other Hispanic groups based on their differing dialect of Spanish or on their ethnic background. And Suzanne Oboler (1997) presents a conversation among a group of women from Latin American countries who disliked being referred to as "Hispanic." They found it odd and annoying that Euro-Americans should call them all by this term, when they belong to different nationalities and different ethnic groups.

TRADITIONAL GENDER ROLES

Why, then, do Euro-Americans use a single term to characterize such a culturally, nationally, and ethnically diverse group of people? Most immediately apparent is the Spanish language that all Latinos share (or share as an ancestral memory), and that so few Euro-Americans master, despite years spent in elementary Spanish classrooms. The other shared characteristic is the core of cultural traits that Latin America inherited from the Iberian Peninsula (Portugal in the case of Brazil, and Spain in the case of the rest of the Latin New World). In every country these traits developed somewhat differently because of the indigenous cultures with which they initially came into contact. Still, it is possible to identify a patriarchal core of the Hispanic cultural construction of gender.

Before we describe this patriarchal cultural construction, it is important to make two points. First, this core is a diffuse traditional ideal that has historically underlain much of Latino life, but always in varying degrees of consciousness and power. It is not a set of specific regulations of which everyone is equally aware or equally observant. Second, as Latino populations gain greater wealth and education and become more assimilated to Euro-American values and behaviors, there is usually a decline in the power of the patriarchal tradition. Culturally conservative Hispanic populations, like those near the Mexican border, for example, are far more likely to be strongly influenced by the patriarchal tradition than are more assimilated populations, like Hispanic groups in Los Angeles or New York City. There is often a difference based on social class, with less middle-class than working-class Latino participation in a traditional patriarchal pattern. Even within a single family, older members, especially those with little education, are more likely to have followed patriarchal norms than younger members.

The common core of traditional Hispanic gender construction is patriarchy, or domination by males. Males derive their status primarily from their control of subsistence, through which they fulfill their primary cultural obligation, the economic support of their wives and families. Females, on the other hand, derive their status primarily from the production of offspring, and the nurturance of their husbands and children. This entitles them to support and protection from their husbands and love (and later care) from their children. Because of a husband's economic support and because of what is perceived as the inherently different natures of men and women, husbands are entitled to their wives' obedience, service, and respect, which includes the acceptance of extramarital sexual activities if any should occur. And they may occur, because both men and women consider men's sexual appetites to be greater and more irresistible than women's. Further, many men consider nearly all encounters with any but the oldest, youngest, and most closely related females to be potentially sexual.

This cultural construction of masculinity is referred to in Spanish as machismo (adjectival form: macho), but it has other dimensions and greater complexity than mere sexual interest. At least as important is a man's sense of honor and pride, much of which, especially among poor men, is derived from his ability to support and protect his family. The ideal man, one who is truly macho, will not accept affronts to his pride nor challenges to his authority, especially within his family. This does not necessarily mean that machismo requires exaggerated aggression, despite the popular Euro-American stereotype. It does, however, mean that the ideal of male behavior may be very difficult for lower-class men to achieve in the public world. Many Hispanics occupy a place near the bottom of the social and economic ladder, where they are subjected to personal and institutional threats to their pride and restrictions on their authority, as well as limits to their ability to support and protect their families. In such a situation, some men find that the only outlets for the expression of the culturally required machismo are either in suppressing the autonomy of wives and children, or in establishing sexual relationships outside of marriage. For middle- and upper-class men with the required wealth, extramarital relationships have long included the casa chica, or "little house" of the mistress, who may (like the mother of Eva Perón) have produced a second family, not entitled to any of the wealth or privilege of a man's first and legitimate family.

Cultural expectations of machismo on the part of men are complemented by expectations of self-effacing obedience and nurturance on the part of women, a complex of behaviors sometimes referred to as *marianismo,* after the assumed personality of the Virgin Mary. Where men are expected to maintain a vivid, lifelong interest in sex, women's (or at least good women's) interest in sex is assumed to be minimal to nonexistent, and for them sex should be confined to marriage. A woman's psychological fulfillment is expected to derive primarily from her relationship with her children, since in more traditional marriages a husband may not interact much with his wife or involve her in his nondomestic life. She should run the household efficiently and smoothly and make sure that her husband and children have the care they need without intruding on her husband's activities or interfering with his authority. Obviously, for the many impoverished Hispanic women, this role is as difficult to achieve as the male role is for poor Hispanic men. The lower the income level the more poignant the words of a poor Mexican woman in Oscar Lewis' *Children of Sanchez,* who said in desperate admiration of her even more destitute aunt, "she was the kind of woman who knew how to suffer" (Lewis 1961, 312).

A construction of gender roles that assumes that men will or may likely have extramarital sexual partners and that women will not or should not do so is, of course, based on a fundamental contradiction: Where are those sexually available women coming from, if women are not having sex outside of marriage? This contradiction should hardly surprise us, since it has also been one of the underlying assumptions of the dominant Euro-American system of gender roles. It is, however, more pronounced in Latino culture, and gives rise to greater negative judgments against women whose sexual activities fail to conform to culturally approved norms. Sexually active women always have the potential to make a misstep and through illicit sexual activity humiliate the men who have responsibility for them (their husbands or fathers), thus "betraying" them. As a result, these women are often regarded with suspicion and mistrust.

Hispanic culture at its most traditional and orthodox is therefore sometimes said to consider all women as belonging to one of two categories, the whore or the madonna (or virgin). Madonnas are those women who are not sexually active—young girls and old women—or who are demonstrably faithful wives; whores are all others. The Mexican term *malinchista* reflects one Latino culture's deep-seated mistrust of women as potential betrayers. The term is derived from the name of Malinche (or Malintzin), a slave given by Moctezuma II to Cortez as part of an enormous gift of riches, intended as a bribe to encourage him to leave Mexico. Malinche was baptized with the name of Marina and became Cortez's concubine, translator, and advisor. As a woman (the Aztec were as patriarchal as the Spaniards), a slave, and a member of a conquered group, Malinche had, of course, no effective choice in her cooperation with Cortez. Nonetheless, in Mexico she has long been considered a faithless woman who used sex to betray the Mexican people, and her name is a metaphor for traitor.

Not surprisingly, any woman may go through several passages from "madonna" to "whore" and back again, as she goes from girl to young woman to old woman. And one man's whore may be another's madonna. A woman whose husband has come to mistrust her will almost certainly be whole-heartedly loved by her children, whose affection for their mother and loyalty toward her are likely to increase as they grow up. In disagreements between their parents, most children are inclined to defend and protect their mothers against verbal or physical aggression on the part of their fathers. To the extent that the whore/madonna dichotomy is useful in understanding gender relations in some traditional Hispanic families, children's views of their mothers nearly always fall on the madonna side of the split. A Mexican American friend once told McKee that his father used to warn his numerous sons "A la mujer ni todo su dinero ni todo su amor" (To a woman give neither all your money nor all your love). It seemed to the sons an unremarkable piece of advice, until it occurred to them that their father was also indicating his mistrust of his wife—their beloved mother.

The emotional and psychological centrality of the mother in a Hispanic family, despite her subordination to her husband, was strikingly demonstrated by responses to a series of interviews that McKee (1985) conducted with impoverished Mexican American residents of the border city of Laredo, Texas (see Figure 5.1 on page 132). In the course of routine questions about family composition, respondents were asked if their parents were living, and if not, when they had died. Some people could provide the dates of death of both parents, while others had only a vague idea of when their fathers had died. But no one had forgotten the date of death of a mother, and maternal death dates were often supplied in great detail, including the day of the week, even if the death had occurred fifty or sixty years earlier. Just referring to a mother's date of death sometimes triggered an outpouring of emotion, as respondents recalled their grief at the loss of their mothers and their own accompanying illness or psychological prostration. "My life has never been the same since she died," one middle-aged woman said. Men's responses were as emotional as those of women.

Latino gender roles and family structure as presented here are constructions that most Latinos recognize as traditional, but that are useful primarily as models of what behaviors and relationships were like a generation or more ago. As mentioned earlier, numerous elements of this construction are, of course, still influential and operational within many of today's more traditional (and often rural) Hispanic families. But a large number of contemporary families, especially those who have lived for several generations in the United States or who have achieved middle-class status, have modified or abandoned many aspects of the earlier Latino gender roles and relationships. Instead of a submersion of the individual in the traditional

FIGURE 5.1
A scene in Laredo, Texas. (*Nancy P. McKee*)

patriarchal family structure, they have become increasingly assimilated to such Euro-American behavioral conventions as the cultivation of individualism, including increasing autonomy for women.

THE MODERN LATINO FAMILY

Like all cultural ideals, the classic Hispanic family structure has never been fully reflected in reality. Norma Williams, in her book, *The Mexican American Family* (1990), points to a great diversity in the extent of male domination in both working-class and professional households. Williams also reported that though there is likely to be greater spousal equality in today's professional families, most of her informants pointed to their mothers' greater dependence and their fathers' greater authority.

Within the home, however, even traditional families have often reflected considerable female power. Men rarely interfere with the running of the household. Whether the husband gives his wife money for food and other expenditures or turns over his entire paycheck to his wife (which has always been common), or whether (as is increasingly true in Hispanic families) women are earning their own salaries, the household is the wife's domain. Men rarely participate in cooking, cleaning, or child care. They are believed by many women and many believe themselves to be incapable of domestic labor, a perspective that is reinforced by the general view that doing women's work is demeaning to men. Working wives thus have a heavy second shift to contend with when they come home from work. On the other hand, Williams reports a negotiated shift over time in the willingness of many Mexican American wives to assert limited independence in such matters as voicing disagreement, going out with friends, or making major household purchases. The words of one woman illustrate this change: "Whatever he said went like that. I'm not so timid now. I have some say. If I don't like what he does, I'll tell him so. Before we did not communicate with each other" (Williams 1990, 91). Though some of Williams' informants described their mothers as important forces at home, many comments were similar to those of the following man, who associated his mother's lack of authority with her lack of education (and ultimately lack of money):

> I think my father and I are totally different persons. I am better off because I have this and that, and he never got us anything. My parents were poor. My mother was very limited because she did not go to school. My father made the decisions because he earned the money. But they didn't have enough money for the bills. (Quoted in Williams 1990, 85)

Everyday control of children in Latino families is likely to be handled by the mother, and this control is likely to last as long as children continue to live with their parents. Since it is still relatively uncommon for unmarried children, especially females, to live independently, parental control of their children's daily activities can last well into the children's adulthood. A middle-aged Laredo mother of eleven children told McKee that she chaperones all of her daughters' social activities: "Si no voy yo, pues no van ellas" (If I don't go, then they don't go). Her two youngest daughters are now in their twenties and working in a bank but living at home.

As a grandmother and mother-in-law, this formidable woman continued to monitor her grandchildren's behavior and kept a disapproving eye on her more modern daughters-in-law, who, she suspected, had not been as well-brought-up as her own daughters. One of these daughters-in-law, a woman who has had a well-paid job for most of her married life, recounted the story of a large family party she had attended with her husband and children— wearing shorts (in an area where summer temperatures frequently rise above 112 degrees). Her mother-in-law said nothing, but after everyone was seated she went into the house and came out with a towel, which she dropped over her daughter-in-law's knees. These anecdotes illustrate the kind of domestic power exerted by even the most traditional women (in this case born in the United States). They also illustrate the concern most Latino families continue to have for their daughters' safety and reputation, though such vigorous chaperoning is not common in more middle-class families.

One of the traits most frequently cited for Hispanic families is *familism*, the psychological, affective, communal, and structural focus of the family, including the extended family, in the lives of Hispanics. While this may be seen as a cultural characteristic of Latino peoples, it may also be considered an adaptive strategy for the many Latinos who live in or near poverty.

In the impoverished neighborhoods of Laredo, familism, especially in the form of kin networks, is essential to survival. Most individual households in Laredo do not contain members of an extended family, partly because houses are extremely small. Nevertheless, any of the poor neighborhoods in the city could be mapped to demonstrate that nearly every household has one or more related families living within walking distance.

These families are frequently the source of small loans of food, money, tools, and labor, from child care to auto repair. They also function to circulate information and to provide emotional support and allay loneliness and despair, especially in the lives of impoverished, house-bound women. A final function of these kin networks is the care of older family members, who might otherwise have to resort to institutional care, something most Latino families resist with greater vigor than Euro-Americans. In one such case in Laredo, the granddaughter of a large family moved with her husband and children to take care of her grandmother when her husband lost his job in Corpus Christi, a hundred and fifty miles away. The family moved into a house (vacated by a cousin who had moved to another city in search of employment) next door to the grandmother, from which they supplied her with cooked food several times a day; they also drove her to the doctor and to do her shopping. A great-granddaughter stopped by every day after school to sweep the yard, water the plants, feed the pets, and do any other chores that needed attention.

The economic situation in Laredo often verges on desperate, with the lowest per capita income of any city in the United States and an official unemployment rate that sometimes nears 30 percent. Many of Laredo's inhabitants have lived elsewhere in the United States, and they are well aware of Laredo's numerous disadvantages. They frequently complain about poverty, unemployment, lack of benefits, and political corruption. But, they say repeatedly, "my mother is here," or "my parents are getting old, and they need my help," or "this is where my family is." Though many would like to leave the city (and in fact, some do leave in search of work), the affective importance of the family is hard to overemphasize, and its collective power frequently overshadows the individual interests of young family members.

FAMILY SIZE

Many people believe that Latinos have a lot of children, and that this is because they are overwhelmingly Catholic. Compared to Euro-Americans, Latinos do have more children as a rule, but some Hispanic groups have more than others, and all groups have fewer than they used to. As for the religious motivation, that is far from certain.

It is clear that family size has been declining among Latinos at least since the 1960s, and that Mexican Americans as a group have more children than other Hispanics, while Cuban Americans have the fewest. The reasons for the downward trend in family size and the ethnic variation are largely economic. In the days when most Latinos lived in rural areas and did agricultural work, large numbers of children were an economic advantage. While it cost something to feed, house, and clothe them, they could begin contributing to the family income very early. And little or no schooling was necessary for agricultural work. There were, of course, other occupations available, including domestic service for girls, but none of them required much formal education. These occupations were not specific ethnic characteristics of Hispanic life; they were at one time characteristic of most people's lives, regardless of ethnicity, and particularly characteristic of the lives of the poor. As we have seen in the case of African Americans in the Southeast, when agricultural technology changed and more machinery came to be used, there was less and less employment for agricultural workers, and small farmers found it increasingly difficult to compete with huge, well-funded holdings. At the same time, employment everywhere began to rely on more complex technology and to require more education. This has been as true for the Hispanic population as it was for the African American or any other population. The large numbers of children characteristic of Hispanic (and other) families were no longer economically advantageous; in fact, they were now a serious liability.

Like Euro-Americans before them, some Hispanics did begin to reduce family size in the 1960s, as is evident from census figures. In middle-class Latino families, children cannot contribute to family income at an early age, because middle-class occupations require years of expensive support, education, and training. Thus these families had downsized their families ahead of poor Latinos.

Though people all over the world make decisions on family size primarily out of economic considerations, these decisions are not simple, nor are they made in isolation from other cultural considerations. Latinos are overwhelmingly Catholic, and the Catholic church teaches that artificial birth control is a sin. This factor cannot be ignored in analyzing Hispanic family size, but it should not be overemphasized, either. After all, in the last third of the twentieth century most non-Hispanic Catholics in the United States—in fact, most Catholics in most places—have ignored the church's teachings on birth control.

In a set of questions about family size and birth control asked of impoverished Mexican Americans in Laredo, people's responses indicated four things: a general approval of limiting family size, a sense of conflict with the church's teachings, change from earlier patterns of family size, and some difference between male and female responses (McKee 1985, 226–229). Half of the respondents simply said outright that they believed birth control was essential. "You have to think how many can I support, feed, educate, protect, and defend against everything," said one young woman, while an eighty-three-year-old mother of five sons responded, "I tell my grandchildren that they must limit their children to one or two—or three." And a woman whose husband had been unemployed for some time responded, "If a person knows that he is poor, he can't have too many children. If you accept what God sends, he could send a bunch." Some informants reflected the church's teachings on birth control, though they had finally decided to ignore them. "They say, 'Have faith,'" one older woman remarked bitterly, "but it's too many." And one father of ten children under sixteen responded similarly: "They say it's a sin, but I say you can't support them."

About a quarter of those interviewed said that one must limit one's family size, but they regretted it, and wished for the vanished time when one could support huge families. One older woman said regretfully, "Before, you could have twelve, fifteen, twenty children. Now everything is so expensive, you can't maintain them."

Finally, just over a quarter of the respondents said that they favored not limiting the size of their families at all. This group was interesting in that it included some men and some older women, both married and never married, but only five (out of sixty) women of childbearing age. Older women in this group usually stated their objections to birth control by reference to their own children ("No, I don't like [it] because I had fifteen, myself"), though a few mentioned religion ("To limit [one's children] would be a mortal sin"). The men in the group did not elaborate on their feelings, and the interviewers, all women, did not press them to do so. But when the sizes of their families were checked, it was clear that the situation was more complex than their responses indicated. In thirteen years of marriage one of these men had had two children, who were eleven and twelve years old, while another had had two in seven years, and a third had had three in seventeen years. It seems clear that either these men were responding to the interviewers according to a culturally approved model while acting according to economic self-interest, or they believed they were acting according to cultural rules while their wives were acting according to economic self-interest.

In sum, despite a nostalgic affection for large families among many Hispanics, particularly those in the working class, most people of Laredo, including nearly all women of childbearing age, have decided that economic reality demands small families—though aware that this conflicts with the teachings of the Catholic church. Some men (who have less to do with the actual caretaking of children than women) may continue to say that they prefer large families, possibly in part as proof of virility. However, even if their wives are young enough to produce children, these men do not in fact have large families.

EDUCATION

The level of education of Hispanic Americans varies dramatically. As was mentioned earlier, nearly 60 percent of Cuban Americans have twelve or more years of schooling, while well under half of Mexican Americans have not completed high school (Ortiz 1994, 26). This has primarily to do with the social class of the groups involved, though it may have something to do with their ethnic composition as well. The Cuban American middle class is overwhelmingly European in appearance, since it has been a disproportionately middle-class population that fled the Cuban revolution. By contrast, other Hispanic Americans, including Puerto Ricans and Mexican Americans, seem more likely to be of mixed ancestry. Whatever social class they now occupy, their immigrant ancestors were likely to have been from the largely non-European working class. In the United States this appearance almost certainly had a negative effect on their educational success and chances.

Adding the variable of gender to the Latino educational picture shows further complexity. Traditionally, education was a luxury for most poor Hispanic families. Children were needed at home or for the family's livelihood; clothing appropriate for school was expensive; and, especially in rural Texas, there might not be a school near enough for children on a ranchito to attend. Even if a school was available, girls were frequently kept home all or part of the time to help their mothers care for the household. Eldest daughters were most likely to become baby tenders and cooks. The general feeling was that education might benefit boys, who, after all, would get jobs and support their families. Girls, on the other hand, would always stay home and education would be of little use to them.

Many poor women in Laredo who were born in the United States in the first third of the twentieth century are wholly or functionally illiterate. Some can write their names and recognize a few words, but others must sign legal and financial papers with an X. Most of these women spent their early years on tiny ranches beyond the reach of a school. Other women, born later in the century, are usually literate, but they have often had much less education than their brothers, and they may have had less education than younger sisters. Part of this is due to their utility as deputy mothers in large families, and part of it is due to a change in the way their families saw education as they were growing up.

As discussed in the preceding section, it has not been lost on Hispanic families in Laredo and elsewhere that there are fewer and fewer unskilled jobs available. They have also come to recognize that more and more women will be working both before and after marriage. In addition, public school systems have begun to take more seriously laws requiring all children to attend school, regardless of ethnicity or gender. Though Hispanic families continue to be concerned about the reputations and behavior of their daughters, few of them now consider schools as threats to a daughter's honor as they once did. Finally, as family size has declined and fewer Latino families are farm-based, the need for young girls to stay home as surrogate mothers and farm help has sharply lessened. So for the past forty years or so Latino families have sent their daughters to school along with their sons.

Raised in a generally patriarchal atmosphere, Hispanic girls have found that their traditionally quiet, obedient demeanor is successful in school. Here they often do well and are rewarded for behavior that would likely pass unnoticed at home. Hispanic boys, on the other hand, often have difficulty in school as they enter adolescence. Eager to demonstrate their independence and manhood, they frequently find the restrictions of school intolerable. Though their families urge them to stay in school, many young men are anxious to work, both to prove themselves and to lighten the economic burden on their parents, to whom they frequently turn over all or most of their paychecks. The result (though Cuban Americans are again the exception) is that in many poor enclaves there are now more Latino girls than boys who graduate from high school. More Latino men than women still graduate from college (Ortiz 1994, 26), but the proportion of women graduating has greatly increased. This has serious implications for employment and family dynamics, as we will see in the next section. It also presents a striking parallel to what we have seen within the Native American and African American communities, in both of which women acquire more education than men.

When poor Laredoans were asked for their opinions on education, they universally manifested an overwhelming belief in the efficacy of education in unlocking the doors of poverty. Old and young, men and women, they echo the words of a fifty-year-old widow with a son and two daughters: "Children must stay in school and study hard so that they can get a good job and protect themselves" (McKee 1985, 209). The need to be able to defend oneself and one's children was the most frequently cited reason given for the nearly unanimous opinion that education is as important for girls as for boys. "If a woman has no education, she can't defend herself," said one fifty-three-year-old man whose Mexican-born wife had never been to school, while a thirty-five-year-old woman said "Girls need education because they, too, have to work. If they marry without education, they cannot defend themselves." Indeed, the wife of a disabled janitor responded that "Education is more important for the woman, because something can happen to the man, and she'd have the kids." This sentiment was echoed by an unmarried eighteen-year-old high school girl who felt that "Education is at least as important for girls, because if you get married and have bad luck, you can take care of yourself."

The conviction that education pays is well-established in Latino communities, both for males and for females. The ineluctable realities of life often intervene, and both sexes may interrupt their education. But to men and women alike, education is the key to prosperity, success, and even survival itself. Indeed, to women, it is the only pathway to economic security.

EMPLOYMENT

The traditional Latino perspective on employment has been that it is the realm of men, and that a working woman is a demonstration of her husband's failure to support her adequately and an affront to his authority. In fact, however, large numbers of Latino women work outside their households— 52 percent of all Mexican American women and nearly 57 percent of Cuban women (Ortiz 1994, 28). In many households, especially middle-class households, this employment of married women has meant the same shift to two-earner families now so common in American families of all ethnicities.

For some households in poor neighborhoods in the Texas-Mexico border region, women's employment has made for serious upheavals. The border region of the U.S. Southwest has a precarious economy, and in Texas the situation is particularly difficult. Partly because of competition from Mexican nationals who live in Mexican border cities and commute to work in the United States every day, and partly because of the region's dependence upon Mexican wholesale and retail trade, which fluctuates with value of the peso, unemployment in the area is very high. In 1998 the official unemployment rate was 14 percent, and the effective, unofficial rate is probably substantially higher. Underemployment is widespread, with many residents of the area working at several part-time jobs. Frequently these jobs are very poorly paid, often off the books and virtually always without benefits. But even along the border, increasing numbers of jobs, especially those that pay well and offer benefits, require a high school diploma and good skills in English. And this means that many of these jobs go to women, while working-class men are more likely to be unemployed or underemployed.

This situation can have a devastating effect on the traditional gender relationships within a Mexican American family, since it erodes the most essential basis of male authority, the ability to support a family. So shameful can this situation be that several unemployed young men in Laredo refused to acknowledge that they were at home during the day. Because their wives were working they had to remain at home looking after the young children, but they would not answer the door or the telephone or leave the house for any reason, despite the sweltering heat, until their wives came home from work. This way they were spared the shame of being seen by their neighbors in their humiliating role as househusbands. The neighbors, of course, were all aware of the men's situation, and discussed it at length. The men's wives were frantic. All of the women wanted to work, and even more than that, they had to work, since they were the sole support of their households. But they were concerned about their husbands' feelings of shame, frustration, and anger, which they feared might destroy their families.

In a comparison of employment in the garment trades of Cuban women in Miami and Mexican American women in Los Angeles, M. Patricia Fernández Kelly (1990) points out that their reasons for working (aside from making money), are quite different. The Cubans are attempting to regain the middle-class status they had before emigration; the Mexican Americans are struggling to survive and perhaps achieve middle-class status for the first time. Because they operate within a cohesive Cuban immigrant subculture marked by vigorous solidarity, the Cubans are generally able to improve their social and economic situations. The Mexican Americans, however, partly because of their "proletarian" origins and partly because the labor market upon which they depend is controlled by a generally unsympathetic Euro-American power structure, are rarely able to prosper.

As the Cuban women's situation becomes economically more secure, usually because their husbands are achieving their own successes as entrepreneurs, these women frequently quit working in an outside shop, but do piecework at home, often at their husbands' request. By contrast, the Mexican American women, if they go to "homework," do so in order to increase their autonomy and economic success. Fernández Kelly points out that the Mexican American women have usually been pushed into the labor market "as a result of men's inability to fulfill their socially assigned role." If they achieve economic success through their own work, it often develops into "a desire for individual emancipation, mobility, and financial independence as women." By contrast, Cuban women "see no contradiction between personal fulfillment and a strong commitment to patriarchal standards" (Fernández Kelly 1990, 188). One Cuban woman had worked to support her family but then retired to "homework" at her husband's request when his business began to prosper. She made the following remark:

> There's no reason for women not to earn a living when it's necessary; they should have as many opportunities and responsibilities as men. But I also tell my daughters that the strength of a family rests on the intelligence and work of women. It is foolish to give up your place as a mother and a wife only to go take orders from men who aren't even part of your family. What's so liberated about that? (Fernández Kelly 1990, 192)

LATINAS AND FEMINISM

The response to feminism varies widely among Latinas. Of Cuban women immigrants who have participated extensively in the U.S. labor force, Fernández Kelly writes, "They are bewildered by feminist goals of equality and fulfillment in the job market" (1990, 193). For these women the patriarchal family provides security and a meaningful existence, and their incursion into paid work has occurred only so that their husbands could reestablish themselves as the primary or sole support of the family. They are happy to move from work in a factory to "homework," or to retire altogether once their husbands' incomes are high enough. For lower-class women the patriarchal family is a much less rewarding environment, particularly when a patriarch is compensating for his economic failure with abuse or unreasonable demands at home, or when he has abandoned the family altogether. Though the actual employment available to these women may be arduous, unpleasant, and poorly paid, it provides them with an income that, if they are unmarried, they may dispose of wholly or partially themselves, or if they are married, they can use as a bargaining chip for greater influence or autonomy within their families. In Fernández Kelly's words, "The absence of economic underpinnings for the implementation of patriarchal standards may bring about more equitable exchanges between men and women, and may stimulate women's search for individual well-being and personal autonomy as women" (1990, 191).

But do these realities turn Latinas into professed feminists? Those for whom the traditional patriarchal structure has proven rewarding, either psychologically or economically, generally find feminists and feminism foolish or unseemly. But those who have found patriarchy oppressive do not necessarily identify themselves as feminists. They may be faced with the same dilemmas that plague many Native American and African American women: To condemn the men of one's own group for sexism may be perceived (even by oneself) as betrayal. Once again the men of the New World and their whole culture are betrayed into the hands of Europeans by the continuous treachery of faithless women. The words of Gloria Anzaldúa, a Chicana poet and feminist activist from the Texas border, make this dilemma clear:

> Not me sold out my people but they me. So yes, though "home" permeates every sinew and cartilage in my body, I too am afraid of going home. Though I'll defend my race and culture when they are attacked by nonmexicanos, conozco el malestar de mi cultura [I know the malaise of my culture]. I abhor some of my culture's ways, how it cripples its women, como burras [like donkeys], our strengths are used against us, lowly burras bearing humility with dignity. The ability to serve, claim the males, is our highest virtue. I abhor how my culture makes macho caricatures of its men. No, I do not buy all the myths of the tribe into which I was born." (Anzaldúa 1987, 21–22)

In addition, for many Hispanic women feminism appears to be the agenda of privileged white women. Thus, even a convinced feminist like Martha Cotera complains of the classism of Angla feminists, who have a "certain air of arrogance, insensitivity to need or incomprehension of need to poor women, regardless of race" (Cotera 1977, 41).

ASIAN AMERICANS: THE "MODEL" MINORITIES

Of all minority groups discussed here, Asian Americans are the most diverse and perhaps the least understood. Many Euro-Americans think of them as the "good" immigrants, who work hard, save their money, and do well at science and math. Chinese or Japanese, Korean or Filipino, Vietnamese or Indian, many outsiders see them as pretty similar, though in fact they are culturally quite diverse. But to understand Asian Americans it is necessary to know something about their early history in the United States, which to a great extent is an artifact of U.S. immigration policies.

THE EARLY YEARS

The first Asians who arrived in the United States in any large numbers were the Chinese laborers who came to work the gold fields of California in 1849. By the time of the Chinese Exclusion Act of 1882, some three hundred thousand Chinese, 90 percent of them male, had entered the country (Daniels 1988, 9). By the end of the first quarter of the twentieth century, nearly a million Asians had entered the country from China, Japan, Korea, the Philippines, and India (Espiritu 1997, 16), all recruited as cheap labor, and nearly all of them male. Though Japanese women could immigrate to the United States until 1924, nearly all Chinese women were prohibited as immigrants until 1943. Those Chinese women who did arrive on American shores were nearly all prostitutes, most of them tricked or forced into their occupations.

The American opinion of Asians, generally, was to a great extent formed by the American reaction to these early Chinese immigrants, who looked different, spoke an unintelligible language, ate food that smelled strange, and worked unimaginably hard for incredibly low wages. The *Marin Journal*, a newspaper published near San Francisco, in 1876 offered vicious objections to the Chinese immigrant, on the grounds that he

> is a slave, reduced to the lowest terms of beggarly economy, and is not a fit competitor for an American freeman. That he herds in scores, in small dens, where a white man and wife could hardly breathe and has none of the wants of a civilized white man. That he has neither wife nor child, nor expects to have any. That his sister is a prostitute from instinct, from religion, education, and interest, and degrading to all around her.... That health, wealth, prosperity, and happiness of our State demand their expulsion from our shores. (Quoted in Daniels 1988, 52–53)

The Chinese and other Asian immigrants were not, in fact, driven out of the United States; their labor was too valuable to railway, mining, agricultural, and other interests. But various restrictions on Asian immigration, particularly an almost total ban on the immigration of Chinese women, insured that nothing like a normal family life would be possible for Asians in the United

States. In fact, many Chinese men did have wives and children, but they were virtually all at home in China. Men visited their families as they were able to afford passage, sometimes returning with sons or "paper sons" (young men they falsely claimed as sons, often for substantial payments, so that the youths could take advantage of the immigration status of their "fathers").

But virtually no Chinese women were permitted as immigrants. Most Euro-Americans felt that the Chinese were simply "too foreign." If they brought wives to the United States and established families here, they would cease to be merely labor. And if wives arrived, the Chinese population would grow. New schools and other institutions would have to be built and funded; living quarters for families would have to be devised; and households with wives and children would soon have a significant impact on the population as a whole.

The restriction on female immigration had a number of far-reaching effects. At home in their villages the wives of emigrants had a degree of autonomy and independence unusual in China. Though these women were initially subject to their husbands' families, this authority faded with time, as the parents-in-law aged and died. The husbands returned for visits if they could, and planned to retire to China in old age. Some did, but after many years in the United States other men preferred to end their days in the New World.

The restriction on Chinese women coming to the United States (accompanied by a legal prohibition on marriage to Euro-American women) created an almost totally male community of Chinese residents in the United States. It was necessarily a community in which men took on many of the occupations that only women occupied in China, and a community in which traditional Chinese patriarchal roles were largely irrelevant. Thus not only did Chinese (and other) Asian men learn to cook, clean, and wash for themselves in the absence of women, but they also performed these jobs professionally, for pay. The occupations were not traditional for men in Asia (particularly in Japan), but in the absence of sufficient Euro-American female labor, especially in the frontier western United States, Asian immigrant men filled the vacuum. In this case we see the inequities of gender, ethnicity, and class all rolled into one. Taking on "women's work" both grew out of and reinforced the lower-class status of Asian men (see Figure 5.2 on page 144).

These Asian men became subject not only to Euro-American male elites, but Euro-American female elites as well. In her remarkable account of Asian American immigrant life, Yen Le Espiritu (1997) describes the despair, resentment, and humiliation many Asian immigrants experienced in their roles as cooks, housemen, laundrymen, and (in the case of Filipinos) military stewards. She provides the following moving narrative of a Japanese domestic servant:

> Immediately the ma'am demanded me to scrub the floor. I took one hour to finish. Then I had to wash windows. That was very difficult job for me. Three windows for another hour!... The ma'am taught me how to cook.... I was

FIGURE 5.2
Asian men doing women's work. (*Joint Publishing [Hong Kong] Company Limited*)

sitting on the kitchen chair and thinking what a change of life it was. The ma'am came into the kitchen and was so furious! It was such a hard work for me to wash up all dishes, pans, glasses, etc., after dinner. When I went into the dining room to put all silvers on sideboard, I saw the reflection of myself in the looking glass. In a white coat and apron! I could not control my feelings. The tears so freely flowed out from my eyes, and I buried my face with both my arms. (Ichioka 1988, 25–26, quoted in Espiritu 1997, 35)

Until 1924, roughly 150 Chinese women per year were admitted to the United States. After a change in the immigration laws in 1924, no Chinese women at all were admitted until 1930, after which perhaps sixty women a year were admitted until restrictions were lifted in 1943. Roughly 88 percent of the families of Chinese immigrants were thus "mutilated," with the wives outside the United States (Daniels 1988, 96–97).

The situation for Japanese and Korean immigrants was somewhat different. Until 1924 a much larger proportion of Japanese and Korean women had been allowed into the country as wives of immigrants. Most of these immigrant brides had never met their husbands. The couples had been married by proxy in Japan or Korea, and knew each other only from

the photographs they had exchanged. These so called "picture brides" arrived in the United States in large numbers, most of them to find that their
husbands were substantially older than they and might not correspond to
their photographs. Some men were also disappointed, but with few exceptions the marriages persisted, in large part because there were no other options (Espiritu 1997, 28).

Because Asian men earned so little in the race-stratified job market that
prevailed in the United States, their wives' labor was essential to family
survival, whether paid factory work or domestic service or unpaid work on
the family truck farm or small business. Married men were thus able to
prosper more rapidly than those without wives. But a patriarchal tradition
prevailed in these marriages. After a full day in the tomato fields or laun-
dry, Asian wives had to attend to the "second shift": the cooking, cleaning,
and child care that their husbands left entirely to them, unless there was a
mother-in-law at home to help.

THE WAR AND ITS AFTERMATH

The beginning of World War II changed everything in the lives of Asian immigrants, most of all for the Japanese. Regarded by the government and
most of the American population as unassimilable and untrustworthy aliens,
roughly 120,000 Japanese residents, more than half of them American citizens by birth, were removed from their homes and herded into concen-
tration ("relocation") camps. This injustice affected all Japanese Americans,
but it tended to damage men more than women and adults more than children. Young children had little idea of what was going on, and often enjoyed
the freedom from parental supervision that the camps provided. Adults, on
the other hand, were profoundly angered, bewildered, and shamed. Men,
particularly, experienced not only the loss of their work, but loss of authority within their families as well. Some reacted with petty familial tyran-
ny, but more responded with withdrawal and depression. Women, on the
other hand, though also shocked by the incarceration, were relieved of
their deadening round of double shift labor for the first time in their married lives. American born (Nisei) women often found relatively well-paid
work within the camps that offered them more status and autonomy than
had previously been available to them. As for adolescents, when educational opportunities away from the camps and their parents presented themselves, many high school graduates took advantage of them. This was
particularly true of women, who saw this as a way to escape the traditional family patriarchy (Matsumoto 1989; Espiritu 1997, 43–49).

The war had an effect on Chinese immigrants as well. Because of their
role as allies of the United States, exclusionary immigration and natural-
ization laws were rescinded in 1943. After the war, additional legislation was
passed to allow the immigration of "war brides," both of Chinese American

soldiers and of Euro-American soldiers. The ultimate result of this legislation was the arrival in the United States of thousands of Asian women. Among them were the recent brides of soldiers, as well as the long-married wives of Chinese men, some of whom had not seen their husbands in many years. Many mutilated families were healed at long last, and the Asian American gender imbalance, including even the seriously skewed Chinese American gender balance, began to right itself (Daniels 1988, 191).

THE PRESENT

Three final pieces of immigration legislation bring us to the Asian American communities of the present. In 1948 the Displaced Persons Act and in 1953 the Refugee Relief Act brought to the United States some twenty-three thousand well-educated refugees from the Communist victory in China. These immigrants were not only employable in academic and other scientific occupations, but were also familiar with the English language and Western ideas (Espiritu 1997, 58). The 1965 Immigration Act, which equalized rights to immigration for all countries, was the final brick in the building of contemporary Asian American communities. Census figures indicate that the Asian American population has grown from 1.5 million in 1970 to 7.3 million in 1990. Some of this increase is due to the collapse of U.S.-supported regimes in Southeast Asia, as a result of which more than a million refugees from Cambodia, Laos, and South Vietnam fled to the United States after 1975.

These new immigrants are different from those who arrived fifty or a hundred years ago. First, they are more diverse, coming from more countries and representing a much wider range of education, training, and social background than the mostly Chinese, Japanese, and Filipino laborers who preceded them. Second, most new immigrants arrive with the intention of remaining permanently, rather than returning to their home villages after having amassed sufficient wealth. Because of these two factors, and because of a change in attitude of the American majority population, the new immigrants and their children are less oriented toward their culture of origin, and become more easily integrated into mainstream U.S. society. Finally, the overwhelming majority of new immigrants arrive with their families, in contrast to the Japanese and especially Chinese immigrants of fifty to a hundred and fifty years ago.

Though many non-Asian Americans look at contemporary Asian Americans as forming a largely undifferentiated mass of uniformly successful individuals, postwar (and especially post-1953) Asian American families represent a much greater range of socioeconomic status. Among the least privileged are those who have arrived with little or no facility in English, little education, and no skills useful in the United States. Among these immigrants are many Southeast Asians, especially Cambodian, Hmong, and

Laotian refugees, whose educational attainments rank lowest among all Asian Americans.

Many Southeast Asian women, along with recent immigrants from China, Korea, and the Philippines, work at poorly paid, repetitive, sometimes hazardous, dead-end jobs in the garment or electronics industries, while their husbands are likely to work at insecure jobs in service industries. Though these women are almost wholly responsible for the domestic "second shift" duties, their work is essential for family survival, and this gives them a certain amount of power and authority within the family that challenges traditional Asian ideas of patriarchy. Indeed, women in this segment of the workforce, though poorly paid, may make more money than their husbands, and they are often more employable. The greater employability of women does not lead up a career ladder, as the hiring philosophy of a (white male) electronics assembly shop manager makes clear:

> Just three things I look for in hiring … small, foreign, and female. You find those three things and you're pretty much automatically guaranteed the right kind of workforce. These little foreign gals are grateful to be hired—very, very grateful—no matter what. (Hossfeld 1994, 65)

At home, however, the "little foreign gals" may have difficulty reconciling their new role as an essential breadwinner with their old role as housewife and supporter of their husbands' patriarchal authority. This frequently causes anger and depression in men whose roles are thus threatened and eroded, and sometimes leads to quarreling, violence, and divorce. The words of a recently divorced Vietnamese man make clear the difficulty of the situation:

> Back in my country, my role was only to bring home money from work, and my wife would take care of the household. Now everything has changed. My wife had to work as hard as I did to support the family. Soon after, she demanded more power at home. In other words, she wanted equal partnership. I am so disappointed! I realized that things are different now, but I could not help feeling the way I do. It is hard to get rid of or change my principles and beliefs that are deeply rooted in me. (Luu 1989, 68, quoted in Espiritu 1997, 79)

A social worker from Vietnam offers a professional intermediary's view of the renegotiation of gender roles within Asian American families:

> [A]fter the family comes to the United States, many of the men can't get a good job, and they are disappointed because they used to hold high positions in the government or in the military.... Here they feel useless even

for the family let alone the community because of the lack of language. Some women can get jobs in factories, and those with a high school education can go for vocational training so in many families, the woman has become the bread winner. They not only make more money than the husband, they very often have better jobs. And of course, if a woman takes a job, she has a certain amount of a social life. Sometimes she goes to a party in the office or she goes out to do business with men and the husband becomes jealous. I have many cases where the husband becomes jealous and abuses his wife by beating her. (Quoted in Lee 1991, 88–89)

Children, too, may threaten old patriarchal norms. Cao O, an ethnic Chinese from Vietnam, is an example of a son who has accepted part of his family's expectations for him (academic success) but is also determined to plot his own course:

Being a Chinese male in Vietnam, the expectations from the family were different than for the male in this country. In Vietnam my role was defined by the family. We were expected to study hard, to get a degree, to get married, to get a job, and to carry on the family tradition—such as the family name, honor, and heritage.... Now I don't want my family to tell me what to do. I control my own destiny. I see myself as having a role in this country.... I see myself as someone who can make a contribution, and I don't care what my family says about what I do. (Quoted in Lee 1991, 105–106)

The resentful young social worker quoted above illustrates the greatest challenge mainstream Euro-American society presents to Asian Americans: the constant pressure of U.S. egalitarianism and individualism on traditional Asian patriarchal authority and family orientation. Where Euro-American families expect that their children will act in accordance with their own self-interest in choosing an occupation, a course of study, or a spouse, many Asian American families continue to expect their children to act in accordance with the interest of the family as a whole in making those choices.

The emphasis on the family rather than the individual applies not only to children but to other family members as well. In many wealthier Asian American households, mothers, though well educated, do not work but devote themselves to the education and extracurricular activities of their children. In less privileged households women work long hours at no pay and with little authority in the family business, so as to ensure its success and the future benefit of the family as a whole. Without this huge investment in unpaid labor, many small Asian American retail businesses, notably the ubiquitous Korean groceries and South Asian motels, would not survive. Not only do the women who work in these family businesses (including in many cases the grandmother who watches the small children while their mother is at the cash register) not receive a paycheck, but they have all the housework and child care to do as well, and they are isolated from nonfamily activities and individuals (Espiritu 1997, 80–81).

Most Asian immigrant families in the late twentieth century manage to negotiate new gender roles without serious conflict or radical restructuring of the family. An (Asian) Indian woman from an immigrant farming community in central California echoed the words of many of the Mexican American women described in the preceding section, when she told an interviewer, "Now, my husband, he listens to me when I say something; when I want to buy something, I do; and when I want to go in the car, I go" (Williams 1989, 157, quoted in Espiritu 1997, 76). This woman's words are particularly interesting in light of the fact that of all Asian immigrants, those from India are least likely to feel that they can do without cultural reinforcement from home. Thus they frequently send one or more children (often daughters) to India to complete their upbringing, or they arrange marriages for their children with spouses from India (Nandi 1980).

Sexual permissiveness, freedom of children, and poor treatment of the old are often cited by Asian immigrants as worrisome individualistic aspects of American culture. But most feel that the traditional Asian family orientation provides adequate resistance to the most damaging practices of U.S. society. One of the most powerful techniques for gaining family security and for protecting it when gained is the much-vaunted Asian educational achievement, illustrated graphically in Table 5.1.

TABLE 5.1   ASIAN ATTAINMENT OF BACHELOR'S DEGREE
OR HIGHER BY GENDER AND ETHNICITY (1990)

	MALE	FEMALE
Total Population	23%	18%
Total Asian	43	33
Chinese	47	35
Filipino	36	42
Japanese	43	28
Indian	66	49
Korean	47	49
Vietnamese	22	12
Cambodian	9	3
Hmong	7	3
Laotian	7	4
Thai	48	25
Other Asian	48	34

Source: Adapted from Espiritu 1997: 66.

As Table 5.1 indicates, five Asian ethnic groups have a higher percentage of bachelor's degrees (or more) for both men and women than is true of the U.S. population as a whole. What the table does not show is that, as a group, Asians also achieve a higher proportion of graduate degrees than is true for the general U.S. population. Thus, 14 percent of the Asian American population possesses a graduate or professional degree, compared with only 8 percent of the white population (Ong and Hee 1994, cited in Espiritu 1997, 65). It is, however, important to recognize two points. First, not all Asian ethnic groups are equally represented among college graduates. Those, like Cambodians, Laotians, and Hmong, who do not come from a family background of education, are less likely to achieve higher education themselves. Second, the figures do not distinguish between older and younger generations. Thus they do not point out that the higher education that is now so common for young Asians was a dream beyond the reach of many of their parents and grandparents.

Like all women in the United States, Asian American women earn less per year of education than men of their own ethnic group (and men, generally), and like other women in this country, they do more housework than their husbands. The higher the educational level of the household, the more likely men are to participate in domestic labor, but never (as is true of all other ethnic groups) to the extent of women's involvement (Espiritu 1997, 69).

As might be expected, between the high level of education for Asian American women and Asian patriarchal culture has emerged a critical and confessional tradition of popular Asian American literature written by and largely for women, in which damage to women is feelingly rendered. Though such work (for example, the novels of Maxine Hong Kingston and Amy Tan) shows both the injuries involving gender (male to female) and those involving ethnicity (Euro-American to Asian American), Asian American males have frequently chided the authors for selling out their ethnic group through adherence to the largely white concern with gender. As we have seen, this is a concern for all other ethnic minorities who find an almost inextricable intertwining between racism and sexism and a parallel complexity of loyalty and self-interest.

SUMMARY AND DISCUSSION

In Chapters 4 and 5 we saw how ethnicity, class, and gender have been interrelated within and around four American ethnic minorities. These last two chapters have also looked at feminism within the four ethnic minority groups. Many Euro-American women have reached out to women of color, believing that in the feminist movement all women would be sisters. Though the women's movement has sometimes crossed ethnic barriers, many women of color, as we have seen, do not ally themselves with it. For these women, the transcendent category is not gender but ethnicity. They point out that the feminist movement addresses the interests of white, privileged women.

At the same time, as black anthropologist Johnetta Cole (1986) has pointed out, all groups of women in America really do share some common forms of subordination. For example, women typically work in sex-segregated jobs and receive less pay for comparable work than men; women generally have a greater share of housework; and women have less political power and are more subject to sexual violence than men. And finally, although most American women of all ethnic minorities are reluctant to identify themselves as feminists, they have increasingly accepted as their due much of the legacy of feminism: more education, increased access to employment, the right to limit the size of their families, and greater autonomy in general.

DISCUSSION QUESTIONS

1. In the opening paragraph to this chapter we point out that Latinos and Asian Americans contrast with Native Americans and African Americans because "they were neither conquered nor enslaved." Technically this is true, but the statement glosses over the experiences of Latinos and Asian Americans, especially in the nineteenth century and the first half of the twentieth. In what ways would you say the experiences of Latinos and Asian Americans, especially before the 1960s, might be said to parallel those of Indian peoples and African Americans? Do you think that gender is significantly different for the populations discussed in this chapter compared to the populations discussed in Chapter 4? How? Why? Is there a significant difference between Latino gender issues and those of Asian Americans? Why (or why not)? What are these differences (or similarities)?

2. What is machismo? Because the concept is designated by a specific term in Spanish, it is easy to point to and discuss. Does it seem to you that machismo is uniquely found among Latinos, or that it exists also among other ethnic groups? Where else do you see it, and what form(s) does it take? How might machismo fill a psychological need among impoverished Latinos in the United States?

3. At the end of the twentieth and the beginning of the twenty-first centuries, social, economic, and technological changes have had profound effects on gender roles in all segments of American society. Describe the specifics of these changes and the way they have affected Latino and Asian American families, pointing out the similarities and the differences. How have these changes and their effects been felt in other ethnic groups in the United States? Do you think it is possible to say whether the results have been beneficial or detrimental? For which segments of society? Why?

4. One striking change for many Asian American families as a result of living in the United States is a shift away from a focus on the needs and interests of the family as a group and toward an emphasis on the needs and desires of the individual members of the family. Why has this shift occurred? It is not enough to point to a Western focus on the individual; discuss the specific social and economic institutions and practices that have fostered the shift. How has the change affected gender relationships among Asian Americans?

REFERENCES

Anzaldúa, Gloria. 1987. *Borderlands/La Frontera: The New Mestiza.* San Francisco, CA: Aunt Lute Books.

Cole, Johnetta B. 1986. "Commonalities and Differences." Pp. 1–30 in *All American Women: Lines That Divide, Ties That Bind,* ed. Johnetta B. Cole. New York: Free Press.

Cotera, Martha P. 1977. *The Chicana Feminist.* Austin, TX: Information Systems Development.

Daniels, Roger. 1988. *Asian America: Chinese and Japanese in the United States since 1850.* Seattle, WA: University of Washington Press.

Espiritu, Yen Le. 1997. *Asian American Women and Men: Labor, Laws, and Love.* Thousand Oaks, CA: Sage Publications.

Fernández Kelly, M. Patricia. 1990. "Delicate Transactions: Gender, Home, and Employment among Hispanic Women." Pp. 183–198 in *Uncertain Terms: Negotiating Gender in American Culture,* ed. Faye Ginsburg and Anna Lowenhaupt Tsing. Boston, MA: Beacon Books.

Hossfeld, Kareb J. 1994. "Hiring Immigrant Women: Silicon Valley's 'Simple Solution.'" Pp. 65–93 in *Women of Color in U.S. Society,* ed. Maxine Baca Zinn and Bonnie Thornton Dill. Philadelphia, PA: Temple University Press.

Ichioka, Yuji. 1988. *The Issei: The World of First Generation Japanese Immigrants, 1885–1924.* New York: Free Press.

Lee, Joann Faung Jean. 1991. *Asian American Experiences in the United States: Oral Histories of First to Fourth Generation Americans from China, the Philippines, Japan, India, the Pacific Islands, Vietnam, and Cambodia.* Jefferson, NC: McFarland and Co.

Lewis, Oscar. 1961. *The Children of Sanchez: Autobiography of a Mexican Family.* New York: Random House.

Luu, Van. 1989. "The Hardships of Escape for Vietnamese Women." Pp. 60–72 in *Making Waves: An Anthology of Writings by and about Asian American Women,* ed. Asian Women United of California. Boston, MA: Beacon Books.

Matsumoto, Valerie. 1989. "Nisei Women and Resettlement during World War II." Pp. 115–126 in *Making Waves: An Anthology of Writings by and about Asian American Women,* ed. Asian Women United of California. Boston, MA: Beacon Books.

McKee, Nancy P. 1985. "Living in La Fabrica: Environment, Opinion, and Strategies for Survival of Low Income Mexican-Americans in Laredo, Texas." Doctoral dissertation, Washington State University.

Nandi, Proshanta K. 1980. *The Quality of Life of Asian Americans: An Exploratory Study in a Middle-Size Community.* Chicago, IL: Pacific/Asian American Mental Health Research Center.

Oboler, Suzanne. 1997. "Language, National Identity, and the Ethnic Label Hispanic." Pp. 54–62 in *Race, Class, and Gender in a Diverse Society*, ed. Diana Kendall. Boston, MA: Allyn and Bacon.

Ong, Paul M. 1984. "Chinatown Unemployment and the Ethnic Labor Market." *Amerasia Journal* 11:35–54.

Ong, Paul M., and S. Hee. 1994. "Economic Diversity." Pp. 31–56 in *The State of Asian Pacific America: Economic Diversity, Issues, and Policies*, ed. Paul M. Ong. Los Angeles, CA: LEAP Asian Pacific American Public Policy Institute and University of California at Los Angeles, Asian American Studies Center.

Ortiz, Vilma. 1994. "Women of Color: A Demographic Overview." Pp. 13–42 in *Women of Color in U.S. Society*, ed. Maxine Baca Zinn and Bonnie Thornton Dill. Philadelphia, PA: Temple University Press.

Williams, Marcelle. 1989. "Ladies on the Line: Punjabi Cannery Workers in Central California." Pp. 148–159 in *Making Waves: An Anthology of Writings by and about Asian American Women*, ed. Asian Women United of California. Boston, MA: Beacon Books.

Williams, Norma. 1990. *The Mexican American Family: Tradition and Change*. Dix Hills, NY: General Hall, Inc.

CHAPTER 6

GENDER ON THE
COLLEGE CAMPUS

In some respects the American campus is a microcosm of gender patterns in the broader society. For example, on most campuses among the nonstudent population (faculty, staff, administrators), the males generally hold the higher-paying, more prestigious jobs. Students, too, bring influences from the broader society with them when they arrive on campus. We can see, for example, that on some campuses the muscle-building males and the tanning, dieting females are almost a caricature of American cultural obsessions with ideal male and female body types. But, as we emphasize throughout this chapter and as we mentioned in Chapter 1, human actors do not merely absorb and reflect cultural patterns from external sources; they participate in cultural constructions of their own. College students are no exception. Although influenced by their families and their high school experiences, most of those in college are away from home, exposed to new ideas, forming their own friendships and romances, deciding their majors, and generally getting on with their lives as independent adults. In the process they are continually constructing their own student subculture within which they generate ideas and behaviors with respect to gender.

In this chapter we take a look at American gender on the college campus. How are today's students thinking about gender? How are they positioning themselves for their later world of work, marriage, and parenthood? Here we will discuss how students' own cultural constructions (of romance, marriage, motherhood, and the family) affect gender differences in their life courses after graduation.

Most of the material in this chapter is based on our own study of gender and students' perspectives on their futures at a university in the Northwest. This study was guided by a disturbing question that has become increasingly pressing during the years we have been teaching at a large public university: Why is it that more of our women students do well in class than their male colleagues, but more men go on to prestigious, well-paying jobs? In exams and papers, and in discussions in and out of class, women students indicated not only their awareness of the disparity in pay of men and women but their anger and resentment at the disparity. Even among the twenty-five-year-old to thirty-four-year-old age group, male college graduates earn just under $40,000 annually, while female college graduates earn just under $30,000. If we look at the salaries of all college graduates regardless of their ages, we see that this $10,000 difference grows into a $17,000 difference: Taken all together, male college graduates earn on average nearly $51,000, compared to female college graduates' average of slightly more than $33,000 (U.S. Bureau of the Census 1993).

Most of the "gender gap" in earnings can be accounted for by gender segregation in the workplace (Reskin 1984; Roos 1985). Women are generally clustered in relatively (or absolutely) poorly paid occupations, and there are fewer of these female-dominated occupations than there are male-dominated occupations. Segregation in the workplace is brought about by employers hiring on the basis of gender, but it is also fostered by women themselves who orient their training and self-images toward lower-paying, less prestigious careers. This is the case despite the fact that female students, from elementary school through graduate school, generally have better grades than male students (though their performance on standardized tests is lower). There is a general, largely unexamined assumption on the part of both students and faculty that academic performance is predictive of future vocational performance. Yet this does not seem to be the case, or at least not the case across gender lines. One contributing factor is that women students' educational and occupational goals frequently decline as they move through their college years (Astin 1977, 1993; Holland and Eisenhart 1990).

A number of theories have been proposed to explain why women college students lag behind men in their career ambitions and achievement levels. Probably the most influential theory for women college students' lower career aspirations and/or their restriction to lower-paying, less prestigious careers has been that institutions of higher education discourage or discriminate against women (among the more recent works are Hall and Sandler 1982; Sadker and Sadker 1994). Though there are variations on this theme, we refer to this central idea as the "chilly climate" theory, after Roberta Hall and Bernice Sandler's influential report, *The Classroom Climate: A Chilly One for Women?* (1982).

Some chilly climate theorists have taken a Marxist position, arguing that all schools, from kindergarten through universities, perpetuate the hierarchies of both social class and gender that are essential to capitalism. These people see capitalism as a patriarchal system that ensures male superiority primarily through gender segregation in the workplace (Hartman 1976). According to this view, educational institutions help to channel women into domestic roles, through which they maintain and produce workers (as wives and mothers), and/or channel them into the ranks of cheap labor.

Other chilly climate theorists have taken a broader cultural view. These writers (Firestone 1970 and Lerner 1986, for example), see universities simply as pieces of society as a whole. And since American society is generally patriarchal, they argue, its educational institutions will also be patriarchal, and will foster the interests and values of Euro-American men and, by definition, will discriminate against women.

Many investigators of the chilly climate perspective (Hall and Sandler 1982, and Sadker and Sadker 1994, to name only a few) have focused specifically on the dynamics of education. These investigators point to the greater attention and constructive criticism given to male students than to female students at all educational levels, and to the lack of mentoring and appropriate role models for women students in universities.

Certainly all of the factors discussed by chilly climate theorists have been important in shaping women's decisions and choices. Together with sexual harassment and more overt forms of sexism they may continue to chill the educational climate for women. But there is an important limitation to chilly climate theories: They tend to depict women students as thoughtless pawns, manipulated by social institutions into passive subordination. We maintain that female students are not merely empty vessels, waiting to be filled with the values and attitudes of the schools and colleges they attend (Holland and Eisenhart 1990; Montgomery 1997; Stone and McKee 2000). Rather, they are continually creating, modifying, discarding, and reinventing ideas about gender, work, marriage, family, and self that guide their life choices. In addition, it is important to remember the many nonacademic sources from which women students draw information and influence.

In addition to our study, an earlier study of college students also took the position that students are active participants in their own cultural constructions (Holland and Eisenhart 1990). Before looking at the student cultural constructions we found in our study, we will discuss this earlier one that uncovered a student "culture of romance." This construction powerfully shapes college students' ideas about gender and influences students' own postgraduate futures as well.

THE CULTURE OF ROMANCE

As we noted earlier, compared with men college students, more women students lower their career aspirations during their college years. Some, for example, come to college wanting to be doctors or lawyers but midway through opt for careers in nursing or decide to work as legal secretaries instead. In many cases they actually wind up in lower-paying, less prestigious occupations than these.

What happens to these women in college that results in the downscaling of their ambitions? Anthropologists Dorothy Holland and Margaret

Eisenhart address this question in their book, *Educated in Romance* (1990). The Holland and Eisenhart study took place on two southern campuses, one having primarily white students and the other enrolling mostly black students. On both campuses these anthropologists selected for their study women students who came to college with relatively high career aspirations and good academic backgrounds. They talked to these women (there were twenty-three altogether) periodically over the years of their college experience and beyond into their postgraduate years. This study showed that in the end, two-thirds of these previously ambitious, career-oriented, and academically qualified women had either abandoned their careers entirely or had subordinated them to the career interests of their husbands.

Holland and Eisenhart found on both campuses a student "culture of romance"—a world of flirtations, boyfriends, thoughts about marriage, and women's concerns about their physical attractiveness—that effectively subverts the career development of many young women. Some women fall into the culture of romance as they become discouraged in their studies, largely because they find their schoolwork too hard and too boring. They then become absorbed in this culture of romance, devoting considerable time and energy to its demands. Even more, their very self-identification moves away from their anticipated careers and becomes enmeshed in their romantic relationships. In Chapter 2 we heard Simone de Beauvoir's (1953, 287) observation, made more than fifty years ago, on American college women: "I saw that college girls cared only about men...." The student culture of romance forces us to ask: Has so little changed?

A cardinal principle of the student culture of romance is that a woman's prestige, in the eyes of her peers, is determined by her attractiveness to men. If a woman can publicly demonstrate that she is attractive to men (for example, by receiving male attention or by securing a boyfriend who treats her well) she is rewarded with prestige. Indeed, once in the romantic culture, women place themselves on a "sexual auction block," come to see their own worth in terms of their attractiveness to men, and increasingly come to view their career aspirations as less important than their romantic involvements.

Men are involved in the student culture of romance, too, but their position within it is very different. Of most importance is that, although men also gain prestige by being attractive to women, they have other sources of prestige and other measures of self-worth. For example, they can acquire prestige through success in sports, school politics, or other activities. For women involved in the culture of romance, by contrast, there are no other sources of prestige than attractiveness to men. As a result, men students are not as caught up in the culture of romance in terms of time, energy, self-identification, and emotional investment. Certainly their participation in it does not result in their downsizing their career aspirations!

There is another way, too, in which men tend to have a position of privilege, or to keep the upper hand, in the student culture of romance. This way

concerns a "double standard," or the different evaluations of male and female sexuality in the student subculture. Both male and female students may
desire physical intimacy in a relationship, but still,

> ... physical intimacy is something the woman gives and the man gets. "Good
> treatment" (primarily being respected and valued as a unique person) is what
> the man gives and the woman gets.... Female sexuality is interpreted in the
> framework of how the man treats the woman in return for her "sexual fa-
> vors"; male sexuality is subjected to no such interpretation. (Holland and
> Eisenhart 1990, 105–106)

With all this, it sounds as though we have not moved very far from the
1950s "dating game" era we discussed in Chapter 2. A woman's popularity
used to be measured by the number of dates she had; now her prestige is
measured by assorted forms of male attention and by "good treatment" from
a boyfriend. And a double sexual standard still holds; sexual intimacy is still
something women are "giving" men. Yesterday's smart women "set the
boundaries" to safeguard their reputations; today's wise women "give" sexual intimacy only when they see signs of "good treatment." As a result of this
double sexual standard, as Holland and Eisenhart show, a woman can experience particular humiliation when her attraction to a man is publicly
well-known while he responds with bad treatment—ignoring her, not showing respect, not giving gifts, and so on. The effect of bad treatment is to lower
the woman's status, and the ultimate in bad treatment, according to these
authors, is rape.

Another interesting finding of this study is that the student culture of romance is quite similar among both black and white students. But the authors
did find one difference between the black and white women whose lives they
followed: Over the course of their lives, the black women were less likely to
expect economic dependence on husbands than were the white women.

An important question is, to what extent does the culture of romance
exist on other campuses around the United States? In our own study of a
northwestern university (to be detailed in the next section), we found that
in the eyes of students a culture of romance exists but is largely confined to
sorority women and fraternity men. One sorority woman we interviewed
said that in her house, a woman's ability to attract men is made quite public. She reported that women of this sorority share one central phone that
they take turns answering, with the call taker yelling out that so-and-so has
a call. They have a code to announce whether a woman's caller is male or
female. Thus, if the call taker yells out "Jennifer, you have a *phone*, this
means it is a man calling. If she calls out, "Jennifer, you have a *tele*phone,"
this signals that the caller is a mere female. This is called out publicly so that
everyone within earshot will know whether or not Jennifer is receiving male
attention. Often, the woman added, when it is a *phone* call, the other sorority women will give out a cheer or clap. A stronger affirmation that in this

sorority a woman's prestige among her peers is measured in terms of her receiving male attention could hardly be imagined! The woman interviewed also added she did not think any fraternity had a similar phone-announcement code system.

Even if a true culture of romance is largely restricted to sororities and fraternities, it may be that some of the basic tenets of this culture are more widespread among young college students. While possibly not as socially absorbed in romance and peer prestige as sorority women, many college women in dorms or apartments may very well feel that their prestige and self-worth depend on their attractiveness to men and that sexual intimacy is something they "give" romantic partners. There is also evidence that young college women's concern for their physical attractiveness to men is quite widespread and exceeds men's concerns for their physical attractiveness to women. One national survey of college freshmen found that men in general are more confident about their appearance: Higher proportions of men at all types of colleges and universities rated themselves as above average in physical appearance than did women (Cooperative Institute Research Program [CIRP] 1995, 76). A woman student of the Holland and Eisenhart study captured the spirit of women's anxieties over physical attraction with her following comments that, we suggest, are echoed among young women students on many campuses:

> [When I'm with my girlfriends] we always talk about our boyfriends, or how we wish we had boyfriends, or how fat we are—we all say that.... None of us have to lose weight, but we just want to be thinner ... I'm gonna lose weight and clear up my face and [grow] my hair out, so I'll be all beautiful this summer. (Quoted in Holland and Eisenhart 1990, 105)

Two aspects of the Holland and Eisenhart research are significant. First, it is clear that the culture of romance entails male privilege. Second, the culture of romance is less imposed on students than generated by them. It is, in Holland and Eisenhart's view, a cultural construction that students themselves create and perpetuate. This is not to say that the culture of romance is unaffected by currents in the larger society or even by sexism in academia. Since male privilege pervades the larger society, it is not surprising that the students' own subculture reflects it. The point rather is that the culture of romance is primarily rooted in and perpetuated by the student peer group, within which students themselves are active agents, not mere pawns of broader social forces. Holland and Eisenhart conclude it is "not that the sexism of the university and society at large is irrelevant but rather that the most effective mediation or communication of male privilege to girls and young women is through the peer group" (1990, 222). Holland and Eisenhart point out that some individual women resist the culture of romance. This raises a question that goes somewhat beyond their study: Given women's inferior position within the culture of romance and given the cost to their careers which, at least initially, are very important to them, why don't more of them resist?

A third aspect of the Holland and Eisenhart study is that it pinpoints what first triggers the fall in women's career aspirations and their subsequent lapse into the culture of romance. In their view, as noted earlier, these college women become discouraged in their studies because they find their classes too hard and too boring. Some women in their study did complain of sexism in their educational institutions—for example, some said that their male professors did not take them seriously. They found this gender discrimination annoying but not really discouraging;[1] rather it was their experience of classroom boredom and/or feeling unable to do well in class that left them vulnerable to the culture of romance. But why do women students find their classes too hard and boring? Do they encounter these problems more than men do? Probably not. Certainly it is well known that around the country women on average get better grades in college than do men. It is also known that many of today's high schools do not adequately prepare students for college and that both male and female freshman college students report feeling overwhelmed by schoolwork. A national survey shows that more students than ever before report the experience of boredom in the classroom (CIRP 1995). Yet it is women, more than men, who then lower their aspirations. Apart from their position of privilege in the culture of romance, what keeps men students going on a track that leads them into better-paying, more prestigious careers? We offer some insights on this question in the next section in relation to our own study of male and female students.

GENDERED FUTURES: A CASE STUDY

Our study was conducted at a large, moderately selective, land grant university located in a small town in the Northwest—we will call it Northwest Public University (NWPU). Though the location of NWPU is rural and isolated, the majority of the students on its main campus come from cities and suburbs in the state's more populated western region. Nearly all of the students live on or very near campus. Many students are attracted to NWPU because of its programs in engineering, architecture, communications, and business. Others come because their older siblings, parents, or even grandparents have attended NWPU; for a public university, NWPU has an unusually high proportion of students from alumni families.

Our study at NWPU consisted of two parts. One part was a series of open-ended, in-depth interviews with thirty-six undergraduate NWPU student volunteers. Half of these were men and half women; we also selected students who represented a range of different majors, grade point averages (GPAs), living arrangements, and class standings. All of the students were between the ages of eighteen and twenty-two, and, like the NWPU student population generally, most were Caucasian. We did interview one black male, one Hispanic female, and two Asian Americans (one female and one male). Students were interviewed by the authors and by their research assistant in a range of locations four times throughout the academic year.[2]

The second part of our on-campus investigation used a questionnaire mailed to a random sample of 3,000 undergraduate students. After eliminating students over twenty-six years old, we had 1,181 questionnaires.[3] It is interesting that 60 percent of the students who responded were female. Either women are more prone to respond to mailed questionnaires or they are more likely to find questions of the sort we asked sufficiently interesting to respond to—or both. Stone did receive a phone message from an irate male student who complained about receiving such a "blatantly biased, feminist" questionnaire.

It was essential to us to have both quantifiable information from a large number of students and detailed, qualitative information from a smaller number. From the students we interviewed we gained insights we could never have extracted from the fixed responses of a questionnaire. With the questionnaire we could obtain information from a larger number of students and also see to what extent our data from the interviews coincided with data from the larger sample.

As we were accumulating data from NWPU, we became interested in seeing to what extent the results of this study might apply to other campuses, which led to a third part of our research. For this we selected eight additional campuses. Nonrandom samples of students were surveyed on these campuses and on a few of them we conducted discussions with small groups of students. At both Northwest Public University and on the other campuses our study uncovered interesting differences in how male and female students plan their futures. In the process of uncovering these differences, our study also gives insights into other gender issues among today's college students.

THE STUDENTS

At NWPU nearly all students were born or raised in the northwestern state in which NWPU is located. About half live in rented housing, a third live in residence halls, and the rest live in sorority or fraternity houses. Overwhelmingly, they are young (only 10 percent of NWPU's undergraduates are older than twenty-five), white (fewer than 25 percent are non-Caucasian), and mostly middle class. As groups, both our surveyed students and our interviewed students fit this profile. In almost all cases, one or both parents of these students had attended college. Most students' mothers (84 percent) had worked, usually in a clerical capacity or in the fields of education, health care, or counseling. Fathers' occupations varied much more widely. In terms of age, class, campus residence, and parents' education, the students of our study show parallels with those in a survey of entering freshmen at public universities in the United States conducted at about the same time (CIRP 1995).

The students of our study, like the larger NWPU student population, appear to come from largely middle-class socioeconomic backgrounds. What variation we did find in students' socioeconomic backgrounds did not coincide with any differences in how students are thinking about and planning for their careers and domestic futures. For example, the survey found no significant correlations between the level of students' parents' education and the students' choices of majors, careers, domestic aspirations, and so on. Among the thirty-six interviewed students, we considered that seven of them came from "working-class" backgrounds, based on parents' education and occupation and students' descriptions of their earlier lives. We did not find relationships between these students' socioeconomic backgrounds and their decisions and plans for their futures.

Most of the surveyed students reported that they were very positive about the university. Only 3 percent of the men and 2 percent of the women thought they were getting a "poor" education, while 33 percent of the men and 43 percent of the women rated their NWPU education as "excellent." They did, however, show significant differences in their academic performance: 47 percent of males surveyed reported GPAs of 3.1 or higher, compared to 59 percent of females. Both women's better grades and their greater satisfaction with their university education have been typical of U.S. universities for several decades, and it is possible that these findings are related. National surveys also show that women students trust the university administration more than male students do (Astin 1993).

Along with their higher grades, women students generally spent more time on their studies. Surveyed students, both men and women, who were part of established heterosexual couples agreed that the woman partner worked harder than the man. And interviewed students felt that women "take their work more seriously," while men "tend to party more." On the other hand, among the surveyed students, three-quarters of the men in heterosexual relationships reported that they take "harder" classes than their partners, whereas slightly more than half the women claimed that they are the ones who take harder classes.

CHOICE OF MAJORS

In contrast to their attitudes toward their educational experiences, NWPU students showed some variation by gender in their decisions and rationales concerning selection of a major. In very general terms, notably more males than females were majoring in physical sciences, engineering, architecture, business, and economics. Half the males had selected one of these majors, whereas only 25 percent of the females had done so. Significantly more females (15 percent) than males (4 percent) had selected either nursing or education. Little contrast by gender was found for majors in the biological sciences, social sciences, and humanities.

A majority of the students surveyed said they chose their major because they "enjoy it," but the female majority of 83 percent with this opinion exceeded the male majority of 70 percent. By contrast, 20 percent of the males surveyed said they chose a particular major because it would lead to a highly paid job, while only 13 percent of the females surveyed gave this answer.

In the interviews as well as the survey, women appeared less motivated by income in their choice of majors than did men. There may be several factors behind this, but one prominent reason was uncovered in the interviews: Many women assume that their husbands' earnings will make it unnecessary for them to concern themselves with the matter. We will return to this issue later.

Compared to reasons for choice of major, a more dramatic gender difference was seen in the percentages of men and women who believed that some majors are more suited to one gender or the other. Men were fairly evenly divided on the issue, whereas substantially more women disagreed (60 percent) than agreed (27 percent with 14 percent unsure). Of those students who felt that some majors suit one gender better than the other, more than half of both men (64 percent) and women (56 percent) believed this is due to "basic sex differences" rather than to "tradition."

Over time, the interviews indicated that students' ideas on these questions are somewhat more complicated than the questionnaire responses indicate. Many students interviewed took an initial position that anyone can do well at any major (possibly in deference to the female interviewers), yet over the course of the interviews they often modified this position. Justin,[4] a premed honors student, stated firmly that he believed no major was more suited to one gender or the other. As the interviews went on, however, he said he thought that because women were "more nurturing, open, and empathetic," they would do better in some majors than in others, while males, "just because they are trained that way," are more likely to excel in physics and engineering. Joy, an education major, also said she thought either gender could do well in any major. Later she said she does not do well in mathematics, "like most girls." It appears that some students have a general, diffuse commitment to the contemporary idea of gender equality; at the same time they are also influenced by the general, diffuse traditional idea of gender difference. As long as these notions are not forcibly juxtaposed, they appear to coexist comfortably.

CAREER CHOICES, PERSPECTIVES, AND STRATEGIES

Most students in our study appeared strongly career oriented. The survey and the interviews consistently showed that nearly all males and females planned to have a career and that they felt their careers were important to them. There were, though, striking gender differences in students' current career choices. Women students (31 percent) were much more likely to choose service occupations (teacher, nurse, social worker, at-home parent) than men (8 percent).

Consistent with these choices and opinions, Table 6.1 shows gender differences in students' reasons for choosing a particular career. Thus a substantial number of women surveyed (41 percent) said they were attracted to a prospective career because it offered them a chance to help others, something that attracted only half as many men. The appeal of time to spend with one's family was a dominant reason for a career choice among very few students, but among these there are twice as many women as men. High salaries and the prospect of exciting experiences were more commonly given by men than women as reasons for choosing a specific occupation.

In the questionnaire survey, more than half of both men (57 percent) and women (63 percent) reported some experience with their ideal careers. However, among the women surveyed, job-related experience was more likely to have been as a volunteer than as a paid employee. Both in high school and in college, women students performed volunteer work much more often than men, and they were consistently less likely to have worked for wages in high school. During their college years the gap in paid work closed, but the gap in career-oriented employment intensified.

Our student interviews showed that women have had far less experience with their ideal careers than men. Women interviewed seldom had job experience that related to the careers they hoped for, while men planned their summer and even school year work with a much more careful eye toward future employment. Rich, a twenty-two-year-old architecture major, had already spent one summer working for an architecture firm and planned the

TABLE 6.1   MOST FREQUENTLY CITED REASONS
FOR CHOOSING A CAREER BY GENDER OF STUDENT

REASON	MALE (N=471)	FEMALE (N=705)
It will allow me to help others.*	21%	41%
It will allow me to spend time with my spouse/children.**	7	14
It is a well-paid field.***	23	13
It is exciting or adventurous.****	24	17
It will allow me to be creative.*****	21	15

Note: Percentages for other reasons were very low and are not shown on the table.
*p ≤ .001
**p ≤ .001
***p ≤ .001
****p ≤ .004
*****p ≤ .004

next summer working in construction to increase his understanding of how physical structures are built. Similarly Rob, a twenty-four-year-old engineering major, had already had several summer positions with power companies, which he believed would be essential in his quest for a job after he graduates. A final example is Justin, a twenty-two-year-old pre-med major, who had worked during the summer as a hospital orderly, and who volunteered his time during the school year as a participant in the university "wellness" teams, providing health advice to undergraduate students.

Though there were a couple of highly motivated female students interviewed who planned their undergraduate work experience to enhance their chances in their chosen careers, most of the women had not done this. Willa, a nineteen-year-old biology major who wished to be a research scientist, has never had any career-related work experience, having worked only at service jobs in restaurants and hotels. At twenty-one, Tammy was vacillating between a major in psychology or sociology. She had worked for a parks and recreation service and at a dry cleaners, but she has never had a job related to her planned career as a social worker. Dru and Linda, both education majors in their early twenties, had sold fast food and clothing and cleaned the athletic stadium, but have never had any education-related employment.

Women students expected to earn less than men. When asked how much they expect to earn at their first jobs, 36 percent of the women surveyed indicated $20,000 or less, compared with only 23 percent of the men. By contrast, 43 percent of the men expected to earn $31,000 or more, while a mere 17 percent of the women expected a salary that high. The students interviewed in person manifested the same pattern. In addition, these men showed far greater awareness of the salary structure of the career they planned to enter. Justin, for example, had researched the average incomes of several different medical specialties. Women, on the other hand, usually had no idea what their proposed occupation was likely to pay.

Women's lack of information about the nature of their chosen careers extended beyond salaries. Ginger, a participant in the preliminary study, said she wanted to be a hostage negotiator because she felt it would leave her plenty of time to be with her children, a stunningly unrealistic perspective. Danielle, a one-time pre-med major who decided on nursing instead, said she could "always get my MD later" if she decided to do so, apparently unaware of how difficult this could be. Men had researched not only salaries, but also the kinds of expectations employers and graduate programs have in the occupations in which they were interested. Male students, but not usually female students, often chose minors or double majors that they expected would offer them alternative opportunities, in case they failed to qualify for their first career choice. Thus Justin's chemistry major will prepare him to be a high school teacher, like his father, should he fail to qualify for medical school. And Rich, the architecture major who was struggling for certification in that department, had a fallback minor in computer science.

Though both male and female students had differing levels of enthusiasm about their majors, only women expressed ambivalence about actually working. Nearly all of the women, but none of the men interviewed, planned to curtail or cease their paid employment after their children are born, something discussed in greater detail later in this chapter. And some women planned a career because they believed it would be necessary for survival, but shared the largely covert feelings of Joy, who said, "Well, I'd really just like to get married and stay home all the time, like my mom did when we were young, but I know I can't." As we will see, Joy was somewhat more realistic about her options than other women interviewed.

DOMESTIC ASPIRATIONS

One of the women we interviewed at Northwest Public University was Susan, a graduating senior with a GPA of 4.0. Susan was a biology major supported by two scholarships. She was strongly career oriented and was actively taking steps to secure a career as a genetic counselor. Twenty-two years old at the time of our study, Susan said she did not want to marry until about age twenty-seven. An obviously successful student, Susan spoke with enthusiasm about her career plans and preparations. She seemed a model of high achievement, autonomy, and self-identification with a professional trajectory—that is, until the subject of children came up. With children, the picture of Susan's life changed dramatically. Susan was adamant that she would quit working entirely when her first child was born and would not return to work. She hoped to begin childbearing at about age thirty and to have between two and four children. She appreciated that her own mother (previously an elementary schoolteacher) was there for her when she grew up. She very definitely believed that children suffer if their mothers work outside the home.

Susan's position on the necessity of full-time motherhood was stronger than that of most other women students, but her case exemplifies what we saw over and over again with the majority of women students in our study: strong career orientation up to but not encompassing reproduction. We heard repeatedly in one way or another from both female and male students that careers and motherhood do not go together. Women as mothers are incompatible with women as workers outside the home. The breaking up of American womanhood into incompatible parts, as we explored historically in Chapters 2 and 3, is apparently continuing at Northwest Public University.

Most of the women we interviewed planned to interrupt their careers for children but very few went as far as Susan in her determination to terminate her career once she has a child. More typical was the remark of Kate: "Once I'm a parent my career is on hold," or the comments of others who felt they would stop working when they had young children or would reduce their work to part-time, but might go back to full-time work when the children are older. Only two of the eighteen women interviewed claimed that they would pursue full-time, uninterrupted careers with or without children.

What was more interesting in our discussions with most women, however, was that they frequently expressed ambivalence and contradiction when discussing careers and children. For example, many said at one point in an interview that they wanted to contribute half of the income for their future families, but in another interview said that they wanted to stay home with their children and not work. Some women expressed strong interest in a full-time career at one point but at another point said they wanted children and were strongly against leaving them in day care.

A married woman's decision to interrupt or terminate a career, or to reduce her workload, will have a number of consequences. One is that she will be wholly or significantly financially dependent on her husband. Another is that she will likely face some difficulties or setbacks in leaving and then reentering the workforce. How did these women feel about these issues? Our finding is that they were largely unconcerned with the first one and somewhat unrealistic about the second. Regarding the first, nearly all the women we talked to believed they will be financially dependent on husbands once children arrive. Diane, who planned to pursue a Ph.D. in psychology and to have two or three children, reported that she wants a husband who

> ... can support me if I need to stay home having children. I don't want to have to worry about the bills. I don't want to depend on him but I have to have children to be a woman. I need extra support. The men can't have that.

Note that Diane said "I don't want to depend on him." This was the exception. Most of the women we talked to did not express concern about being financially dependent on a husband. More typical was the comment from Stacy, who planned to have two children and to interrupt a career in accounting: "If I have kids I will be totally dependent on my husband; I don't expect the responsibility of income to fall on me." Wanda, when asked how much a person makes in her chosen field of teaching, gave a figure and added, "... but I don't care 'cause the guy I'm going to marry is going to make about $50,000." In another interview, when asked to describe an ideal husband Wanda said, "... kind of well off; he can be materialistic so I don't have to [be]."

Women with children who are financially dependent on husbands are understandably fearful of divorce (Hochschild with Machung 1989). Our women students, too, were aware that the divorce rate in the United States is rather high (a number of them have divorced parents) and that divorce leaves many women as poor, single mothers who must go out to work. Indeed divorce is the primary cause of downward mobility for American women, or for the pattern we now see of middle-class women rather abruptly falling not only into financial difficulties but often into true poverty. The economic impact of divorce on most men is by comparison negligible, primarily because men tend to be higher earners and do not need jobs or workforce re-entry upon divorce (Newman 1988). Yet our interviewed women students were comfortable about financial dependence on husbands. Most did not envision having to face divorce for themselves; divorce is something that happens to other people, through immaturity, rushing into marriage, or financial problems. Only two of the females and one of the males expressed concern that they might ever have to face divorce.

As for reentering the workforce, our female students were overwhelmingly optimistic. Very few were concerned that interrupting a career would in any way limit their employment opportunities, earning power, or opportunities for advancement. Kate, who planned a career in the media, simply claimed that by the time her children arrive (she hoped to have two before age thirty), she will have made a name for herself; hence, she contended, it will be easy to resume her career when her children are older. Alice, who planned a career in social work and wanted between two and five children, said that by the time she has children (before age thirty), "I will have enough credibility to be gone for pregnancy, illnesses, etc."

The general picture we have, then, of the women students in our study is one of strong career orientation mixed with an equally strong commitment to be home with their young children. Considerable ambivalence and contradiction surrounded their discussions of an issue they will inevitably face— the balancing of careers and motherhood. Despite their ambivalence, they appeared in general to be comfortable with the idea of financial dependence on husbands and optimistic about the stability of their future marriages and the ease of workforce reentry.

An expression of ambivalence, or of women students' struggles to cope with and make sense of their futures, came from Karen, a student who was not a part of our study but who came to us for academic advising during the year of our study. In the course of the advising session, Karen mentioned that after graduation she hoped to work as a physical therapist. When we asked how she might look for a job, she vaguely mentioned a few possibilities, ending her remarks half-jokingly with, "And if that doesn't work, I guess I can always make babies."

On the one hand Karen's comment seems to completely reverse what middle-class women of fifty years ago (our own mothers' generation) expressed. These women, expecting to be nonworking wives and mothers, felt they should get an education so that they "would have something to fall back on" should they ever have to work, as might happen should a husband die or become disabled. Karen, by contrast, saw her career as a top priority at this stage in her life, and her fertility, or potential motherhood, as "something to fall back on" should she fail in the marketplace. It seems something has changed in the past half century; or has it? After all, these two very different generations of women are both expressing the idea that a career and motherhood are mutually exclusive propositions. They are also both suggesting that women, unlike men, have an alternative to earning a living.

Now how do men students fit into this picture? To begin with, the men in our study (both those we interviewed and those in the sample survey) did not differ from women in terms of their domestic aspirations. Like the women students, nearly all of these men were currently single but planned to marry and have children. Like the women, the men hoped to have on average about two children. The men we interviewed seemed to plan for and want children as much as did the women. We did not find, then, any difference by gender in students' interest in having children.

A dramatic gender difference emerges, however, when we look at how children will affect students' careers. None of the males (or females) we interviewed ever suggested that men should stop work or reduce their workloads once children are born. Both men and women saw the balancing of careers with parenthood to be a problem for women, not men. No males in our study ever expressed concern with balancing fatherhood with careers.

How did these men feel about their future wives working and what do they expect of them in terms of child care? Only two of the males interviewed said that they would prefer nonworking wives. Most expected their wives to work, but in many cases males' attitudes toward working wives seemed to be detached and indifferent: A frequent response to the idea of a future working wife was, "she can work or not as she likes" (compare Machung 1989). Only one male interviewed (an African American student) felt that his future family will have to depend on two incomes. But when the issue of children was raised, nearly all males interviewed said that they would prefer that their wives be home with the children, at least when they are young. These men saw themselves as primary breadwinners for their families and expected their wives to be economically dependent on them. Thus, males and females did not differ in their priorities regarding parenthood, yet it is parenthood that, in their own eyes, will make all the difference in their career paths.

In contrast to the women, the men in our study did not express ambivalence and contradiction with regard to the intersection of their careers with parenthood. However, our study did uncover one area in which both males and females expressed a curious contradiction. In the survey we asked students whether or not their own mothers had worked when they were growing up. In many cases they had (82 percent for males and 84 percent for females). The questionnaire next asked these students whether the mother's working had had a positive, negative, or neutral effect on them. Overwhelmingly, males and females felt that the effect had been either positive or neutral; only 7 percent of both males and females reported a negative effect. At the same time, the survey (see next section) showed that higher proportions of both men and women (50 percent and 31 percent respectively) believe that children are harmed if both parents work. And, as we have seen here, interviewed women wished to stay home with children and interviewed men wished their own wives to do so. Why? If not from their own negative experience with working mothers, from what source were these students constructing the idea that mothers (but not fathers) should stay home with children? This seems to be another example of coexisting contradictory points of view. We will return to this question in the final section of this chapter.

REACTIONS TO FEMINISM

In the survey, men and women students showed a significant difference in their attitudes toward feminism: 42 percent of the males thought that feminism has had a negative impact on U.S. society, while only a quarter of the females thought so. On this question, the students we interviewed showed about the same variation by gender as seen in the survey. However, with these students we discussed the concept of "feminism" at length. We found that although both male and female students praised the feminist movement for progress toward goals such as equal pay for equal work, about half of the females and nearly all of the males had formed negative associations with the terms "feminism" and "feminist." These students defined feminists as "extremists," "antimale," and "troublemakers." One male went so far as to say that feminists are "like White supremacists." Some male and female students blamed feminists for the breakdown of the American family. Only four students (two females and two males) said they themselves are feminists.

Negative student attitudes about feminism were also captured in an article in the university newspaper in the semester following our study. Written by a woman student columnist, the piece was entitled, "Feminism Confusing, Pointless" (*The Daily Evergreen*, Thursday, October 10, 1996). In it the author complained that "Women are made to believe by other women they [sic] are oppressed, enslaved and weakened by men and other women who do not realize how bad things are." The article goes on to say that "the glass ceiling is the exception" and asks women in power who feel disliked or ignored to ask themselves "is it because I'm a woman or is it because I really am a bitch?"

POSTGRADUATES

In the course of our study we became curious to see how perspectives on life among NWPU postgraduates may have changed during the years following graduation. To find out, we mailed a questionnaire to a random sample of about two hundred people who had graduated from NWPU either five or ten years ago. Very few of these postgraduates mailed the questionnaire back (only twenty-two females and sixteen males) so that the results of the postgraduate survey are not statistically significant. Nevertheless we present what we learned from those postgraduates who did return the questionnaire. Most of these postgraduates were between twenty-seven and thirty-four years of age. Most of the women (76 percent) were married; more than half (59 percent) of them had children. Fewer men (56 percent) were married and fewer (44 percent) had children.

Interestingly, only 5 percent of these postgraduate women claimed that while at NWPU they considered being an at-home spouse/mother as their ideal career, but at the time of the survey a third of them were at-home spouses/mothers. By contrast, virtually all of the males were working full time, just as they had expected they would be while at NWPU. Fewer than half (45 percent) of these women compared to nearly all of the men expected to have a full-time job five years from now. Among those postgraduate women who had children, 82 percent had either terminated or interrupted their careers in order to be home with their children. Thus, in this sample, the women were less likely to maintain careers than men and the turning point in these women's working lives came with their reproduction.

OTHER CAMPUSES

Many of the findings of our study at Northwest Public University are similar to those of a 1985 study of Berkeley undergraduates (Machung 1989). From interviews with senior students, Anne Machung found that most of the women were strongly career oriented, yet they planned to interrupt their careers when their children were young. They saw their future husbands as primary breadwinners for their families and felt that a husband's career should come first. They saw their own careers as economically optional or a luxury.

A later study by Laura Montgomery (1997) reported results very similar to ours at NWPU. Montgomery's results are based on extensive interviews conducted with students at a small, private college where most of the students come from upper-middle-class families and strong Christian backgrounds. Like our students at NWPU, most of Montgomery's students said they chose their majors primarily because they "just like" them, though at NWPU this was more common among women than men. Women students in Montgomery's study planned to work after graduation, just as they did at Berkeley and NWPU, and most men said their wives' work should be their own choice. But the women interviewed by Montgomery almost universally planned to quit working permanently or temporarily after they have children. And men generally believed that this is not only acceptable but preferable. The response of two male students to the question of expectations about their wives' working demonstrate this:

> Jack: … I don't really think I have expectations. I don't really think so. But at least I know what my girlfriend thinks, and I know that she wants to stay home with the kids. And that's what I'm used to. My mom worked and then she quit when she had kids. And then she went to work after, again after we were old enough.

> Mike: … if she'd like to work I think that's wonderful until there's kids. And then at that time, I really think that the actual, proper place would be at home raising kids because the truth is they can do a better job, usually. (quoted in Montgomery 1997, 12)

FIGURE 6.1
University students, 1996. (*Robert Harbison*)

Looking at these other studies and our own, we next sought to explore gender and students' future plans on a variety of other campuses. We were particularly interested in seeing to what extent we would obtain similar or different results from our student questionnaire. For this part of the study we constructed nonrandom student samples by contacting colleagues at colleges and universities around the country and asking them to administer a slightly modified version of our questionnaire[5] in their classes (see Appendix A). With this, we received survey data from classes at eight different institutions. We selected these institutions to span a wide variety of geographical regions and educational contexts.

Table 6.2 lists each institution we covered by a descriptive pseudonym and gives its level of selectivity.[6] The table then gives the classes at each institution from which student respondents were recruited, the number of student respondents, and the total enrollment of each class. Because we relied on the cooperation of our professional colleagues, most of these classes are in the social sciences, and anthropology classes are particularly common.

Unlike Northwest Public University, all of the other campuses are located in urban areas. Most of the public institutions have large numbers of commuting students. On all of the campuses the students are predominantly white though some, especially West Coast Public University, show considerable ethnic diversity. The private institutions are relatively small and the public ones are large.

TABLE 6.2 CHARACTERISTICS OF STUDENT CLASS SAMPLES

INSTITUTIONAL PSEUDONYM	INSTITUTIONAL SELECTIVITY	COURSE	NUMBER OF RESPONDENTS	TOTAL
Southern Public University	low	Introduction to Anthropology	66 (45f, 21m)	104
		Introduction to Biology	54 (43f, 11m)	118
		Women in Society	26 (all female)	29
Southern Private University	moderate	Introduction to Anthropology	55 (33f, 22m)	79
Midwest Public University 1	low to moderate	Introduction to Anthropology	43 (31f, 12m)	75
Midwest Public University 2	low to moderate	Criminal Justice	59 (23f, 36m)	65
Northwest State College	low	Introduction to Social Science	17 (10f, 7m)	33
West Coast Private Christian College	high	World Civ., Psychology	52 (38f, 14m)	60
West Coast Public University	high	Film Criticism	25 (12f, 13m)	32
East Coast Private University	high	Anthropology Seminar	11 (all female)	42
Total Respondents			408 (272f, 136m)	

As seen in Table 6.2, the number of student respondents in each sample is quite small. These small sample sizes plus the fact that all student respondents were nonrandomly selected means that in no case can the results of a class sample be considered representative of any student population. What the data does do, however, is, first, show that from sample to sample there are fairly consistent gender differences in student responses to the survey questions; and second, this nonrandom survey suggests that Northwest Public University is not unique in how female and male students think about and plan for their futures.

RESULTS

Needless to say, there was variation in the survey responses among students taking different classes on the eight campuses of our study. But our overall finding was that many of the patterns we saw in the Northwest Public University study were also evident in the class samples from the other campuses. Appendix B includes tables showing the survey results. Where possible we have included data from our Northwest Public University study for comparison. Here we provide a description of the results of the investigation of the other campuses along with one of the more interesting tables.

In general we found that men students are more conservative in their opinions on most gender issues than are women students. For example, with the exception of the students at Northwest State College, significantly higher proportions of males than females agreed that feminism has had a negative effect on the United States.

Many women in the Northwest Public University study (about a third) and many men (half) indicated agreement with the belief that children turn out less well when both parents work. As mentioned earlier, we feel that this result contradicts the survey finding that among students whose own mothers worked when they were growing up, most felt this had had either a positive or a neutral effect on them. The same contradiction was found in the samples from the other campuses. In these samples most students reported that their mothers had worked while they were growing up,[7] while very few of them reported that their mothers' working had a negative effect on them. In most of the class samples, negative effects were indicated by fewer than 10 percent of male or female students.

When asked, "After marriage, do you expect your spouse will work outside the home?" the males of the class samples responded in a way similar to those in the Northwest Public University study. With few exceptions a third to one-half of the males in all samples indicated indifference ("don't know, up to spouse"). This result suggests that what we saw at Northwest Public University, namely that today's male students are tolerant of working wives but see themselves as primary household breadwinners, may be widespread.

Women students in the class samples were strongly career oriented but were far more willing than males to interrupt their careers, reduce their workloads, or change jobs in order to be at home with children. This parallels what we found in the Northwest Public University study: While in many contexts women students appeared strongly career oriented and did not indicate a greater interest in children than did men, it was women students who were already contemplating career adjustments for children.

From our interviews at Northwest Public University, we saw that many men prefer their future wives to stay at home with young children and that most women plan to interrupt their careers to stay home with young children. We found similar results on all the other eight campuses as seen in Table 6.3. The table shows that in most cases, well over half of all males preferred their wives at home with young children. Large percentages of women either planned to interrupt a career for children or, if already married with children, did interrupt a career. In addition to these figures, in some samples a few additional women indicated that they would terminate (or did terminate) a career when they have (or had) children. The table also shows that the male preference for wives at home with children is generally stronger than the female plan to interrupt a career for children.

TABLE 6.3   DOMESTIC PLANS AND PREFERENCES
AMONG STUDENTS MARRIED OR PLANNING MARRIAGE

CLASS SAMPLE (INSTITUTION AND COURSE)	FEMALE PLANNING TO INTERRUPT CAREERS FOR CHILDREN	MALE PREFERRING SPOUSE STAY HOME WITH YOUNG CHILDREN
Southern Public U		
Anthropology		
(N=43f, 16m)	77%	75%
Biology		
(N=41f, 10m)	76	90
Women in Society		
(N=26f)	68	—
Southern Private U		
Intro. Anth.		
(N=30f, 18m)	77	89
Midwest Public U 1		
Intro. Anth.		
(N=28f, 9m)	71	67
Midwest Public U 2		
Crim. Justice		
(N=18f, 29m)	72	72
Northwest State College		
Intro. Soc. Sci.		
(N=10f, 7m)	70	86
West Coast Private		
Christian College		
World Civ., Psyche.		
(N=37f, 13m)	92	85
West Coast Public U		
Film Crit.		
(N=11f, 11m)	55	45
East Coast Private U		
Sem. Anthro.		
(N=10f)	80	—

A majority of men in the class samples indicated that they expect to earn more than their wives; very few women indicated that they expect to earn more than their husbands. Most women and men in most samples thought that they would share housework and child care equally with their spouses, but by far more women than men felt they would do more of the housework and child care (see Appendix B).

ETHNICITY

An obvious question for our study is this: Did students show notable variation in their survey responses according to their ethnic affiliation? To see, we
put all the student class samples together in one pool and then divided it up
by ethnic group and by gender. This produced some categories with very few
people in them. For example in the whole study of 408 students there were
only four Asian American males and eleven Asian American females. Blacks
were more predominant with twelve males and forty-three females. Whites
were a clear majority (107 males and 199 females). All other ethnic groups
consisted of nineteen females and thirteen males.

A general finding of the study was that women students showed fewer
differences between ethnic groups than did men students. For women, for example, about the same proportion of blacks (73 percent) as whites (75 percent) planned to interrupt careers for children. However, one interesting
finding was that considerably greater proportions of white women (36 percent) than black women (14 percent) felt that children turn out less well
when both parents work. All the women of other ethnic groups were also well
below the white proportion on this question. Another difference between
black and white women students was that a larger proportion of black women
(57 percent) claimed that having a career was most important to them in the
long run than did white women (38 percent). In turn, more white women
(36 percent) than black women (19 percent) ranked marriage or a love relationship as most important in the long run. These differences appear to reflect the general contrasts between black and white women's perspectives on
work, motherhood, and marriage that we noted in earlier chapters.

For males we found that on a number of survey questions all nonwhite
groups were fairly similar to one another while the white males stood out as
a strong exception. For example, a high 81 percent of the white males preferred
that their wives stay home with young children. For all the other ethnic groups
taken together, the percentage with this preference was 56 percent. Among
these groups black males (30 percent) expressed this preference in the lowest
proportion. Also interesting is that nearly half (44 percent) of the white males
said feminism has had a negative effect on U.S. society compared with less
than a quarter (24 percent) of the nonwhite males. Finally, half of the white
males held that children turn out less well if both parents work while only a
quarter of the black males agreed. Adding all nonwhite males together, the percentage of men who agreed was 34 percent. White males were also relatively strong in expecting to contribute the most to household income (52 percent
compared, for example, with 40 percent of black males).

Another kind of study would be needed to determine whether these ethnic differences hold up among college students generally. But what we can
suggest from our study is that white males may have stronger leanings toward
more traditional gender roles and more conservative opinions on gender issues than nonwhite males.

SUMMARY AND DISCUSSION

Our study has shown that women students at NWPU and other surveyed institutions are making decisions and choices that will lead them toward lower-paying, less-prestigious careers than their male counterparts. This pattern is seen in women's choices of majors, their current career choices, and, most particularly, in their plans to interrupt their careers or reduce their workloads once children are born. At NWPU this orientation is also reflected in women students' lack of knowledge about salary structures and job requirements.

Our study and those of others have shown, further, that this difference between male and female students exists within a larger context of shared ideas and attitudes concerning education, work, and gender. Although males and females show some significant differences in their attitudes toward specific gender issues, what is as striking is the cultural values they hold in common. Overall, males and females share values and attitudes concerning their college experiences, and they have very similar domestic aspirations and priorities. Most important of all, many agree that gender roles should be different when it comes to the intersection of careers with parenthood. Husbands should be primarily responsible for family income, while wives should be primarily responsible for child care. The men and women of this study are planning their futures in contrasting ways within a shared ideology of gender difference.

Where does all this leave today's students with respect to the women's movement? Our impression is that the most recent wave of the women's movement has clearly affected the women students in our study. Most obviously, virtually all women students expect to work, at least initially, and, like men, most of them say their careers are very important to them. But women differ from men in their views on several important issues, and these differences, too, can probably be attributed to the influence of the women's movement:

1. Women are more likely to say that women and men are equally able to do well at any academic major.
2. Of those students who do feel that some majors are more suited to a specific gender, more women than men attribute this to tradition rather than to biological sex differences.
3. Fewer women than men feel that two working parents would have negative consequences for children.
4. Fewer women than men see feminism as a negative force in the United States.

On the other hand, many of the women students we interviewed and surveyed manifest perspectives at odds with the goals of the women's movement:

1. Women students continue to choose majors and plan for careers that, because of their lower prestige and lower pay, will perpetuate women's social and economic disadvantage with respect to men.

2. Many women students ensure an inequitable future for themselves by their assumption that they will and should assume an ancillary economic role and a dominant domestic role, particularly after their children are born.

3. A majority of the women we interviewed have accepted the notion that motherhood (but not fatherhood) is incompatible with a serious commitment to a career, a position with which most men agree.

At NWPU, about a third of the women surveyed and a quarter of those interviewed hold a belief that children are harmed when both parents work. Taken all together, about a third of the women in the class samples from the other campuses agree. The idea that children suffer when both parents work is common in American society generally, despite a huge literature to the contrary, as well as historical and cross-cultural evidence that extended family members, and, for elites, paid child-care providers, have for millennia cared for children other than their own without negative results. In most cultures, childrearing is shared among women and shared with older children (Hays 1996). In one study it was found that mothers are primary caretakers of children in only 20 percent of the cultures sampled (Weisner and Gallimore 1977). In this respect our society is the exception.

As we have seen, many students say they make academic choices according to personal preference, and plan future employment, and unemployment, because they believe it will be best for their families. But many are apparently unaware that in these decisions they are following traditional gender stereotypes, and that these decisions may be at odds with the economic and social realities of twenty-first century America. As Montgomery points out from her study, students describe their decisions according to the rhetoric of individual choice, a currently powerful expression of American individualism, as we discussed in Chapter 3. She further suggests that "language that explains one's place in life as individual choice obscures structural choices of social inequality," here, in the form of gender inequality, and asks "is it that the language of individual choice makes more palatable the reality of cultural prescription?" (Montgomery 1997, 16, 19).

In terms of the theme of American individualism developed in Chapters 2 and 3, it is interesting that today both male and female students express individualism through the modern rhetoric of free choice. We do not find a gender difference in this expression. But when we look at what students are choosing, we do see a gender difference; furthermore, we see that the expression of "individualism," in its older sense of extradomestic autonomy and achievement, still remains more a male than a female expression. From the students' perspectives, their decisions about their futures are individual choices; for example, a major is chosen "because I like it." Nevertheless, gender patterns and cultural prescriptions can be seen in these choices when the choices of many individuals are added together to form a larger picture.

In this chapter, we have seen that for many students motherhood is now a central cultural construction that is perceived to be at odds with work outside the home. We suggest that students' constructions of motherhood derive from two interrelated sources. The first is a larger American cultural model of what Sharon Hays has called "intensive mothering." She notes a number of cultural assumptions embedded in this model as follows:

> The model of intensive mothering tells us that children are innocent and priceless, that their rearing should be carried out primarily by individual mothers and that it should be centered on children's needs, with methods that are informed by experts, labor-intensive and costly. (Hays 1996, 21)

Hays shows how this model historically developed in America, and we have covered some of this development in Chapters 2 and 3. As we saw in those chapters, the idea that women should be the primary childrearers developed in the nineteenth century with the "Cult of True Womanhood." This idea thus grew alongside the fragmentation of middle-class American womanhood into incompatible parts. In the nineteenth century a woman could not be both sexual and motherly; in the twentieth century a woman cannot be both a good mother and an autonomous person out in the workplace. We might call this American peculiarity a cultural refusal to accept a multifaceted conception of women.

The other source we posit for students' constructions is the current "revitalization movement" that is focused on the American family. In the midst of social and economic reconfigurations and difficulties, many Americans long for the ways of their forebears, when Father brought home the bacon and Mother was in the kitchen in an apron and high-heeled shoes, turning out delectable meals for the family of well-scrubbed children who gathered around the table with their parents every evening. In our study at Northwest Public University, Wanda expressed this American nostalgia for the 1950s family when she said, "I am kind of in love with that Donna Reed image," as did Susan, who remarked that she wanted to raise a family "like in *Leave It to Beaver*." Students like these are caught up in the American "nostalgia trap" about which Coontz (1992) has written. As discussed in Chapter 2, Coontz is referring to the ideal 1950s family of husband/breadwinner and full-time, at-home wife/mother. Those who yearn for this sanitized image, kept alive by television reruns, forget that it was an economically viable family form only in the tiny bubble of time between 1945 and 1965, between the end of World War II and the heating up of the conflict in Vietnam. More important, they forget that it was this kind of family, with a captive, educated wife and mother, that helped give rise to the 1960s wave of the middle-class women's protest.

Anthropologists have studied revitalization movements mostly in the context of indigenous groups undergoing rapid modernization at the hands of colonial powers. Frustrated by lives they can no longer control and that have lost meaning and resonance, these groups often long for the lifeways of their ancestors. Revitalization movements usually include prophets preaching the way to the past and rituals that ensure its return, all of this harkening to a time no one really remembers accurately, but which everyone feels must have been better than the present. We suggest that involvement in the "nostalgia trap" by students (and many others) amounts to participation in a "revitalization movement" in American culture that seeks a return to an imagined past or to a reconstructed cultural tradition.

This chapter opened with the question of why women college students wind up in lower-paying, less-prestigious jobs than do men students. To address this question we discussed the influence of students' constructions of the "culture of romance" (Holland and Eisenhart 1990) and, from our study, students' constructions of motherhood and the family. We suggest that a "culture of motherhood" as well as a "culture of romance" may lie behind women students' lower career aspirations. We have seen that many women students, before having any experience with marriage, motherhood, or work, are constructing core ideas—namely, that motherhood and extradomestic work are incompatible and that husbands are reliable lifelong providers—that powerfully influence their choices and decisions as they go through college.

From our study we offer one other speculation—that current women students, although career oriented, are perhaps uncertain about their chances or happiness in the world of work. Constructing motherhood in opposition to work may keep their options open in a way not seen as possible for men. We "raise the possibility that women unconsciously resist the idea of juxtaposing motherhood and work in order to give themselves more room to maneuver as they face the uncertainties of their postgraduate lives," and we suggest that ideas about part-time, supplemental, and interrupted work "may serve as a kind of buffer for this generation of women as they explore their options and shape their identities for the future" (Stone and McKee 2000, 81).

Finally, many of those who have looked at gender and employment have suggested that to help close the "gender gap," other gaps need to be narrowed. Some suggest that the gap between husbands and housework/child care needs to be closed, that husbands need to pick up their share of domestic labor so that their wives can devote more reasonable time and energy to their work outside the home. Others say we need to close the gap between government employment policies and the realities of working women's lives (Hochschild with Machung 1985; Stacey 1996). Thus, working women could benefit from paid maternity leaves, day care centers at the workplace, and so on.

Another suggestion from our findings has to do with bridging the gap between young female college students and those who teach and advise them. The need to recognize this gap was a lesson we learned for ourselves in this study. What we learned is that for many young college women, most of the feminist message is irrelevant or unwelcome. Though they value certain concrete feminist gains, most female students we interviewed see these as faits accomplis, and regard continued feminist discourse as the unappealing rhetoric of bitter, man-hating women. This position fits in with the findings of Elizabeth Fox-Genovese, reported in her book, *Feminism Is Not the Story of My Life* (1996). Fox shows that many women reject feminism because they associate it with the more extreme forms of man-hating political radicalism.

From this study we conclude that for the category of young men students there has been little change concerning marital, reproductive, and career interests and priorities over the past several decades. But young women students have seen changes, and today they face new challenges. The women students of our study are trying to construct ideas that will give meaning and direction to their lives. The fact that their own discussions with interviewers often showed ambiguity and contradiction on the topics of marriage, motherhood, and careers reflects the difficulty of the challenges they will face both practically and ideologically. These women appear to be part of a generation caught between a vision of the liberated "woman as person" and a reviving traditional cultural conception of motherhood. However, their ideas may change and whatever life directions they take, combining these two currents in American society will be no easy task. These women are caught between two images of womanhood in the dominant culture that has for more than two centuries broken "woman" up into incompatible parts. Much like all the king's horses and all the king's men (!), American culture may be unable or unwilling to put "woman" back together again. Yet these women are active participants in this culture and so will themselves have a voice in the fate of American womanhood in the twenty-first century.

DISCUSSION QUESTIONS

1. The concept of the "culture of romance" is helpful in understanding women's experiences in college and their career paths in later life. It also raises an interesting question: Why does the culture of romance affect the aspirations and career paths of women only, and not men? Both men and women derive prestige from sexual attractiveness; both men and women find happiness and fulfillment from establishing romantic relationships; and both men and women college students frequently find that academic success is harder to achieve in college than it was in high school. Why, then, are women so much more likely to lower their academic expectations or give up on them entirely?

2. In Chapter 2, we encountered the nineteenth-century Cult of True Womanhood. The term is not used to describe contemporary society's view of women's nature, nor do women today apply the concept to themselves. But do you see any similarities between the views of modern college students discussed in this chapter and the Cult of True Womanhood? What kinds of differences exist?

3. In discussions with our students about the research reported in this chapter, we have received some interesting comments. First, many students have said something like, "I'm not like the students you surveyed, and neither are my friends. Who *are* these people?" Second, some women students, especially older ones, often point out that even if the women students we interviewed believe that they will drop out of the labor force wholly or completely when their children are young, they will most probably work far more continuously than they think they will.

These responses raise two questions. First, why do a number of students feel so differently from the many hundreds we surveyed? What do you think accounts for this variation? Second, even though it is almost certainly true that most women students will spend more time in the workforce than they expect to, their expectations as college students are very important. Why?

4. Look at Appendix A, the survey questionnaire. Would you change any of these questions, and, if so, how? If we were to use this questionnaire again, what additional questions do you think would elicit interesting and useful information? Why?

NOTES

1. Our student study, discussed in this chapter, also showed that some women students do see gender discrimination at their institutions (see Appendix B). But like the students of Holland and Eisenhart's study (1990), most of those we interviewed said that while this discrimination is annoying, it does not discourage them from academic choices or career pursuits. We grant that this discrimination may discourage women students in subtle ways of which they are not aware.
2. These interviews were tape-recorded. The student volunteers were given an honorarium for their participation.
3. This yields a margin of error of less than 3 percentage points at the 95 percent confidence level for the sample as a whole.
4. This is a pseudonym, as are all student names in this chapter.
5. To construct this questionnaire (see Appendix A), we deleted questions on mothers' and fathers' incomes and some opinion questions on gender issues from the questionnaire we had used at NWPU. We then added questions on expectations about who (self or spouse) will do the most housework and child care after marriage, and about interrupting or changing careers in order to be with children.
6. An institution's selectivity is measured by the average Scholastic Aptitude Test (SAT) scores of a recent entering freshman class. Here, where possible, we followed the selectivity rating given to institutions in the CIRP studies (1995). The CIRP assignments rank universities within particular categories—public universities, private universities, and so on—and not between categories. Two institutions in our study—Northwest State College and Midwest Public University 1—are not included in the CIRP survey; the selectivity rating shown in Table 6.3 for these institutions are the authors' estimates.

7. In only two cases was the percentage of mothers working below 70 percent—among males taking biology at Southern Public University and among males in the class sample from West Coast Private Christian College.

REFERENCES

Astin, Alexander W. 1977. *Four Critical Years: Effects of College on Beliefs, Attitudes and Knowledge.* San Francisco, CA: Jossey-Bass.

Astin, Alexander W. 1993. *What Matters in College?: Four Critical Years Revisited.* San Francisco, CA: Jossey-Bass.

Beauvoir, Simone de. 1953. *America Day by Day.* Trans. Patrick Dudley. New York: Grove Press.

Coontz, Stephanie. 1992. *The Way We Never Were: American Families and the Nostalgia Trap.* New York: Basic Books.

Cooperative Institute Research Program (CIRP). 1995. *The American Freshman: National Norms for Fall 1995.* American Council on Education. Los Angeles, CA: University of California.

Firestone, Shulamith. 1970. *The Dialectic of Sex: The Case for Feminist Revolution.* New York: Bantam Books.

Fox-Genovese, Elizabeth. 1996. *Feminism Is Not the Story of My Life.* New York: Anchor Books.

Hall, Roberta M., and Bernice Sandler. 1982. *The Classroom Climate: A Chilly One for Women?* Washington, D.C.: Association of American Colleges.

Hartmann, Heidi. 1976. "Capitalism, Patriarchy and Job Segregation by Sex." Pp. 137–170 in *Women and the Workplace: The Implications of Occupational Segregation,* ed. Martha Blaxall and Barbara B. Regan. Chicago, IL: University of Chicago Press.

Hays, Sharon. 1996. *The Cultural Contradictions of Motherhood.* New Haven, CT: Yale University Press.

Hochschild, Arlie, with Anne Machung. 1989. *The Second Shift: Working Parents and the Revolution at Home.* New York: Viking.

Holland, Dorothy C., and Margaret A. Eisenhart. 1990. *Educated in Romance: Women, Achievement, and College Culture.* Chicago, IL: University of Chicago Press.

Lerner, Gerda. 1986. *The Creation of Patriarchy.* New York: Oxford University Press.

Machung, Anne. 1989. "Talking Gender, Thinking Job: Gender Differences in Career and Family Expectations of Berkeley Seniors." *Feminist Studies* 15 (1): 35–58.

Montgomery, Laura M. 1997. "'It's Just What I Like': Explaining Persistent Patterns of Gender Stratification in the Life Choices of College Students." Paper presented at the annual meeting of the American Anthropological Association, Washington, D.C., November 1997.

Newman, Katherine S. 1988. *Falling from Grace: The Experience of Downward Mobility in the American Middle Class.* New York: Free Press.

Reskin, Barbara F. 1984. Introduction. Pp. 1–7 in *Sex Segregation in the Workplace: Trends, Explanations, Remedies,* ed. Barbara F. Reskin. Washington, D.C.: National Academy Press.

Roos, Patricia A. 1985. *Gender and Work: A Comparative Analysis of Industrial Societies.* Albany, NY: State University of New York.

Sadker, Myra, and David Sadker. 1994. *Failing at Fairness: How America's Schools Cheat Girls*. New York: Charles Scribner's Sons.

Stacey, Judith, Susan Béreaud, and Joan Daniels. 1974. Introduction. Pp. 13–29 in *And Jill Came Tumbling After: Sexism in American Education*, ed. Judith Stacey, Susan Béreaud, and Joan Daniels. New York: Dell Publishing Co.

Stone, Linda, and Nancy P. McKee. 2000. "Gendered Futures: Student Visions of Career and Family on a College Campus." *Anthropology & Education Quarterly* 31 (1): 67–89.

U.S. Bureau of the Census, 1993.

Weisner, Thomas S., and Ronald Gallimore. 1977. "My Brother's Keeper: Child and Sibling Caretaking." *Current Anthropology* 18:169–180.

CHAPTER 7

AMERICAN GENDER: THEMES AND ISSUES

In this chapter we pull together what we have learned about American gender from the book's various explorations. What has a cultural history of American gender taught us? How do gender patterns vary among ethnic groups? How are gender, race, and class interrelated? And what form does gender take on the college campus? Here we review the most salient themes to emerge in the book. Finally, we take a brief look at national reports on the status of men and women in America, followed by some international comparisons. In the process of covering these topics, this chapter provides the book's summary and conclusion.

THE DISCOMBOBULATED AMERICAN WOMAN

One theme emphasized throughout this book is that American woman-hood historically has been and continues to be discombobulated—cultur-ally broken up into incompatible parts. This has been a white middle-class cultural construction, yet because of the dominance of this group, the con-struction also affects other ethnic and class groups in American society.

According to this construction, American men get to play a variety of roles, but women can only properly play one or two at a time. Both middle-class women and men have within them the capacity to be autonomous, career-pursuing persons, sexual beings, spouses, and parents. But whereas all these roles, or dimensions of self, can fit together for men, they rarely have for American women. We saw that in the nineteenth century women could not both express their sexuality and be considered good mothers. Today, women with children can be sexually expressive; but even today the blatant juxtaposition of female sexuality and motherhood makes some people uncomfortable, as seen for example in the uproar over a popular magazine's photograph of a bare-bellied pregnant movie star on its cover. Today, however, discombobulated womanhood involves the tension or incompatibility between being a mother and having a career outside the home. More and more American mothers are working outside the home, but many people (including many college students) believe that a woman's career (an important dimension of a woman's autonomy) is incompatible with motherhood.

We have suggested that the discombobulated American woman grew out of American individualism set within a capitalist economy. As men in the nineteenth century entered the individualistic capitalist market to perpetually prove their manhood, women were enjoined to stay at home to provide a "haven in a heartless world." With their domesticity, "natural" nurturing qualities, virtue, sexual purity, and an ability to connect with others in a show of selfless caring, women embodied the antithesis of stark American individualism. All this culminated in the Cult of True Womanhood, in which women were placed on a pedestal as paragons of virtue and good motherhood but were devalued as persons in their own right.

In the twentieth century many women went out to work and many sought to express themselves as autonomous persons—in a word, to embrace individualism as men had done. They have challenged their discombobulation, but at great expense. Many people see them as selfish and greedy or as bad, negligent mothers; many working mothers feel guilty about leaving their children in the care of others; most working married women still are primarily responsible for housework and, if they have children, child care. And on top of all that, many of these women in the workforce are largely stuck with lower-paying, less-prestigious jobs than men.

Meanwhile, child care in America is still seen as best done through full-time motherhood. Hays (1996) has called modern American child care "intensive mothering," demanding considerable time, emotional energy, and financial cost. Hays claims that American intensive mothering has actually become more intensive as the outside, public world of work has grown more cutthroat, impersonal, and individualistic. She argues that Americans have constructed motherhood as the new "haven" we all need to soften the blows of individualism and self-interested materialism in the outside world. Since divorce is high and the American family is now more unstable than ever before, Hays contends that the mother-child bond is about all we have left with which to build a "haven." We then construct motherhood as the last vanguard of warm, human, and decidedly nonindividualistic relationships. Thus the tensions Americans feel between, on the one hand, their culture's individualism, materialism, and impersonality in the public sphere and, on the other hand, the need for connection, intimacy, and love are being played out in the cultural construction of intensive motherhood.

GENDER AND AMERICAN BODIES

Throughout this book we have seen how American gender is intertwined with and reflected through ideas and practices concerning the body. This is true in all cultures, but possibly this connection is even more pronounced in America, where the body itself is culturally so emphasized. Chapter 1 opened with a discussion of the Nacirema, for whom the body is inherently ugly and debilitating and the subject of many rituals that can only be seen as bizarre and torturous to an outsider. And that was in the 1950s. If anything, the American obsession with subjecting the body to torturous "rituals" to make it less ugly and debilitating has grown over the past half-century. Americans, especially white Americans, invest so much of their self-identification into their bodies while at the same time they construct unattainable ideals of the body, that a certain amount of frustration and self-denigration is inevitable. Other ethnic groups seem to have handled the American body problem better than middle-class Euro-Americans: They have at least accepted a wider range of body types as attractive.

We have seen in the book how American gender and cultural constructions about the body have been connected over time. We saw, for example, how in the nineteenth century the ideal male body underwent a shift from thin and unobtrusive to big and muscular. Historians have seen this shift as arising from men's stress over having to continually prove their manhood through success in a competitive, individualistic, capitalist public sphere (Bederman 1995; Kimmel 1966). Manly honor receded while a more virile "masculinity" emerged (Bederman 1995), almost as though men came to feel that it would be easier to build visible muscles and stake one's manhood on that than to keep up success as breadwinners in the dog-eat-dog world of the American marketplace.

We also saw how the American ideal female body type has shifted over the decades—round and voluptuous until the 1920s "androgynous" flapper, round and full again after World War II, and now back to thin. Notice how the thin ideal has twice coincided with waves of the woman's movement. Are women really trying to be more androgynous, more like men? Or is it that the ideal super-thin female, a shape that suggests a woman's physical immaturity, set against the ideal big muscular male, is emphasizing a gender difference in strength, authority, and power? (Bartky 1997). Or, does the new thin woman represent a sort of resolution of the conflicts contemporary women face; is it an attempt both to express woman's interest in entering the public, masculine world and yet retain a distinctive "femininity' (Bordo 1997)?

In Chapter 2 we saw how, in the nineteenth century, ideas about physical illness intersected with gender and sexuality. For example, male masturbation was admonished as a lack of manly restraint and as a dangerous loss of male energy that could lead to illness and even insanity or death.

Women's bodies faced other kinds of risks—for example, too much reading or intellectual endeavor was believed to harm women's reproductive organs. Also for women, too much sex was said to be debilitating and physically harmful. And we saw how many of the frustrations of nineteenth-century "ladies" became literally embodied in their fits of hysteria.

For middle-class women of the twentieth century we saw how medical discourse about and treatments of women's bodies fostered their sense of inadequacy and fragmentation. In the same century and continuing into the present, striving to be very thin has led many young women into anorexia. We also saw in Chapter 6 that many young college women are concerned with making themselves physically attractive to men as a means of receiving male attention and hence social prestige. Young men fare somewhat better, at least healthwise, in their current pursuit of muscularity but older men suffer from problems with impotence and the cultural construction of masculinity in terms of sexual performance.

Our bodies, then, speak volumes about gender in our society. Most of us participate in gendered body rituals and body language in a way that is largely unconscious. Many of us consciously uphold a vague ideal of gender equality and yet with our body rituals, postures, and purchasing patterns uphold an image of strong, powerful men and diminutive, deferential women.

GENDER, ETHNICITY, AND CLASS

In looking at gender in the United States, we first drew out the cultural constructions of the white middle class. We did so because these constructions have been influential—they have had an effect on all other U.S. groups, at least to some extent. But, as we have shown in Chapters 4 and 5, alongside this influence from the dominant culture, ethnic minorities have developed their own constructions of gender. And throughout the book we have emphasized that it is impossible to understand gender in America without understanding how it intersects with ethnicity and social class and how those intersections have developed through time.

What we have called the discombobulation of white middle-class American women is based on a conflict of roles, particularly a failure to integrate successfully the roles of mother and of individual, or public person, which in late-twentieth-century and early-twenty-first-century America is closely allied with employment. But for some ethnic minorities these roles have been combined for many generations. Native American and African American women have long acted both as mothers and as workers—providers of subsistence—without any feeling of conflict or fragmentation, and without apparent notice on the part of the white middle class.

For whites in the antebellum south, African American women were supposed to work as slaves. Their labor as mothers was of little interest to white society. In more recent years, it is African American women's income-producing labor that has disappeared from the consciousness of others, especially of many feminists. This is almost certainly because much of the work done by African American women has been exactly the work (cooking, cleaning, and child care for others) that so many white middle-class women, especially feminists, have reviled as repetitive, mindless, and demeaning. In the ongoing attempt by middle-class white women to integrate their various roles into one coherent, satisfying person, the successes of both Indian and black women in this respect have been largely ignored. These women have always combined motherhood and a "career," though the career may have involved a mop and an apron or a hoe and a pair of boots rather than a briefcase and a suit.

What has often been noticed by the white middle class in the past few generations is the family structure practiced by many Native Americans and African Americans. This structure often involves female-headed households. This phenomenon, discussed at length in Chapter 4, is the result of easily ascertainable historical causes, largely produced by racism and socioeconomic oppression. Yet female-headed households have usually been attributed by the majority population to moral failure on the part of ethnic minorities, and, despite the lack of objective evidence, these households have also been considered pathological. Ironically, unmarried mothers on welfare are increasingly chided for their lack of employment by the same members of the white middle class who state that children should be cared for full-time by their mothers.

Many Native American and African American women would prefer to be married. They would like to share their lives with a permanent partner and they appreciate the economic benefits of marriage. Indeed, Robin Jarrett's work with poor, unmarried black mothers convinced her that nearly all of them felt that "legal marriage was the cornerstone of conventional family life," which they wanted. Because of such concerns as independent household formation, economic independence, compatibility, fidelity, and commitment, however, most of these women "were pessimistic about actually contracting family roles as defined in the mainstream manner" (Jarrett 1997, 349, 351).

At all social and economic levels, black women, and to some extent Indian women as well, find that they encounter few men who are able to be supporting and supportive fathers and husbands. But despite a shortage of husbands, these women are not willing to give up children or motherhood. The words of a young, unmarried African American mother of three children illustrate the perspective of many women like her:

> I used to have this in my head, all my kids got the same daddy, get married, have a house. That's a little white girl's dream. That stuff don't happen in real life. You don't get married and live happily ever after. (Jarrett 1997, 352)

Asian and Hispanic women often share with their black and Indian sisters a need to cope with the indignities of racism. But for them the struggle with gender has a somewhat different locus, nearer to that of Euro-American women but perhaps more clear-cut. For many decades in America, Asian and Hispanic women have worked at agricultural subsistence, and also, in the case of Asian women, at family-run businesses. More recently, both Asian and Hispanic women have worked away from home. This, combined with their increasing levels of education, has complicated the definition and articulation of gender roles. Women's work is increasingly performed outside of the household, and it generates cash income. Thus for family members and for the woman herself, it is easier to identify the financial contribution she makes. And it is increasingly likely that the woman will begin to feel that she has a right to an opinion as to how her income should be spent and how her time should be spent, both on and off the job. This increasing autonomy threatens not only the traditional patriarchal orientation of the Asian and Hispanic family, but its collective focus as well. As we have seen, both men and women are likely to cause family distress when they embrace Euro-American-style individualism, but individualism is usually seen as less acceptable and more disruptive when it is expressed by a woman.

GENDER AND HIGHER EDUCATION

This book has discussed American gender in the context of higher education, largely through our study of students at Northwest Public University. In this study, one of the questions we included on our questionnaire for postgraduates concerned whether the former student wished she or he had done anything differently while at this university. Respondents were encouraged to "check all that apply," and many indicated, among others, the response: "I have few regrets." But 40 percent also checked "I wish I had paid better attention, studied more, and got better grades." We pass on this information not only to encourage current students to study more, but also to bring up the topic of American student alienation from higher education. Studies are indicating that today's students are less well-prepared and less enthusiastic about coursework than earlier generations have been. We raise this issue because we believe that this trend is affecting women and men students quite differently. And insofar as the trend continues, it will be more detrimental to women than to men.

The latest nationwide study shows that more students are reporting boredom in the classroom and general alienation from the academic experience (CIRP 1995). As noted in Chapter 6, the Holland and Eisenhart (1990) study showed that women lower their career aspirations because they feel that their coursework is too hard and too boring. Their study does not specify this, but it may be that in many cases the coursework is boring because it is too hard. And yet the women of their study had relatively good grades in high school. Of course, all this brings up the general problem of our country's current educational crisis in high schools and elementary schools. In our own study at Northwest Public University we were struck by the number of students we interviewed who said their high schools had not adequately prepared them for college. Over and over again these students told us, independently, "High school was a joke." We can also report from our own teaching experience that, over the years, more students feel that the content of their coursework is irrelevant to their lives.

The educational crisis in the lower levels of our system has produced a kind of minicrisis in higher education. If students are entering with less and less adequate preparation for college-level work, more and more of them will be frustrated and will come to feel that their coursework is too hard and too boring. Of course we can all recommend that high schools be improved and that higher educational institutions work harder to make their classes more relevant to students, but the point we wish to emphasize now is that the current situation has different repercussions for women and men. Men may find their classes boring and irrelevant and they, on average, do less well than women. Nevertheless, they more often manage to stay on track, they do not lower their career aspirations, and those who finish their degrees go on to higher-paying, more prestigious jobs than women graduates. Women, by contrast, do better than males, on average, in their classes, but they more often lower their career aspirations and go on to less-well-paying, less prestigious jobs than men.

As we have seen, women in some cases fall into a "culture of romance," which draws their time and attention and fixes their identity more within romantic relationships than on their careers (Holland and Eisenhart 1990). Our study has additionally shown that many women are constructing marriage and motherhood in such a way that they are already considering that they will interrupt their careers for children and be financially dependent on husbands. This all happens despite the fact that women appear to be as career oriented as men. For many students, higher education may unfortunately be boring and irrelevant, but the upshot of this is that men more often put up with it and get on with their careers just fine while many women lower their ambitions and gear themselves toward more traditional domestic identities.

Women college students with serious career interests could find that there are many, often gradual, ways in which their lives and orientations may change in the crucial years ahead. If these changes are deliberate, thought out, and conscious, no one should object. But if the changes are subtle and largely unconscious, the consequences may be undesirable.

Whatever trajectory these women take, it remains the case that throughout American history, education for women has been the greatest force behind whatever progress we have made toward gender equality. We saw in Chapter 2 that in the nineteenth century higher education for women was primarily intended to make them better wives and mothers. But once unleashed, educated women became a force for change in America; women increasingly used educational opportunities to pursue new goals and identities for themselves. We also saw in Chapters 4 and 5 that among many black, Native American, and Hispanic women especially, education has brought new economic opportunities. These opportunities give them significant bargaining power, especially with spouses, that their traditional gender roles did not allow.

One gender issue that involves students is the unconscious perpetuation of gender inequality, an issue we saw earlier in the discussion of American gender and the body. Our impression is that most college students, male and female, do uphold at least a vague ideal of gender equality, or the idea that no one gender should enjoy particular privileges, advantages, or opportunities over the other. At the same time, our study and others suggest that today's students are unwittingly perpetuating gender inequality and male privilege. We have seen this work in two ways.

First, on many campuses, or among certain groups on some campuses, a student-generated "culture of romance" boosts male privilege and in many cases deflates women who originally had high career aspirations. Not all college students participate in the culture of romance, though many possibly are affected by it at some point during their college years. We have seen that by the prescriptions of this culture, males have a variety of sources of prestige and avenues through which to build a sense of self-worth. Females, by contrast, have only one source of prestige: male attention, or the demonstration that they are attractive to men (Holland and Eisenhart 1990). The culture of romance also entails a double sexual standard by which male and female sexuality are evaluated differently. Sex is something women "give" men in return for "good treatment." If they give sex and are not treated well, they lose prestige and feel denigrated.

A second way in which students, and here we refer specifically to women students, unconsciously perpetuate gender inequality and male privilege is by shying away from avenues by which they might, themselves, achieve power and prestige. There may be a number of reasons for this. According to some, women students are discouraged from achievement by gender discrimination within academic institutions. This may be true, but based on our own study we would put more weight on four other factors. First, whatever the rewards of a career, they must be deferred, and they fail to provide the same immediate, intense psychological and social justification as, for example, romantic attachment. They also fail to provide the public validation of sexual desirability that American culture and especially the media encourage as a top priority for women. In fact, career success continues to be seen by many Americans as "second best": what women do when they are not winners in the culture of romance.

Second, American women have been socialized to accept a gender-biased dichotomy. Even in the opening years of the twenty-first century, many believe that they must choose either marriage and motherhood or a career. The general culture does not set men up to see a conflict between being husbands and fathers and pursuing challenging careers. Men are not asked whether fatherhood or their career is more important to them, nor are they expected to choose between them. Presumably, all well-balanced people, male and female, if pushed to the wall, would choose their families over their careers. Why then should this be a question that is relevant only to women?

It is not only conservative "family values" advocates that consider the family/career dichotomy legitimate. Some feminist career women seem to consider that career success is impossible for women when they are also concerned with a family. One of our students reported to us that when she asked a prominent woman academic, who had been a guest speaker in her women's studies class, how it would be possible to combine being a mother with being a professor, the guest speaker responded, "Don't even think about it." But, of course, many women have successfully integrated both roles.

Third, some students, male and female, believe that mothers should care for their children full-time, and that to do otherwise puts their children at a disadvantage. Repeatedly, students have told us that they do not want other people to "raise their children," though that seems like a dramatic exaggeration of the realities of paid child care. Certainly very few parents consider that their children's teachers are "raising" them, though children spend many hours at school. As for the widespread but nonspecific idea that children are damaged when they are cared for by someone other than their mothers, there is simply no evidence for it.

As noted in Chapter 6, although many women students mistrust "feminism," they have been affected by it. Nearly all plan to work for at least part of their lives, and many say that when they are married they plan to contribute to household income equally with their husbands. They have a general belief in the moral and intellectual equality of women and men, and are specifically attracted to the feminist doctrine of equal pay for equal work. Finally, they believe that their future husbands should be equally involved in child care and domestic labor.

As we pointed out in Chapter 6, many students are holding simultaneously opposing positions and may be unaware of the contradictions of these opinions. How, for example, can a nonworking mother make any economic contribution to the household? Yet many of the same students who plan to contribute equally with their husbands also plan not to work when their children are born. How can these same women expect equal domestic and paternal labor from their husbands when those husbands are working full-time as the sole support of the household?

We suspect that as they grow older, many of the students we surveyed and interviewed will make choices different from those they now believe they will make. In some cases their lives may diverge significantly from the picture they currently envision. In accordance with national trends, it seems inevitable that most of them will work even when their children are small, and that roughly half of them will divorce. But the distressing reality is that decisions made when one is eighteen or twenty-two constrain decisions made later in life. An undergraduate student (like Danielle of Chapter 6) who opts for a lower-paying career instead of medicine will probably not be able to earn a medical degree "later if I want." She will not have the required undergraduate coursework; she may have lost her undergraduate academic confidence; and medical schools are notoriously unwilling to invest in older, nontraditional students. Similarly, the young woman we interviewed who plans to interrupt her career in public relations to stay home with her children will almost certainly find that it is impossible to resume her career where she left it. Not only will the conventions of the occupation have changed in ten (or even five) years, but, because she dropped out, she is likely to be perceived as less than serious about her work.

More and more "returning" students appear every year on college campuses, in both undergraduate and graduate programs. Most of them are women, and most of them are very good students. They are studying now with a clear vision of the career they considered expendable years before, and they may do well at these careers. But, as they well know, they have lost many years that cannot be regained.

WHERE ARE WE NOW?

As we look toward American gender in the future it may be useful to take a quick glance at where we are now in terms of some simple, straightforward parameters. Here we use a method of assessing gender equality that we mentioned in Chapter 1, namely, taking items that are both generally valued in a society and measurable, and seeing how they are distributed in that society according to gender. For this we can look at measures of health, education, and income.

Women slightly outnumber men in America and tend to live longer. Life expectancy at birth is now about eighty years for women and seventy-three years for men. Women throughout our history have consistently increased their presence in higher education. Now, more women than men earn postsecondary degrees, except for the doctoral degree. Looking at both gender and ethnicity, black women have, since the 1970s, shown the greatest increase in schooling. Compared to the past, many women are now earning degrees in business and biology, but still relatively few earn degrees in the physical sciences, engineering, and computer science (Herz and Wootton 1996).

In contrast to life expectancy and education, women lag behind men in earnings, as we discussed in Chapter 6. In 1994, women working full-time earned only 76 percent of what men earned. The gap in male and female income increases with age. After retirement, at age sixty-five and over, men earn, on average, a little over $20,000 a year, while women earn an average of about $11,000 (Costello and Krimgold 1996, 307). However, over the past few decades the gender gap in earnings has narrowed. Yet it is not certain that this trend will continue, and in fact recently it has begun to widen again.

A lot of the gender gap in earnings is due to the fact that women are over-represented in lower-paying jobs in service, sales, and clerical work. In fact, nearly six out of ten working women held these kinds of jobs in 1994. But even within the same occupations, men tend to earn more than women. Considering gender and ethnicity, white males earn the most, followed by white women and black men. Black women and Hispanic men and women have the lowest average earnings. Along with their depressed earnings, women of all races are far more likely to experience poverty than men (Galinsky and Bond 1996). Particularly vulnerable to poverty are single women and their dependent children.

Gender in America is being affected by several national trends. The age at first marriage has been rising, but the divorce rate remains quite high; about half of all first marriages end in divorce. Another partly interrelated trend is that more and more women are entering the workforce; now about 46 percent of the total workforce is female. More than half of all women with very young children are working, and about 60 percent of those with children under age six are working outside the home. Along with all this the American family is changing, too. Today less than 20 percent of all families have a Leave-It-To-Beaver-style husband/breadwinner with a non-working wife. Nearly 20 percent of all families are now female-headed. The message for women is clear: "The combination of these social trends has meant that women have increasingly relied on themselves for their own support and that of their families" (Herz and Wootton 1996, 48).

It is also interesting to note that working mothers really do experience a "second shift" of domestic work when they come home. Our student surveys showed that the women are optimistic: With only a few exceptions, most of the women in our student class samples expect that housework and child care will be shared equally with their spouses. Right now, however, national surveys show that over 80 percent of all women who are married with children report that they are primarily responsible for cooking, cleaning, and shopping. Nearly 70 percent of working mothers report that they are primarily responsible for child care. Compared with working fathers, working mothers also report greater job stress and greater dissatisfaction about how their children are doing (Galinsky and Bond 1996).

AN INTERNATIONAL COMPARISON

The focus of this book has been the articulation of gender within American culture (or cultures). But a comparison with other industrial countries can give us an idea of areas in which the United States is unique and those it shares with other countries that have a similar technoeconomic base. We will look first at seven countries of Western Europe (Belgium, Denmark, France, Germany, the Netherlands, Sweden, and the United Kingdom), primarily through Hettie Pott-Buter's (1993) comparative study, and then at Japan.

WESTERN EUROPE

Marriage in Europe has been the cultural ideal throughout history. This has been particularly true for women, since until very recently it was the only way for them to achieve security and respectability. The notion that men and women had "naturally" different roles was accepted by most people well into the twentieth century. Nonetheless, though men were seen as the family breadwinners, women of all but the upper classes worked, not only at home in their nurseries and kitchens, but side by side with their husbands in agriculture and small family businesses. Girls and young women of the working classes were frequently employed as domestic servants and, after industrialization, as factory workers. Middle-class girls, however, had virtually nothing to fall back on if they found themselves unmarried and without male support except work as companions and governesses. Eventually, better-paid work as schoolteachers and nurses became available. But at least until the end of the nineteenth century, public opinion generally opposed offering females educational or occupational choices that would lead to well-paid, secure employment for fear that this would encourage them not to marry (Pott-Buter 1993, 70).

Before World War II, married women throughout Europe were most likely to be employed if their husbands' incomes were low. Indeed their employment was an indicator of family economic distress. Because their occupations were usually precarious, onerous, and poorly paid, "working class culture adopted the image of the married woman at home as the sign of the health, stability, and prosperity of a household" (Tilly and Scott 1987, 274, quoted in Pott-Buter 1993, 199).

Indeed, in many "respectable" female occupations, marriage meant the end of employment. Dutch women employed in the national postal, telephone, and telegraph services were by law fired upon the occasion of their marriage, as were French telephone operators, who, in any case, could not work past the age of twenty-five (Pott-Buter 1993, 197, 223). In most European countries, including England, schoolteachers and nurses were usually unable to work after marriage. This was also frequently the case in the United States, a country in which airlines stewardesses were grounded at marriage as late as the 1960s.

In the twentieth century, compulsory schooling increased employment opportunities for women in Europe, and women took immediate advantage of their new options. By 1990, labor force participation rates for women from ages twenty-five to forty-nine are shown in Table 7.1.

In the same year, women's labor force participation rate in the United States was similar to that of France and the United Kingdom. By 1994 in the United States this rate was 75 percent of women aged twenty-five to fifty-four (Costello and Krimgold 1996).

In Europe, gender segregation in the newly expanded workplace was immediately established. This began to erode after the end of World War II, but it took sexual discrimination legislation in the 1970s to alter it significantly. Thus, Europe managed to legislate the equivalent of the Equal Rights Amendment, which is still being debated and remains unpassed in the United States.

By the 1960s enrollment in postsecondary education had increased all over Europe, and the rates of participation by women began to equal or even exceed those of men. However, their additional education has not appeared to provide women with "further preparation for employment," in the

TABLE 7.1 WOMEN AGED TWENTY-FIVE TO FORTY-NINE
IN THE WORKFORCE IN SELECTED EUROPEAN COUNTRIES

COUNTRY	PERCENTAGE
Sweden	91
Denmark	89
United Kingdom	73
France	73
Germany	65
Netherlands	62
Belgium	57

Source: From Hettie A. Pott-Buter, *Facts and Fairy Tales about Female Labor, Family, and Fertility: A Seven-Country Comparison 1850–1990* (Amsterdam: Amsterdam University Press, 1993), 155. Used by permission of the publishers.

words of a document prepared by the Organization for Economic Cooperation and Development (Pott-Buter 1993, 152). In vocational education females have also benefited less than males. Fewer female students are involved, and those who are usually enroll in programs that are shorter and lead to fewer skills and lower pay. One 1970 study on apprenticeship programs in Britain noted that of the girls participating, 75 percent had opted for training in hairdressing. As a result of this trend, the European Community in 1988 began a program of female vocational training that encourages girls to make vocational choices without regard for traditional gender stereotypes (Pott-Buter 1993, 226).

In many European countries, marriage and fertility patterns have changed dramatically since the 1970s. The number of couples living together without being married is increasing, especially among younger people (aged twenty to twenty-four). Now these unions span a high of 75 percent in Sweden and 60 percent in Norway, to a midrange of 30 percent for France and 25 percent for Belgium, to a low of 7 percent in the United Kingdom. Many of these unions evolve into marriage, but many also result in out-of-wedlock births. In Germany and the Netherlands, out-of-wedlock births amount to only 10 percent, but they are nearly 50 percent of the total births in Sweden and Denmark (Pott-Buter 1993, 175).

In terms of the promotion of gender equality, perhaps the most amazing feature of Europe from the perspective of American eyes is the statutory paid maternal leave of at least fourteen weeks in every country in Pott-Buter's study. Indeed the United States is practically the only advanced industrialized country in the world not to offer any maternal leave by law. While each European country has its own policy as to how the leave should be divided, they all provide remuneration for the prospective mother of roughly 90 percent (or more) of her salary. Sweden, Belgium, Germany, and Denmark also provide paternal leave. The availability of child care varies from country to country: The Netherlands and the United Kingdom offer the fewest options, while France, Belgium, Sweden, Denmark, and Germany offer a range of institutionalized child-care providers.

There has been great improvement in gendered pay equity in Europe since the days when Dutch women received an average wage that was 60 percent of men's. This situation prevailed from the end of World War II until the passage of the Equal Pay Act in 1975, despite increasing complaints beginning in the 1960s (Pott-Buter 1993, 248). The notion of equal pay for equal work has now been largely officially accepted and legislatively implemented, but primarily in those occupations in which the encroachment of women threatened to erode the male salary base. Those occupations still dominated by women, and in which it would be more difficult to assess "equal work," are still, as they are throughout the world, less well paid than male-dominated occupations.

JAPAN

Most Americans believe that, in Japan, men work long hours at the same company for a lifetime and women stay at home as compliant wives and compulsive mothers. Though there is some truth to this stereotype, it is a far from accurate picture.

Most important, Japanese women participate in the labor force at an official rate of 42 percent (Saso 1990, 5). This does not include the informal employment sector, in which many women provide such "under the table" services as tutoring in languages, mathematics, music, or the traditional arts, or the addressing of envelopes in elegant calligraphy. Also, though most women who work do so in order to help out with family expenses, they and women who are considering working also cite economic independence and self-reliance as motivating factors—not what one might expect of the submissive female stereotype.

But Japanese women have always worked under disadvantageous conditions, performing continuous, onerous, unacknowledged work alongside their farmer, manufacturer, or shopkeeper husbands or having their labor contracted as adolescent girls by their fathers. Today, women who graduate from first-class universities are likely to be employed at roughly the same rate as men with similar qualifications. It would seem that gender inequities in employment are a thing of the past.

But despite her initial employment, neither the new employee nor her company expects that she will stay with the company long. She will leave after four or five years to marry or in six or seven years to have children. This pattern becomes clear from the first, as the new woman employee is asked to choose whether she will work on the "executive" track, or the "auxiliary" track. Though the executive track leads to promotions and salary increases, women are usually warned that the long hours and frequent transfers their work requires will destroy their family life, while the auxiliary track will be more suitable for them. After several years on the auxiliary track, which is largely dead-end labor, most women are ready for marriage and children. Even for those on the executive track, the birth of children often results in their leaving the company to be full-time wives and mothers.

European and American women frequently combine families and careers, albeit with great effort and some stress. Why is it so much more difficult for Japanese women? First of all, Japanese professional careers require extremely long hours with few holidays or days off. Even though there may be several weeks' annual leave or vacation time, employees in large, prestigious firms feel pressured not to use it all, any more than they would consider leaving their desks at the official quitting time of 6:00 P.M. They use only a fraction of their vacation, and work until 9:00 or 10:00 at night to demonstrate loyalty to their company and a serious investment in their work. This makes it hard to care for young children without a nanny or unemployed family member (like a mother or mother-in-law) at home. Though Japan is well-supplied with *hoikuen* (day nurseries) both private and public (tax subsidized), they do not accommodate the long hours of a career woman on the rise. And professional salaries, though generous, are rarely sufficient to pay for live-in child care. Nevertheless, it is important to note here that Japan, like European countries but unlike the United States, has a government-mandated maternal leave of fourteen weeks, during which a significant portion of the woman's salary is paid by one or more private or government programs.

Once a child is in school a mother may have more time for work, but there is still the problem of children's illnesses, a need to accompany children to their lessons and cram schools, and the numerous and important school meetings that mothers are expected to attend. One solution might seem to be a sharing of child care and other household duties with fathers, but the fathers are themselves locked into careers with long hours and little time off. Unlike women, they have no alternate route to cultural legitimacy, and so the majority of Japanese husbands and fathers leave most family and household labor to their wives.

A newspaper poll carried out in Japan indicated that 80 percent of Japanese women were aware of discrimination in the workplace, which, in any case, is relatively stressful for both men and women (Saso 1990, 52). Further, as turns out to be true also in Europe and the United States, even women who have graduated from prestigious, first-class universities have usually studied subjects that are not vocationally useful. The percentage of women graduating in the arts has been over 35 percent since the 1960s, while sciences and engineering have attracted just under 5 percent, up from only 3 percent in the 1960s (Saso 1990, 36). Finally, the Japanese cultural emphasis on graceful, elegant femininity, coupled with the still prevailing opinion that women with children should be at home, remains powerful. For all of these reasons there are many Japanese women who look forward eagerly to life as a full-time housewife.

Once their children are older, many Japanese women return to the workplace, but virtually never to a job on the executive track. Because of the extreme Japanese emphasis on the seniority-company loyalty system, a returning woman worker cannot hope for well-paid employment with prospects of advancement. Indeed, many such jobs have upper age limits of twenty-three to thirty-five.

There is increasing awareness today in Japan of the employment needs and desires of women. Some major companies are beginning to make a concerted effort to employ women as researchers and software engineers. There is a call for more, better, and more flexible part-time work, with higher pay and greater benefits. But without a modification of the Japanese seniority system and a reduction in the extremely long hours of work expected of professional employees, women who wish to have children will find it nearly impossible to have manageable careers as well.

We can see in this international comparison that as far as gender equality goes, and as measured by the parameters we have used, Europe wins over Japan and the United States. Though beginning in the twentieth century with a similar gender ideology to that of the United States—one stressing domesticity for women and breadwinning for men—European countries have been able to more effectively pass legislation promoting gender equality in the workplace and to facilitate women having both careers and maternal roles. Europe proved to be less rigid than the United States in maintaining traditional gender roles, and in the process these countries have avoided fragmenting womanhood to the extent that we see in the United States. Japan and the United States lag behind, and in both cases we suggest that this is for cultural reasons. But the reasons are very different. In Japan the rather extraordinary demands of the workplace, supported by a cultural ideology that values seniority and company loyalty, results in particular stresses and constraints on women. Of all the countries considered here, it is probably most difficult for women of Japan to pursue prestigious or high-paying careers. In the United States, as we have seen throughout the book, a dominant culture of individualism and self-reliance, a unidimensional view of womanhood, an ideology of "intensive motherhood" (Hays 1996), and the conscious and unconscious choices and actions we all make every day perpetuate our own unique brand of gender inequality.

DISCUSSION QUESTIONS

1. In this book we have discussed changing gender roles and expectations in the United States from the perspective that gender is now at a critical point in American culture. Do you agree with this perspective? If you disagree, why do you think gender issues are now of so much concern to so many people? If you agree, what would you say are the central issues of the crisis? What steps are being taken to promote a successful outcome? Do you think both men and women want to be involved in determining the future of gender issues?

2. Women, including college students, often complain about the feeling that they are being pressured by advertising to present an unattainable physical self: body, face, hair. Why do you think women are so vulnerable to this kind of pressure? Why don't more women simply refuse to accept unrealistic images of physical perfection as models for their own appearance? What would happen if they did? Though men also want to look young, slim, strong, and fit, they do not seem to anguish so much over their physical appearance. Why? This is a question that will be answered in distinctively different ways, depending upon the

respondent's theoretical perspective. How would you characterize yours? Were you aware that that perspective was informing your answer until you saw the last question?

3. Despite their generally higher grades at all levels of schooling, women continue to earn less than men and to occupy less prestigious occupational positions. Since you have now completed this text, you can formulate an answer as to why this is so, an answer that may or may not accord with the discussion of this issue in this book. To what extent, then, do you believe women's failure to achieve at the level of men is the result of social and economic forces beyond their control? Which social and economic forces, specifically? To what extent do you think this failure is the result of decisions and courses of action chosen by women themselves? Or do you see a combination of forces at work? What changes do you expect in women's employment in the next ten years? In the next twenty years?

4. What would you say are the three most pressing gender issues facing the United States in the twenty-first century? How do you think they could be addressed? Do you think they will be? Why or why not? Do all three of your selections center on women? If so, what issues that concern men, specifically, do you think might be important in the coming century?

SOME USEFUL WEB SITES

Much information relevant to gender in America is now available on the Web. Here we provide a brief list of Web sites we have found helpful in exploring further some of the topics and issues covered in this book.

FEMINIST THEORY WEB SITE

This Web site provides bibliographies and links for feminism.
http://www.cddc.vt.edu/feminism

THE WORLD WIDE WEB VIRTUAL LIBRARY: THE MEN'S ISSUES PAGE

This Web site provides articles and links for a variety of men's movements and issues.
http://www.vix.com/pub/men/index.html

GAY & LESBIAN ALLIANCE AGAINST DEFAMATION WEB SITE

This Web site is the home page of the Gay & Lesbian Alliance against Defamation.
http://www.glaad.org/org/index.html

NATIONAL ORGANIZATION FOR WOMEN

This Web site is the home page of the National Organization for Women.
http://63.111.42.146/home

NATIVE WEB

This Web site provides Native American links.
http://www.nativeweb.org

ASIANGURLS: ASIAN AMERICAN WOMEN

This Web site provides articles and links for Asian American women.
http://www.asiangurls.com/cat_home.cfm?catid=48

AMERICAN ASSOCIATION OF UNIVERSITY WOMEN

This Web site is the home page of the American Association of University Women.
http://www.aauw.org/home.html

REFERENCES

Bartky, Sandra Lee. 1997. "Foucault, Femininity, and the Modernization of Patri-archal Power." Pp. 129–153 in *Writing on the Body: Female Embodiment and Feminist Theory*, ed. Katie Conboy, Nadia Medina, and Sarah Stanbury. New York: Columbia University Press.

Bederman, Gail. 1995. *Manliness & Civilization: A Cultural History of Gender and Race in the United States, 1880–1917*. Chicago, IL: University of Chicago Press.

Cooperative Institutional Research Program (CIRP). 1995. *The American Freshman: National Norms for Fall 1995*. American Council on Education. Los Angeles, CA: University of California.

Costello, Cynthia, and Barbara Kivimae Krimgold, eds. 1996. *The American Woman, 1996–1997*. New York: W. W. Norton and Company.

Galinsky, Ellen, and James T. Bond. 1996. "Work and Family: The Experiences of Mothers and Fathers in the U.S. Labor Force." Pp. 79–103 in *The American Woman, 1996–1997*, ed. Cynthia Costello and Barbara Kivimae Krimgold. New York: W. W. Norton and Company.

Hays, Sharon. 1996. *The Cultural Contradictions of Motherhood*. New Haven, CT: Yale University Press.

Herz, Diane E., and Barbara H. Wootton. 1996. "Women in the Workforce: An Overview." Pp. 44–78 in *The American Woman, 1996–1997*, ed. Cynthia Costello and Barbara Kivimae Krimgold. New York: W. W. Norton and Company.

Holland, Dorothy C., and Margaret A. Eisenhart. 1990. *Educated in Romance: Women, Achievement, and College Culture*. Chicago, IL: University of Chicago Press.

Jarrett, Robin L. 1997. "Living Poor: Family Life among Single Parent, African-American Women." Pp. 344–365 in *Race, Class, and Gender in a Diverse Society*, ed. Diana Kendall. Boston, MA: Allyn and Bacon.

Kimmel, Michael. 1966. *Manhood in America: A Cultural History*. New York: Free Press.

Pott-Buter, Hettie A. 1993. *Facts and Fairy Tales about Female Labor, Family, and Fertility: A Seven-Country Comparison 1850–1990*. Amsterdam: Amsterdam University Press.

Saso, Mary. 1990. *Women in the Japanese Workplace*. London: Hilary Shipman.

Tilly, Louise A., and Joan W. Scott. 1987. *Women, Work, and Family*. London: Methuen and Co.

APPENDIX A

SURVEY QUESTIONNAIRE

1. How old are you?
   [ ] a. 18–22   [ ] b. 23–26
   [ ] c. 27 or older

2. What is your gender?
   [ ] a. male   [ ] b. female

3. Are you a foreign student?
   [ ] a. yes   [ ] b. no

4. What is your ethnic group?
   [ ] a. Caucasian   [ ] b. African American
   [ ] c. Asian American [ ] d. Native American
   [ ] e. Hispanic   [ ] f. Other

5. What is your position at your current educational institution?
   [ ] a. freshman   [ ] b. sophomore
   [ ] c. junior   [ ] d. senior or 5th year student

6. Where are you living now?
   [ ] a. sorority/fraternity house
   [ ] b. residence hall
   [ ] c. own home
   [ ] d. rented apartment/house/room/mobile home
   [ ] e. living with parents

7. In general, how would you evaluate your educational experience at your present
   educational institution?
   [ ] a. excellent   [ ] b. good
   [ ] c. fair   [ ] d. poor

8. How much education do you plan to complete?

[ ] a. a few years of college/university

[ ] b. a bachelor's degree

[ ] c. a master's degree

[ ] d. a professional degree

[ ] e. Ph.D.

9. What is your Grade Point Average (GPA) now?

[ ] a. 0–2.0   [ ] b. 2.1–2.5

[ ] c. 2.6–3.0   [ ] d. 3.1–3.5

[ ] e. 3.6–4.0

10. What is your major? Select one category, or select two if you have a double major. Do not indicate a minor. If none of the following apply, skip these and go to Question 11.

[ ] a. humanities (e.g., English, philosophy, foreign languages)

[ ] b. social sciences (e.g., anthropology, sociology, history, criminal justice, political science)

[ ] c. biological sciences

[ ] d. physical sciences (e.g., physics, mathematics, chemistry)

[ ] e. engineering, architecture

[ ] f. education

11. Are you majoring in any of the following? If not, mark "other" or "undecided."

[ ] a. pre-med or pre-vet   [ ] b. business, economics

[ ] c. nursing   [ ] d. communications

[ ] e. other   [ ] f. undecided

12. What one factor influenced you the most in your selection of this major? Please mark only one.

[ ] a. I just enjoy this field of study.

[ ] b. I get good grades in this area.

[ ] c. It will help me to get a well-paying job.

[ ] d. It is a well-respected field.

[ ] e. It fits in with my family plans.

13. Are there certain majors that you feel are more suited to one gender or the other?

[ ] a. yes, because of basic biological differences between men and women

[ ] b. yes, because of years of tradition

[ ] c. no

[ ] d. not sure

14. Ideally, what kind of career would you like to have? Please mark only one. If none of the following categories apply, skip these and go to Question 15.

    [ ] a. at-home spouse/parent

    [ ] b. accountant/business person/banker

    [ ] c. stockbroker/engineer/lawyer

    [ ] d. elementary or secondary school teacher

    [ ] e. college or university professor

    [ ] f. specialist in public relations/advertising/communications

15. Do any of the following categories indicate your ideal career? If not, mark "other."

    [ ] a. nurse

    [ ] b. clinical psychologist/social worker/therapist

    [ ] c. physician, dentist, veterinarian

    [ ] d. police officer/post office worker/fire fighter/civil service employee/military

    [ ] e. owner of your own business

    [ ] f. other

16. What one factor attracts you most to the career you have chosen? Please mark only one.

    [ ] a. It is a well-paid field.

    [ ] b. It will allow me to help others.

    [ ] c. It is a well-respected occupation.

    [ ] d. It is exciting, adventurous or creative.

    [ ] e. It will give me time to spend with my children.

    [ ] f. It is my family's business.

17. Do you expect that your career will be related to your major?

    [ ] a. yes   [ ] b. no

18. Have you had any experience in the career you would like to have?

    [ ] a. yes   [ ] b. no? Go to Question 20.

19. If you answered yes, how did you get this experience? Please mark all answers that apply.

    [ ] a. volunteer work during high school years

    [ ] b. volunteer work during college years

    [ ] c. paid work during high school years

    [ ] d. paid work during college years

    [ ] e. college internship

    [ ] f. other

20. Do you expect to find a job in your chosen field within one year of graduation?

[ ] a. yes

[ ] b. no

[ ] c. I will not be looking for a job in the first year after graduation.

21. How much do you expect to earn annually in your first job after graduation?

[ ] a. under $15,000	[ ] b. $15,000–$20,000
[ ] c. $21,000–$30,000	[ ] d. $31,000–$40,000
[ ] e. over $40,000	[ ] f. I do not plan to work

22. What was the highest level of education your mother completed?

[ ] a. elementary or junior high

[ ] b. high school

[ ] c. some college

[ ] d. bachelor's degree

[ ] e. master's degree

[ ] f. professional degree (law, MD, DDS, DVM, RN) or PhD

23. What was the highest level of education your father completed?

[ ] a. elementary or junior high

[ ] b. high school

[ ] c. some college

[ ] d. bachelor's degree

[ ] e. master's degree

[ ] f. professional degree (law, MD, DDS, DVM, RN) or PhD

24. Were your parents ever divorced?

[ ] a. yes	[ ] b. no

25. While you were growing up, and before you graduated from high school, did your mother ever work outside the home?

[ ] a. yes	[ ] b. no? Go to Question 27.

26. If you answered yes, what effect did your mother's working have on you?

[ ] a. generally positive effect	[ ] b. generally negative effect
[ ] c. no effect	

27. Which one of the following is most important to you right now? Please mark only one.

[ ] a. preparing for a career

[ ] b. getting a good education

[ ] c. having friends and a good social life

[ ] d. being married or having a love relationship

[ ] e. being a parent

28. Which one of the following is most important to you in the long run? Please mark only one.
    [ ] a. having a career
    [ ] b. having money
    [ ] c. being a parent
    [ ] d. having friends and a good social life
    [ ] e. being married or having a love relationship

29. What is your marital status?
    [ ] a. never married
    [ ] b. living with partner but not married
    [ ] c. divorced or separated
    [ ] d. widowed
    [ ] e. married now; living with spouse? Go to Question 31.

30. If you are not currently married, do you expect to be married later on?
    [ ] a. yes   [ ] b. no? Go to Question 36.

If you are married or expect to marry, please answer Questions 31–35. If not, skip these and go to Question 36.

31. After marriage, do you expect that your spouse will work outside the home? (Or, if married, does your spouse work?)
    [ ] a. yes
    [ ] b. no
    [ ] c. don't know; my spouse can work or not as she/he likes

32. If you have children, would you prefer that your spouse stay at home when they are young?
    [ ] a. yes   [ ] b. no
    [ ] c. I do not plan to have children.

33. Who do you think will contribute most to your family income? (Or, if married, who does contribute most?)
    [ ] a. I will.
    [ ] b. My spouse will.
    [ ] c. My spouse and I will contribute equally to family income.

34. Who do you think will do most of the housework? (Or, if married, who does it?)
    [ ] a. I will.
    [ ] b. My spouse will.
    [ ] c. My spouse and I will share housework equally.
    [ ] d. I expect to have hired help.

35. If you have children, who do you think will do most of the child care? (Or, who does or did?)

    [ ] a. I will.

    [ ] b. My spouse will.

    [ ] c. My spouse and I will share child care equally.

    [ ] d. I do not plan to have children.

If you are male and currently married or have a girlfriend, or if you are female and married or have a boyfriend, please answer Questions 36–38. If not, skip these and go to Question 39.

36. Who gets better grades?

    [ ] a. I do.   [ ] b. My partner does.

    [ ] c. We get about the same grades.

37. Who takes harder classes?

    [ ] a. I do.

    [ ] b. My partner does.

    [ ] c. We are about the same in this respect.

38. Who spends more time on coursework?

    [ ] a. I do   [ ] b. my partner does

    [ ] c. we spend about the same time

39. Do you have children?

    [ ] a. yes   [ ] b. no

40. Whether or not you have children now, how many children would you like to have in all?

    [ ] a. 1

    [ ] b. 2

    [ ] c. 3 or more

    [ ] d. I do not plan to have children? Go to Question 45.

If you expect to ever have a career, please answer Questions 41–43. If not, skip these and go to Question 44.

41. When you have children, do you plan to interrupt your career for several months or years in order to stay home with them when they are young? (Or, if you have children, did you interrupt a career to stay home with them?)

    [ ] a. yes

    [ ] b. no

    [ ] c. I plan to terminate my career completely when I have children.

42. When children arrive, do you think you might reduce your workload to part-time work? (Or if you have children, did you do this?)

    [ ] a. yes   [ ] b. no

43. When children arrive, do you think you might change your job in order to spend more time with them? (Or, did you do this?)

    [ ] a. yes   [ ] b. no

44. How old would you like to be when your first child is born? (Or, if you already have children, how old were you when your first child was born?)

    [ ] a. 20 or under   [ ] b. 21–26

    [ ] c. 27–30   [ ] d. 31 or over

45. Which category best describes the domestic situation you believe you will have about five years after graduation?

    [ ] a. married with one or more children

    [ ] b. married with no children

    [ ] c. single with one or more children

    [ ] d. single with no children

    [ ] e. involved in a long-term relationship with children

46. Which category best describes the work situation you believe you will have about five years after graduation?

    [ ] a. full-time job

    [ ] b. part-time job

    [ ] c. no job

    [ ] d. graduate school/continuing education

47. While at your present educational institution, have you ever experienced sexual harassment or other gender-based discrimination?

    [ ] a. yes   [ ] b. no

For the next 3 questions, please mark whether you agree or disagree with the opinion statements shown.

48. "Females in general have lower self-esteem than males."

    [ ] a. agree   [ ] b. disagree

49. "In general, feminism has had a negative effect on U.S. society."

    [ ] a. agree   [ ] b. disagree

50. "In general, children raised in households where both parents work full-time turn out less well than children raised in families where one parent stays home or works only part-time."

    [ ] a. agree   [ ] b. disagree

APPENDIX B

TABLES SHOWING
SURVEY RESULTS

Each class sample in the tables on pages 214–225 (see also the sample summary in Table 6.2 of Chapter 6) has its own particular profile. Students taking Introduction to Anthropology at Southern Public University are mostly between eighteen and twenty-two years old and represent a wide range of years in school. They are almost all Caucasian and most live in rental units or residence halls. The students taking Introductory Biology at the same institution are also largely eighteen to twenty-two years old; they are mostly freshman or sophomore students living in residence halls. More than two-thirds of the males are Caucasian but 42 percent of the females are black. The women students taking the course Women in Society at Southern Public University are largely young, Caucasian, unmarried, and living in dorms or apartments.

The Midwest Public University 1 students in the Introduction to Anthropology class are on average a little older than those in most of the samples and they span a range of years in school. Nearly a quarter of these students are black. Almost half of them live in rental units and most are unmarried. Students at Midwest Public University 2 were recruited from a lower-division course in criminal justice. They closely resemble those at Midwest Public University 1 except that most are juniors or seniors and fewer are black.

The Introduction to Social Science course at Northwest State College was a night course, with many of the students working during the day. Here the students are older than in other samples (30 percent of the women and 57 percent of the men are twenty-seven or older). Most of the women are currently unmarried whereas 43 percent of the men are married. Twenty percent of the women and 14 percent of the men are divorced. More than half of the men and nearly half of the women have children. These Northwest State College students are largely Caucasian, though 20 percent of the women are Native Americans. Northwest State College is a four-year college.

The questionnaires of students at West Coast Private Christian College were merged from three classes. Most (thirty-five) were in a lower-division course, World Civilizations; the rest were in one of two upper-division courses in psychology. We kept these questionnaires together in one sample because the students were remarkably homogeneous in terms of background and responses. Nearly all of the West Coast Private Christian College students are young, unmarried, and Caucasian; none have children. Most of them are juniors or seniors living in residence halls. This same description also characterizes the Southern Private University students taking Introduction to Anthropology.

At the highly selective institutions, the West Coast Public University sample shows students who are a little older on average than are students in most other samples. Most are unmarried. About half of these students are Caucasian. More numerous than in all other samples are Asian Americans and Hispanic students. The women students at East Coast Private University are all graduating senior anthropology majors. The majority are Caucasian but nearly a quarter are African Americans; nearly all are unmarried.

Where possible we have included data from our study at Northwest Public University (NWPU) in these tables for comparison.

TABLE A.1   PERCENTAGE OF STUDENTS AGREEING THAT FEMINISM
HAS HAD A NEGATIVE EFFECT ON U.S. SOCIETY

CLASS SAMPLE (INSTITUTION AND COURSE)	FEMALE	MALE
Southern Public U		
Anthropology		
(N=44f, 21m)	25%	42%
Biology		
(N=42f, 11m)	33	45
Women in Society		
(N=26f)	4	—
Southern Private U		
Anthropology		
(N=33f, 22m)	30	55
Midwest Public U 1		
Anthropology		
(N=30f, 12m)	17	33
Midwest Public U 2		
Criminal Justice		
(N=22f, 35m)	9	46
Northwest State College		
Social Science		
(N=10f, 7m)	30	29
West Coast Private		
Christian College		
World Civ., Psych.		
(N=38f, 14m)	21	50
West Coast Private U		
Film Criticism		
(N=12f, 13m)	8	15
East Coast Private U		
Seminar in Anthropology	0	—
Northwest Public U		
Sample		
(N=689f, 465m)	25	42

TABLE A.2   STUDENT OPINIONS ON WHETHER SOME MAJORS
            ARE MORE SUITED TO ONE GENDER

	YES, DUE TO BIOLOGY		YES, DUE TO TRADITION		NO		UNSURE	
	FEMALE	MALE	FEMALE	MALE	FEMALE	MALE	FEMALE	MALE
Southern Public U								
Anthropology								
(N=45f, 21m)	9%	24%	11%	5%	73%	43%	7%	29%
Biology								
(N=43f, 11m)	5	36	7	9	79	55	9	0
Women in Society								
(N=26f)	0	—	12	—	85	—	4	—
Southern Private U								
Anthropology								
(N=32f, 22m)	6	27	19	14	63	45	13	14
Midwest Public U 1								
Anthropology								
(N=30f, 12m)	7	8	7	25	73	50	13	17
Midwest Public U 2								
Criminal Justice								
(N=23f, 33m)	0	22	17	11	83	58	0	8
Northwest State College								
Social Science								
(N=10f, 7m)	30	0	0	0	40	57	30	43
West Coast Private								
Christian College								
World Civ., Psych.								
(N=38f, 14m)	5	14	5	21	79	57	11	7
West Coast Public U								
English								
(N=12f, 13m)	0	8	17	8	67	69	17	15
East Coast Private U								
Anthropology Sem.								
(N=11f)	0	—	27	—	72	—	0	—
Northwest Public U								
Sample								
(N=704f, 471m)	15	27	13	15	59	43	13	16

TABLE A.3   STUDENTS AGREEING THAT CHILDREN
TURN OUT LESS WELL WHEN BOTH PARENTS WORK

CLASS SAMPLE (INSTITUTION AND COURSE)	FEMALE	MALE
Southern Public U		
Anthropology		
(N=43f, 21m)	30%	43%
Biology		
(N=42f, 11m)	26	64
Women in Society		
(N=26f)	15	—
Southern Private U		
Anthropology		
(N=33f, 22m)	48	68
Midwest Public U 1		
Anthropology		
(N=28f, 12m)	29	17
Midwest Public U 2		
Criminal Justice		
(N=22f, 35m)	27	34
Northwest State College		
Social Science		
(N=9f, 7m)	56	29
West Coast Private Christian College		
World Civ., Psych.		
(N=38f, 14m)	61	71
West Coast Public U		
English		
(N=12f, 13m)	17	46
East Coast Private U		
Anthropology Seminar		
(N=11f)	9	—
Northwest Public U		
Sample		
(N=695f, 465m)	30	50

TABLE A.4   EFFECT OF OWN MOTHER WORKING
OUTSIDE THE HOME ON STUDENT

CLASS SAMPLE (UNIVERSITY AND COURSE)	POSITIVE		NEGATIVE		NEUTRAL	
	FEMALE	MALE	FEMALE	MALE	FEMALE	MALE
Southern Public U Anthropology (N=41f, 19m)	51%	53%	2%	5%	46%	42%
Biology (N=41f, 8m)	49	38	0	25	51	38
Women in Society (N=25f)	60	—	0	—	40	—
Southern Private U Anthropology (N=27f, 16m)	37	44	22	13	41	44
Midwest Public U 1 Anthropology (N=28f, 11m)	61	45	18	27	21	27
Midwest Public U 2 Criminal Justice (N=21f, 35m)	52	40	5	6	43	54
Northwest State College Social Science (N=9f, 6m)	56	50	22	17	22	33
West Coast Private Christian College World Civ., Psych. (N=31f, 10m)	48	50	19	10	32	40
West Coast Public U English (N=10f, 10m)	50	20	10	20	40	60
East Coast Private U Anthropology Sem. (N=9f)	89	—	0	—	11	—
Northwest Public U Sample (N=590f, 391m)	52	40	7	7	41	53

TABLE A.5   MALE STUDENT EXPECTATIONS ABOUT
SPOUSES WORKING OUTSIDE THE HOME

CLASS SAMPLE (INSTITUTION AND COURSE)	SPOUSE WORK	SPOUSE NOT WORK	DON'T KNOW, UP TO SPOUSE
Southern Public U			
Anthropology			
(N=16)	38%	6%	56%
Biology			
(N=10)	40	10	50
Southern Private U			
Anthropology			
(N=19)	47	5	47
Midwest Public U 1			
Anthropology			
(N=10)	30	20	50
Midwest Public U 2			
Criminal Justice			
(N=31)	87	3	10
Northwest State College			
Social Science			
(N=6)	67	0	33
West Coast Private			
Christian College			
World Civ., Psych.			
(N=14)	64	0	36
West Coast Public U			
English			
(N=12)	75	0	75

TABLE A.6 FEMALE STUDENTS' SELECTION
OF ONE ITEM MOST IMPORTANT TO THEM IN THE LONG RUN

CLASS SAMPLE (INSTITUTION AND COURSE)	HAVING A CAREER	HAVING MONEY	HAVING FRIENDS	MARRIAGE OR A LOVE RELATIONSHIP	PARENT-HOOD
Southern Public U					
Anthropology					
(N=45)	47%	9%	4%	29%	11%
Biology					
(N=43)	47	14	5	26	9
Women in Society					
(N=26)	38	0	15	42	4
Southern Private U					
Anthropology					
(N=33)	21	24	6	42	6
Midwest Public U 1					
Anthropology					
(N=31)	52	6	3	23	16
Midwest Public U 2					
Criminal Justice					
(N=23)	48	13	0	26	13
Northwest State College					
Social Science					
(N=10)	50	0	0	30	20
West Coast Private Christian College					
World Civ., Psych.					
(N=34)	21	0	15	47	18
West Coast Public U					
English					
(N=11)	55	9	18	9	9
East Coast Private U					
Anthropology Sem.	40	10	20	30	0
(N=10)					

TABLE A.7   MALE STUDENTS' SELECTION
OF ONE ITEM MOST IMPORTANT TO THEM IN THE LONG RUN

CLASS SAMPLE (INSTITUTION AND COURSE)	HAVING A CAREER	HAVING MONEY	HAVING FRIENDS	MARRIAGE OR A LOVE RELATIONSHIP	PARENT-HOOD
Southern Public U Anthropology (N=21)	33%	10%	5%	48%	5%
Biology (N=11)	27	27	18	9	18
Southern Private U Anthropology (N=22)	32	23	0	32	14
Midwest Public U 1 Anthropology (N=12)	25	0	8	67	0
Midwest Public U 2 Criminal Justice (N=34)	50	12	0	29	9
Northwest State College Social Science (N=7)	29	14	0	29	29
West Coast Private Christian College World Civ., Psych. (N=14)	7	0	14	43	36
West Coast Public U English (N=12)	8	17	25	50	0

TABLE A.8   WOMEN STUDENTS WHO THINK THEY MIGHT (OR WHO DID) REDUCE WORKLOAD OR CHANGE JOB TO SPEND MORE TIME WITH CHILDREN

CLASS SAMPLE (INSTITUTION AND COURSE)	REDUCE WORKLOAD	CHANGE JOB
Southern Public U		
Anthropology (N=41, 42)	66%	38%
Biology (N=41)	56	29
Women in Society (N=25)	60	24
Southern Private U		
Anthropology (N=30)	73	40
Midwest Public U 1		
Anthropology (N=29)	66	28
Midwest Public U 2		
Criminal Justice (N=18)	67	44
Northwest State College		
Social Science (N=10)	70	60
West Coast Private Christian College		
World Civ., Psych. (N=37, 36)	100	58
West Coast Public U		
English (N=11, 10)	73	10
East Coast Private U		
Anthropology Sem. (N=9)	67	33

Note: Very few males indicated they would either reduce workload or change a job to be with children. However, relatively high proportions at Southern Public University (41 percent) and West Coast Private Christian College (43 percent) indicated they would change a job to be with children.

TABLE A.9   STUDENTS EXPECTING THEMSELVES
TO CONTRIBUTE MOST TO HOUSEHOLD INCOME

CLASS SAMPLE (INSTITUTION AND COURSE)	FEMALE	MALE
Southern Public U Anthropology (N=33f, 16m)	06%	50%
Biology (N=34f, 10m)	6	50
Women in Society (N=25f)	8	—
Southern Private U Anthropology (N=30f, 19m)	7	84
Midwest Public U 1 Anthropology (N=28f, 10m)	4	20
Midwest Public U 2 Criminal Justice (N=20f, 31m)	20	35
Northwest State College Social Science (N=10f, 7m)	20	86
West Coast Private Christian College World Civ., Psych. (N=34f, 14m)	3	50
West Coast Public U English (N=12f, 12m)	0	33
East Coast Private U Anthropology Sem. (N=10f)	20	—

TABLE A.10   STUDENTS EXPECTING THEMSELVES
TO CONTRIBUTE MOST TO HOUSEWORK

CLASS SAMPLE (INSTITUTION AND COURSE)	FEMALE	MALE
Southern Public U		
Anthropology		
(N=33f, 16m)	27%	0%
Biology		
(N=34f, 10m)	24	0
Women in Society		
(N=26f)	23	—
Southern Private U		
Anthropology		
(N=30f, 19m)	47	5
Midwest Public U 1		
Anthropology		
(N=28f, 10m)	39	10
Midwest Public U 2		
Criminal Justice		
(N=20f, 31m)	30	0
Northwest State College		
Social Science		
(N=10f, 7m)	60	14
West Coast Private		
Christian College		
World Civ., Psych.		
(N=35f, 14m)	26	7
West Coast Public U		
English		
(N=11f, 12m)	18	17
East Coast Private U		
Anthropology Sem.		
(N=10f)	09	—

TABLE A.11   STUDENTS EXPECTING THEMSELVES
TO CONTRIBUTE MOST TO CHILD CARE

CLASS SAMPLE (INSTITUTION AND COURSE)	FEMALE	MALE
Southern Public U		
Anthropology		
(N=33f, 16m)	24%	0%
Biology		
(N=34f, 10m)	21	10
Women in Society		
(N=25f)	40	—
Southern Private U		
Anthropology		
(N=30f, 19m)	53	0
Midwest Public U 1		
Anthropology		
(N=28f, 10m)	29	20
Midwest Public U 2		
Criminal Justice		
(N=20f, 31m)	25	0
Northwest State College		
Social Science		
(N=10f, 6m)	50	0
West Coast Private		
Christian College		
World Civ., Psych.		
(N=35f, 14m)	31	0
West Coast Public U		
English		
(N=11f, 12m)	27	0
East Coast Private U		
Anthropology Sem.		
(N=11f)	0	—

**TABLE A.12   WOMEN STUDENTS REPORTING SEXUAL HARASSMENT
OR GENDER DISCRIMINATION AT EDUCATIONAL INSTITUTION**

CLASS SAMPLE (INSTITUTION AND COURSE)	FEMALE
Southern Public U	
Anthropology	
(N=44)	23%
Biology	
(N=43)	28
Women in Society	
(N=26)	50
Southern Private U	
Anthropology	
(N=33)	12
Midwest Public U 1	
Anthropology	
(N=30)	23
Midwest Public U 2	
Criminal Justice	
(N=22)	27
Northwest State College	
Social Science	
(N=10)	20
West Coast Private	
Christian College	
World Civ., Psych.	
(N=38)	26
West Coast Public U	
English	
(N=12)	50
East Coast Private U	
Anthropology Sem.	
(N=10)	50

GLOSSARY

antebellum   Latin: "before the war." In the United States this usually refers to the time before the U.S. Civil War, 1861–1865.

anti-imperialist   Opposed to forces, ideas, or principles of imperialism (see *imperialial*).

berdache   A word of Persian origin, but popularized through French, that refers to gynemimetics (transgendered men who take on the role of women). The term is applied especially to the gynemimetic role in many Native North American groups, where it had, and sometimes still has, a place of honor. Because the term *berdache* was initially applied contemptuously by European settlers and missionaries, many Indian people prefer the terms "twin spirited" or "twin souled."

bride-price   Wealth given by the groom's family to the bride's family as a way of compensating the bride's family for the loss of the woman and loss of rights to any children she may have.

Calvinist   Having to do with the religious philosophy of French/Swiss theologian John Calvin (1509–1564). The most striking feature of Calvinism was the doctrine of predestination, which stated that God foreknows and ordains who is saved and who is damned.

consumerism   A characteristic often attributed to modern Western societies, according to which people are strongly motivated to acquire material items, especially those that have been publicly advertised, in order to establish a sense of themselves and to increase their status in the eyes of others.

cultural relativism   The position that it is counterproductive to make moral and value judgments about cultures different from one's own. Anthropologists cultivate cultural relativism in order to gain a more objective understanding of other cultures.

culture   The way of life of a group of people. Anthropologists usually think of culture primarily as the often unspoken rules a society has to guide behavior, as well as the society's collection of values and beliefs about the nature of the universe and the place of humans within it.

emancipation   The granting of freedom to a slave. In the United States, this often refers specifically to the emancipation of slaves in slaveholding states as a result of the Civil War.

epitaph   The words written on a gravestone or funeral monument.

ethnic group   A group of people who set themselves apart from others on the basis of sharing distinctive cultural, linguistic, or other characteristics.

ethnocentrism   The notion that one's own culture is the best, the standard, the normal and natural, and that other cultures are inferior and unnatural, the more so the more they vary from one's own. Anthropologists work to avoid ethnocentrism, since it clouds objectivity and the ability to appreciate cultural variation.

ethnography   An account of the characteristics of a culture. Traditionally, ethnographies have been primarily descriptive, but increasingly they also include interpretation and analysis.

evolution   The process by which organisms and populations change through time. Charles Darwin articulated the principle of biological evolution through natural selection. The notion of social evolution (the systematic change of simple social institutions into progressively complex ones) has been influential outside the academic world, despite the fact that it has often accompanied ethnocentric notions of the superiority of the complex over the simple.

familism   The practice in particular cultures of focusing not on the interests and needs of the individual, but on the well-being of the family group, often the extended family group.

feminism   A doctrine advocating the granting of the same rights to women and to men; a position of gender equality.

gay   An individual who is sexually attracted to members of his or her own gender. The term *gay* is usually preferred to *homosexual* for self-identification, especially by men.

gender   The culturally constructed aspects of maleness and femaleness.

hierarchy   A social structure based on stratification or rank ordering.

holistic   Inclusive, global. Holistic judgments are based on considerations of a phenomenon as a whole, rather than upon analysis of its individual, constituent parts.

hominid   A family-level classification of primates that includes modern humans and their ancestors. Though modern humans are the only living hominids, numerous ancestral and collateral hominid species existed in the past.

homosexual   An individual who is sexually attracted to members of his or her own gender. Many homosexual men (and some women) prefer the term *gay*, and many homosexual women identify themselves (and are referred to by others) as *lesbian*.

horticulture   A style of subsistence marked by the raising of plant foods with simple tools and human energy, but without elaborate technology, fertilization, irrigation, or animal traction or fossil fuels.

imperialial Having to do with the attempt by one nation to dominate or control another.

indigenous Native to a particular location. Indigenous peoples are usually thought of as the original inhabitants of an area, as opposed to later immigrants, and often maintain a way of life that preserves elements of tribal or band culture. The terms *native* and *autochthonous* mean essentially the same thing as *indigenous*.

individualism A focus on the rights, interests, and needs of the individual as opposed to the larger group to which he or she belongs. The notion that the essence of humanity is contained within each individual person rather than dependent upon relationships between persons. Individualism is primarily a modern, Western focus, which has increased in significance since its development during the rise of humanism in the European Renaissance. It is often contrasted with a focus on the larger family or kin group, especially in traditional Asian, Latino, and Native American societies.

lesbian A woman who is sexually attracted to other women.

lineage A group of people claiming descent from a common ancestor.

machismo/macho Spanish: "maleness/male." Machismo refers specifically to a style of masculinity characteristic of Latino culture, in which men assume positions of dominance and authority over women and may cultivate a highly sexed persona.

malinchista Spanish: "Malinchelike." Malinche was the Indian translator and mistress of Hernan Cortez, Spanish conqueror of Mexico. Though she had been sold into slavery by her family and given as a gift to Cortez, her cooperation with the Spaniards has been seen by some Mexicans and Mexican Americans as traitorous. Thus a "malinchista" is a cultural traitor or "sellout" to European or Anglo-American culture.

marianismo Spanish: "Marylikeness." Marianismo is a quality, based on the assumed characteristics of the Virgin Mary, of self-abnegation, nurturance, gentleness, and long-suffering, believed suitable to women in many Latino cultures.

matriarchy A society in which women as a group dominate men as a group and control politicoeconomic institutions. Despite sensational stories in magazines, there is no evidence that any matriarchy has ever existed. Neither the presence of high-status women in a society nor the worship of female supernaturals is in itself proof of a matriarchy.

matricentric/matrifocal A characteristic of societies in which families are organized around a senior female, her children, and the children of her adult daughters. Adult males in matricentric/matrifocal societies do not usually set up new households with their sexual partners, though they may live with them sporadically. Instead, their primary residence is likely to be with their mothers or other adult female relatives. Matricentric/matrifocal households are common in impoverished enclaves of contemporary postindustrial societies where unemployment is extremely high and many males find it impossible to support a family.

matrilineal Having to do with reckoning descent through female links only. Though both males and females belong to matrilineal kin groups, only females will pass on their membership in the groups to their children. Children of male members will belong to their mothers' kin groups.

matrilocality   The practice of a newly married husband moving into or near his wife's natal household. Matrilocal societies are nearly always matrilineal. Because women remain with their families after marriage in matrilocal societies, they tend to have higher status than they do in patrilocal societies, where they marry into their husbands' households.

microcosm   Literally, a "little world." The term is usually applied to a situation or phenomenon that seems to sum up salient qualities of the universe as a whole.

orthodox   Based on sound or "true" doctrine or teachings. Orthodox teachings in religion and politics may be contrasted with heretical ("false"), folk, and reform teachings.

patriarchy   A culture marked by pronounced male dominance.

patrilineal   Having to do with reckoning descent through male links only. Though both males and females belong to patrilineal kin groups, only males will pass on their membership in the groups to their children. Children of female members will belong to their fathers' kin groups.

polygyny   A variety of polygamy (marriage to multiple spouses), in which a man has more than one wife at the same time. Though many societies permit polygyny, most marriages within these societies are likely to be monogamous (involve only single spouses at a given time) for reasons of convenience, wealth, or personal inclination.

postbellum   Latin: "after the war." In the United States this usually refers to the time after the U.S. Civil War, 1861–1865.

predestination   A doctrine popularized by theologian John Calvin, though based on the writings of St. Paul and St. Augustine. It stated that God has foreordained all things, especially the salvation of individual souls.

race   A group of people considered to have some physical characteristics in common. The scientific status of the concept of *race* when applied to humans is controversial.

subculture   A specialized subset of rules, values, and behaviors within a larger, dominant culture. Subcultures develop in large, complex societies, and are based on such characteristics as social class, ethnicity, religion, occupation, or gender preference. Some people argue that gender, itself, forms the basis of subculture.

subsistence   As anthropologists use the term, it refers to the activities undertaken in order to survive, particularly the means by which people collect or produce food. In some societies subsistence, by hunting and gathering or by horticulture, for example, is direct, whereas in the industrial and postindustrial societies most people's subsistence provides food only indirectly.

transgendered   An individual who incorporates elements of both male and female gender in his or her identity or self-presentation. Some transgendered individuals are transsexuals, while others may be intersexed, transvestites, or merely masculine-appearing women or feminine-appearing men.

transsexual   An individual who has undergone surgical and/or hormonal alteration from one sex to the other. There are both male-to-female (MTF) and female-to-male (FTM) transsexuals.

transvestite   An individual who cross-dresses (dresses as a member of the other sex). The term is usually applied only to men, most but not all of whom, at least in the United States, are gay. Some transvestites cross-dress only in their work as entertainers, while others cross-dress for private gratification as well.

utopian   Having to do with a socially, morally, and politically ideal situation. The term is derived from the satirical political tract *Utopia*, written by the English statesman and intellectual Sir (later Saint) Thomas More. Utopia (from the Greek *ou*, not + *topos*, place) was a fictitious island on which there was perfection in all human institutions.

INDEX

Fox, Richard, 64
Fox-Genovese, Elizabeth, 181
Foxwoods casino, 103
Fragmentation of women. *See also* Gender roles, conflicting
  career and, 166, 193
  ethnicity and, 188
  medical discourse and, 81
  NRMs and, 84
Fraternities, 158–159, 161
Frazier, E. Franklin, 108
Freedman, Estelle B., 33, 53
Freedom of choice, 64–65. *See also* Individualism
Free love, 83–84
French, Marilyn, 76
Freud, Sigmund, 85
Friedan, Betty, 69
Friends and lovers, 68–69
Futures. *See* Aspirations

G
Gaines, Edmund (Maj. Gen.), 102
Gathering hypothesis, 10
Gay(s), 53–56, 79, 85–90, 227
Gender. *See also* Gender roles; Gender roles, conflicting
  anthropology of, 1–2, 9–13, 18
  and culture, 4–5
  defined, 227
Gender discrimination, 160, 197, 200, 225
Gender equality
  anthropology and, 10
  defining, 6–8
  evolutionary biology and, 12–13
  Great Awakening and, 41
  materialism and, 13–15
  Oglala Sioux and, 106
  Puritans and, 30
  Raelians and, 84
  students and, 192–194
  Victorian women and, 57
  women's movement and, 77
Gender gap, 154–155, 180, 195, 198
Gender roles. *See also* Domestic roles; Economic roles; Gender equality; Gender roles, conflicting
  career choice and, 163–166
  changing, 168
  college and, 192
  colonial, 36
  conflicting, 76–80
  current, 194–196
  dating and, 70–74
  ethnicity and, 99–103, 111–114, 128–132, 149
  homosexual, 90
  impotence and, 82–83

individualism and, 40–42
international, 196–201
social process and, 17
Victorian, 48
Gender roles, conflicting. *See also* Gender; Gender roles
  Cult of True Womanhood and, 47–53
  motherhood and, 166–170, 179
  NRMs and, 83–84
  students and, 193–194
  Twentieth Century, 65–68, 76–80, 185–186
Glick, Paul, 118
God, gender of, 34, 41
Going steady, 72
Golden Age, 34–36, 74–76, 80
Gorer, Geoffrey, 65, 71–72
Government, U.S., 86–87, 117
Graham, Sylvester, 44
Graham crackers, 44
Great Awakening, 40–42
Great Depression, 117
Greeks, Ancient, 54
Guadalupe Hidalgo, Treaty of, 127
Gunsmoke, 65
Gutman, Herbert G., 108–111

H
Hall, Roberta, 155
Hays, Sharon, 179, 186
hooks, bell, 112, 121
Hierarchy, 227
  colonial, 36–37
  Puritan, 31–32
  witchcraft and, 38
Hispanic Americans. *See* Latinos
HIV, 88
Hmong, 146, 150
Hoikuen, 200
Holism. *See* Hierarchy
Holistic, 227
Holland, Dorothy, 156–160, 190–191
Hominid, 227
Homo erectus, 10
Homosexual, 55, 227
Homosexuality, 85–90
  discourse of, 18
  Navajo, 103–104
  Raelians and, 84
  in the Victorian Period, 53–56
Horticulture, 227
Hospitals, 81–82, 86
Household economy, Puritan, 30–31
Hudson, Rock, 72
Human Imunodeficiency Virus. *See* HIV
Hunting hypothesis, 9–10, 11
Hutchinson, Anne, 36
Hysteria, 51, 188